POLITICAL
TERRORISM

PETER LANG
New York • Washington, D.C./Baltimore • Bern
Frankfurt am Main • Berlin • Brussels • Vienna • Oxford

Jeffrey Ian Ross

POLITICAL
TERRORISM

An Interdisciplinary Approach

PETER LANG
New York • Washington, D.C./Baltimore • Bern
Frankfurt am Main • Berlin • Brussels • Vienna • Oxford

Library of Congress Cataloging-in-Publication Data

Ross, Jeffrey Ian.
Political terrorism: an interdisciplinary approach / Jeffrey Ian Ross.
p. cm.
Includes bibliographical references and index.
1. Terrorism. 2. Political violence. I. Title.
HV6431.R675   303.6'25—dc22   2005023783
ISBN 978-0-8204-7949-1 (paperback)
ISBN 978-0-8204-8050-3 (hardcover)

Bibliographic information published by **Die Deutsche Bibliothek**.
Die Deutsche Bibliothek lists this publication in the "Deutsche
Nationalbibliografie"; detailed bibliographic data is available
on the Internet at http://dnb.ddb.de/.

Cover design by Lisa Barfield

Maps of United Kingdom and the world courtesy of www.cia.gov

The paper in this book meets the guidelines for permanence and durability
of the Committee on Production Guidelines for Book Longevity
of the Council of Library Resources.

© 2007, 2006 Jeffrey Ian Ross
Peter Lang Publishing, Inc., New York
29 Broadway, 18th floor, New York, NY 10006
www.peterlang.com

Printed in the United States of America

To Karyn

He was loving, kind and fearless.
I knew he was kidding but it sounded mean.
He went off to work.
I went off to school and then with an explosion he was no more.
I didn't understand but then I cried.
Dakota Ross-Cabrera

Table of Contents

List of Illustrations xi

Foreword by Alex Schmid xiii

Preface xv

Acknowledgments xxi

Chapter One
     Introducing Oppositional Political Terrorism 1

Chapter Two
     Tracing the Historical Trajectory and Contemporary Trends . . . 31

Chapter Three
     Exploring the Causes 77

Chapter Four
     Understanding the Effects 95

Chapter Five
     Three Case Studies: Al-Fatah, FARC, and PIRA 123

Chapter Six
     Terrorism in the United States 143

Chapter Seven
　　　9/11, al Qaeda, and Osama bin Laden 165

Chapter Eight
　　　The Role of the Mass Media 183

Chapter Nine
　　　Combating Terrorism 201

Chapter Ten
　　　Post 9/11: Are We Any Safer Now? 215

Chapter Eleven
　　　The Future of Terrorism 235

Appendix A
　　　Pedagogical Suggestions 251

Notes 253

Bibliography 263

Index 285

About the Author 289

List of Illustrations

Figure 1.   Physical Map of the World   xii

Figure 2.   Map of the UK (Exhibit 8)   37

Physical Map of the World, April 2005

Foreword

Alex P. Schmid
(UN Terrorism Prevention Branch)

Terrorism—the deliberate display of violence in public against civilians and non-combatants to induce and manipulate widespread fear—has been around for centuries and has often caused more damage by the reaction it provokes rather than by its own power. A brief look at history illustrates this.

Placing guillotines on French town squares to decapitate royal persons and other opponents of the Revolution sent shock waves through aristocratic Europe in 1793 and triggered more than a decade of wars. Almost one hundred years later, assassinations of kings and presidents—stimulated by the invention of dynamite—raised fears of an intercontinental anarchist conspiracy stretching from Russia to the United States. After World War I, which was triggered in 1914 by an assassination in the anarchist tradition, fascism and communism emerged, and terrorism as a strategy of social control was used on a grand scale to subdue whole nations. During World War II, crimes against humanity and war crimes terrorized civilian populations in occupied countries. Aerial bombardments put millions of people in fear and killed civilians by the hundreds of thousands.

Following the World War II, national liberation movements in Asia, the Middle East, and Africa used terror tactics in combination with guerrilla warfare to shake off colonialism. In the 1960s, Latin American leftist revolutionaries, inspired by the Cuban revolution and Guevara's *foco* theory, thought they could create rural guerrilla armies out of nowhere. When most of them failed to mobilize poor *campesinos*, these middle-class militant "intellectuals" (who still constitute the majority of terrorist leaders) thought they could continue their struggle in the cities as "urban guerrillas." Instead, they provoked the rise of right-wing death squads, which were even more indiscriminate in their violence. The leftist urban terrorists of Latin America managed, however, to inspire radical elements of the 1968 student generation in Europe and the United States to engage in provocative acts of kidnapping, hostage-taking, assassination, and bombing.

The Palestinians, inspired by the success of the Algerian revolution, turned to terrorism after the third Arab military defeat against Israel in 1967. Expelled from Jordan in 1972, militant Palestinians nested themselves in Lebanon, which led to civil war and foreign intervention. To fight the French, Italian and American peacekeepers in Lebanon, suicide bombers using trucks appeared on the scene. In 2001, the hijacking tactics of the 1960s and the suicide tactics of the 1980s merged in the simultaneous attacks on the World Trade Center and the Pentagon, which, in turn, triggered two wars in Afghanistan and Iraq.

What will be next? Will terrorists employ weapons of mass destruction? There is enough uranium and plutonium in the world to construct more than 300,000 atomic bombs, and some of that material is not as well protected as the almost 30,000 atomic bombs in the arsenals of the nine nuclear powers. Some politicians say it is not a question of "if" but only of "when" terrorists will engage in radiological, chemical, nuclear, or biological terrorism. Should we believe them?

Dr. Jeffrey Ian Ross has written an introduction to terrorism that invites students to think for themselves on the basis of sound conceptual and theoretical tools offered by the author. Dissecting systematically the various facets of contemporary non-state terrorism, Professor Ross' interdisciplinary approach enables readers to develop critical capacities to withstand both terrorist intimidation and the manipulation of fear generated by some advocates of the "Global War on Terror"—a war which in 2005 cost the world close to $200 billion and saw violations of human rights and humanitarian standards in some well-established democracies that seemed inconceivable before 9/11. It is time to rethink terrorism and counter-terrorism, and this book is a good start.

Preface

Most of the political terrorism textbooks of the 1970s and 1980s are now out of print or out of date. Granted, several books have been written in the meantime on the subject of terrorism—not to serve as classroom texts, but rather to describe current events. These treatments, however, are too specific for the advanced undergraduate or graduate student.

The academic field of terrorism studies has grown substantially. Two scholarly journals focus almost exclusively on our subject—*Terrorism and Political Violence* and *Studies in Conflict and Terrorism*—and a number of scholars and research centers devote the majority of their efforts to researching terrorism. Moreover, the following factors have affected the study of terrorism during the past decade:

- a better definition of terrorism has been established;

- more empirical studies of terrorism have been conducted;

- the number of suicide bombings has increased;

- terrorist attacks are more severe and deadly;

- a greater number of religiously motivated terrorist groups have formed;

- many potential and actual targets are now better protected;

- both terrorists and counterterrorist agencies have integrated new technologies into their repertoire;

- more security policies and practices (at airports, schools, and workplaces) have been implemented to prevent terrorism or to respond to it when it occurs;

- one of the most deadliest incidents took place on September 11, 2001; and

- some would say that 9/11 has fostered a paradigm shift in America's response to terrorism.

By taking an introductory course on terrorism, students should learn:

- who the terrorists are and are not;

- what they do (including the tactics they use, how they commit these actions, who they attack, and why they engage in this behavior);

- the relationship between the media and terrorism;

- the importance of research on terrorism;

- the steps that citizens, businesses, and the government are taking to deter, prevent, and respond to terrorism; and finally,

- that terrorism is nothing new—it has been going on since the dawn of human history.

In short, after reading this book, students should be able to more objectively and rationally understand terrorism and government, public, and victim responses to it. By becoming more aware of terrorism at a broader level, readers may also become less afraid of terrorism on a personal level.

To those ends, this book has a number of features not present or emphasized in other textbooks on terrorism, including:

- a greater theoretical focus;

- a critical-thinking foundation;

- a causal model;

- an effects model;

- an application of both of these tools to selected cases of terrorism;

- empirical evidence about terrorism as well as descriptive material;

- confrontation of the myth surrounding "Islamic terrorism" (that it is the dominant type of terrorism); and

- end-of-chapter questions (multiple choice, short answer, and essay).

Chapter 1, "Introducing Oppositional Political Terrorism," reviews the thorny definitional issues connected to terrorism and the different forms terrorism takes. It settles on the consensus definition offered by Schmid (1983) as the most useful, and then argues why the study of terrorism is important, as well as what constituencies are interested in the subject matter. The chapter concludes with a review of the different typologies of terrorism and of current problems with the study of terrorism.

Chapter 2, "Tracing the Historical Trajectory and Contemporary Trends," sensitizes students to the fact that terrorism is not a new phenomenon. In so doing, it outlines three dominant periods in the history of terrorism—ancient, modern, and contemporary—which encompass terrorism motivated by religious, nationalist-separatist, and ideological concerns. It then subdivides the contemporary period into three further blocks and briefly examines state-sponsored terrorism, narco-terrorism, and grey-area phenomena. Finally, the chapter ends with a discussion of trends in terrorism, covering changes that have occurred over the past four decades in terms of the number of incidents, types of actions, kinds of targets, regional dispersion, and terrorist groups that have emerged.

"Exploring the Causes," chapter 3, presents explanations and theories on the causes of terrorism, followed by a model that integrates five psychological and ten structural factors. It divides the causes into precipitants and permissive causes and specifies the linkages among these variables.

Chapter 4, "Understanding the Effects," first reviews explanations and theories concerning reactions to terrorism, beginning by analyzing a conflict model to sketch the responses of terrorists, victims, victims' families and friends, the general public, the business community, and the government. The rest of the chapter integrates five "actor-based" models that outline the responses to terrorism. Topics covered include the response to terrorism at home and abroad, including the reactions of local law enforcement, the Federal Bureau of Investigation, the Central Intelligence Agency, and international political actors.

"Three Case Studies," chapter 5, applies the structural components of the causal models developed in chapter 3 to three different campaigns of oppositional political terrorism to help the reader better understand the dynamics of this form of criminal and political violence. Our three case studies cover al-Fatah, the Revolutionary Armed Forces of Colombia (FARC), and the Provisional Irish Republican Army (PIRA).

Chapter 6, "Terrorism in the United States," reviews the history of terrorism in America. It is divided into four sections: left-wing terrorism, right-wing terrorism, émigré/nationalist-separatist, and single-issue terrorism, with a discussion of those groups that are or were active and fall into these categories. Groups covered include the Weather Underground, the United Freedom Front, the Symbionese Liberation Army, black militant groups (Hanafi Muslim Group and Black Liberation Army), the Ku Klux Klan, and the Aryan Nations, as well as Armenian, Croatian, Cuban, and Puerto Rican organizations. We also examine the actions of individuals, such as Timothy McVeigh, and of groups like the Animal Liberation Army or Front, the pro-life (anti-abortion) movement, and the Jewish Defense League (JDL).

Although domestic terrorism in the United States will always be present, perhaps the greatest threat in the early twenty-first century is foreign terrorist activities. "9/11, al Qaeda, and Osama bin Laden," chapter 7, begins by briefly reviewing the circumstances of September

11, 2001, the victims and perpetrators. It then moves to a larger discussion of terrorism arising in the Middle East, including an examination of the first World Trade Center bombing in 1993 and how American national security agencies ignored the signals about a possible larger attack. We review the history of Osama bin Laden, al Qaeda, and their supporters, and try to identify some of their motivations as well as the short- and long-range effects of the 9/11 attacks. This chapter also discusses the existence of other groups that should be feared; and measures of protecting ourselves.

Chapter 8, "The Role of the Mass Media," examines the relationship between the mass media and terrorism. This chapter takes a more comprehensive approach than is offered in traditional texts by going beyond how the news media (typically newspapers and television) portray terrorism to analyzing how terrorists *use* the media (through, for example, the timing of attacks and the creation of their own websites, video production, and so on) and how popular culture (Hollywood, foreign movies, popular fiction) depicts terrorism. The balance of the chapter will examine if and how public opinion is affected by media reports on terrorism.

Chapter 9, "Combating Terrorism," reviews domestic and international programs and practices, particularly their success or failures in responding to and preventing terrorism. In so doing, we'll look at both proactive and reactive measures. Embedded in this discussion is anti-terrorist legislation, enforcement (including specialized antiterrorism strike forces), efforts at conflict resolution, diplomacy, and the use of international law. Additionally, the chapter will try to outline a new role for local law enforcement in the detection of terrorism and the consequences for democracies of that role, particularly when emergency legislation such as the Patriot Act is passed.

Chapter 10, "Post 9/11: Are We Any Safer Now?" looks at the fundamental changes that have taken place at the individual, community, national, and international levels. Organized along the models developed in chapter 4, this chapter will review, among other topics, the impact of 9/11 on the economy and on the public's faith in government. We will primarily focus on the efforts of the federal government to combat terrorism, including the new regulations concerning transportation, airport security, and the creation of the Department of Homeland Security, but will also look at operations in Afghanistan and Iraq.

Finally, chapter 11 examines the future of terrorism, both in general and in light of 9/11, through an extended discussion of the potential for terrorism through weapons of mass destruction, suicide bombings, cyberterrorism, and globalization. We shall also examine new procedures and technological innovations to combat terrorism. The book concludes with a discussion regarding the potential unintended consequences we might experience with respect to terrorism, including human-rights violations and greater government intrusiveness into our private affairs.

Acknowledgments

Over the past two decades, my scholarly research on terrorism has benefited from the assistance of a number of people. Journal or special issue editors (including Yonah Alexander, James David Ballard, David Charters, Robert Elias, Bruce Hoffman, Harvey Kushner, Graham Turbiville, and Paul Wilkinson) and their publications' anonymous reviewers allowed me to test some of my early ideas and sharpened my thinking. Editors of books in which chapters of mine appeared provided a similar function, and so I acknowledge Lee Muraskin, Alex Schmid, Craig Summers, Kenneth S. Tunnell, and Graham F. Walker. Other individuals, such as Raymond Corrado, Morad Eghbal, Chip Ellis, William Eubank, Ted Robert Gurr, Mark S. Hamm, Chris Hewitt, Mike Gunter, Tom O'Connor, David Mason, Manus Midlarsky, Rueben Miller, Will H. Moore, Norm Rosenberg, Brent Smith, Austin Turk, and Leonard Weinberg, among others, provided input on different papers and conceptual hurdles that formed the backbone of my research on terrorism. My students at institutions where I taught were kind enough to let me subject them to my ideas, often in rudimentary form. Special commendations to Catherine Leidemer, Bridget Muller, and Gretchen Knapp who on separate occasions struggled with my often difficult prose. Thanks to Natasha, my wife, who provided comments on various papers, served as a sounding board for ideas, and tried to keep my feet firmly planted on the ground. And hats off to my children, who often wonder exactly what I do and continue to be a source of inspiration and joy. Special appreciation is extended to Alex P. Schmid for writing a thoughtful foreword.

I would also like to thank Phyllis Korper, an enlightened editor who saw promise in this project and offered me encouragement and constructive criticism through its various stages, and Lisa Dillon, Lang's production and creative director, helping me past the finishing line. This book is dedicated to Karyn; it's now your turn.

CHAPTER ONE

Introducing Oppositional Political Terrorism

Terrorism is not a new phenomenon. However, during the last half of the twentieth century, terrorism became recognized as a major problem in domestic and international politics. Almost every country in the world has experienced this type of violence, although some geographic areas and political actors are more targeted and affected than others. Naturally, as a result, there has been increased attention to this behavior over the past four decades.

Yet a number of issues that had led to persistent political violence subsided after certain critical events: the fall of the Berlin Wall (November 9, 1989); the collapse of the Soviet Union (1991); the Gulf War (1990–91); the election of Nelson Mandela (1991); the signing of the Israeli/Palestinian peace accords in Oslo (September 13, 1993); and the "Good Friday Agreement" between the Provisional Irish Republican Army and the British government (1998) (Stern 1999, 8–10; Ross 2003, chapter 5). Additionally, the capture of the heads of significant terrorist movements—like Abimael Guzman of Peru's Shining Path (September 12, 1992) and Abdulla Ocalan of the Kurdish Workers Party (PKK) (April 15, 1998)—led policymakers and political leaders to believe that terrorism was abating. Finally, it appeared as if the international economy improved, thus bringing wealth to many individuals, nations, and states. Consequently, many observers and analysts hoped that oppositional political terrorism was a thing of the past and that it might even end.

The relatively recent Oklahoma City bombing (April 1995), the sarin gas attack in the Tokyo subway (March 1995), and frequent suicide bombings by Hamas in Israel renewed interest in terrorism among governments, the media, and the public. Then came 9/11, when four planes were hijacked allegedly by members of Osama bin Laden's al

Qaeda network. These planes slammed into the World Trade Center, the Pentagon, and a rural field in Pennsylvania, causing close to 3,000 deaths and more than 6,300 injuries.

In the meantime, although some previously established terrorist organizations disbanded over the past decade, new terrorist groups formed in their place. These entities acquired and used new communications and more destructive technology in their attacks. By the same token, reports—uncovered during the investigations into the causes of 9/11—of poor collaboration among key federal agencies (the Federal Bureau of Investigation, Central Intelligence Agency, and the former Immigration and Naturalization Service) and our allies have indirectly led to both a sense of vulnerability in the United States and elsewhere and to the establishment of the Department of Homeland Security.

Nowadays, we cannot pick up a newspaper or watch or listen to a newscast without seeing or hearing some reference to terrorism. Predictably, many people are becoming exhausted with the continuing coverage of the 9/11 attack, the war on terrorism, and "waiting for the other shoe to drop." Before analyzing this phenomenon, we must ask the logical and necessary question: What is terrorism? Without a widely accepted definition, analysts and counterterrorist practitioners will not agree upon the subject matter, thus wasting resources and jeopardizing their efforts to prevent the needless property damage, injury, and death resulting from terrorism.

Defining Terrorism

The proper definition of terrorism has led to considerable debate. As Sederberg puts it, "A variety of problems . . . impede our efforts to develop an analytically useful definition of terrorism" (1991, 7). We'll examine eight interrelated drawbacks below.

1. Relativity definition

In many quarters, identifying acts as "terrorist" requires something akin to a baseball umpire's reasoning: "I call them as I see them." Indeed, terrorism has become a value-laden term. Phrases such as "one man's terrorist is another man's freedom fighter" are often used by reporters, policy-makers, politicians, and many academics to clarify situations—and, at other times, to muddy them. This approach can be regarded as the *relativity definition*. It implies that "all attempts to formulate the concept will be hopelessly compromised by essentially arbitrary personal or political bias. Consequently, any analysis based on such dubious conceptual foundations will be distorted and most likely vacuous" (Sederberg 1991, 6).

2. Conflation of analysis with evaluation

Because analysts often "intermingle explanation, justification, and condemnation," neutral definitions of terrorism are hard to achieve (Sederberg 1991, 6). Similarly, Mitchell suggests that "the term terrorism itself contains an implicit condemnation . . . [it] is a profoundly heterogeneous phenomenon." He continues to delineate what a definition of terrorism should include when he states that "a definition of terrorism must clearly establish what terrorism is not" (Mitchell 1991, 14).

3. Changing nature of terrorism

Terrorism is a dynamic phenomenon. This has led some observers to suggest that "a definition of terrorism must take into account the constantly changing nature of tactics, targets, and strategies, as well as the impact of technological innovations such as new techniques of media coverage and advanced types of weapons" (Mitchell 1991, 13–14).

4. Emotional response to terrorism

Another reason for definitional confusion is that terrorism evokes extreme emotions such as fear, anger, and rage (Wardlaw 1982, 3), which prevent people from thinking clearly or dispassionately about the subject matter. The graphic images of the World Trade tower attack (September 2001) or the London tube bombings (July 2005) played repeatedly by television stations surely contributes to this problem.

5. Varied forms of terrorism

Another problem, which will be explained in greater detail later in this chapter, is that there appear to be various types of terrorism, which may confuse the casual observer into assuming that no overall unifying theme exists. Mitchell, for example, suggests that "many scholars who undertake research on terrorism tend either to regard the development of a general definition as a hopeless endeavor or simply dodge the issue by embracing" the relativity definition, or "blithely devise a narrow operational definition suitable to the requirements of their specific methodology or approach" (Mitchell 1991, 9).

6. Unique position of terrorism among acts of political violence and crime

Some analysts have suggested that terrorism is so unique that it is almost impossible to define. According to Sederberg, "The confusion between the action (terrorism), the actors (the terrorist) and the effect (terror) detracts from the ability to distinguish between terrorism and the larger class of coercive behavior of which it is a part. In this regard, definitions should focus on the act, and recognize that issues of actors and effects are areas for inquiry, not definitional attributes" (1991, 7).

7. Difficulty of practical application

According to White (1991, 163), "No definition or approach to American terrorism is generally accepted and the practical implications are very real. The lack of a social or legal definition creates problems. . . . American police and security agencies literally do not know what terrorism is. . . . Agencies charged with countering domestic terrorism often have no idea what they are looking for" (see exhibit box 1).

Exhibit Box 1
The different definitions of terrorism used by federal government agencies
The State Department uses Title 22 of U. S. Code, Section 265(f) to define terrorism. For them, "terrorism means premeditated politically motivated violence perpetrated against noncombatant targets by subnational groups or clandestine agents, usually intended to influence an audience."
The FBI relies on the definition provided by the Code of Federal Regulations (revised July 2001), which defines terrorism as "the unlawful use of force or violence against persons or property to intimidate or coerce a Government, the civilian population, or any segment thereof, in furtherance of political or social objectives."

8. Overinclusivity

There is a tendency, as we'll discuss later, to interpret and define many individuals and groups as "terrorist" and their actions as "terrorism" (Bell 1977). Some analysts (e. g., Vetter and Perlstein 1991, 52) use vague, over-inclusive labels to classify actions as acts of terrorism and encourage the reader to infer from their analysis that some social movements—such as pro-choice, gay rights, feminist, and American nationalists—could very well have been terrorists. This kind of approach is problematic in view of the lack of evidence that these groups' actions meet the criteria for most definitions of terrorism. We must also be cautious about affixing the terrorist label to groups more appropriately identified as political organizations, and about linking particular nationalities with terrorism.

In sum, no internationally accepted definition of terrorism exists. Many individuals and organizations have emphasized the need for a clear definition. As Schmid (1996) said, "Only then can we be certain of what is meant by the word and then design laws to punish the terrorists." The desire to reach a consensus on the meaning of the term was clearly critical in 1996—and even more demanding in the wake of the events of September 2001.

Where does this leave us? Perhaps if we understand the context of terrorism, we can better appreciate a definition that has a wide applicability.

A Contextual Understanding

What is political terrorism? One of the earliest distinctions was developed by Hacker. He suggested that terrorists can be divided into three types of perpetrators: criminals, crazies, and crusaders. This categorization distinguishes perpetrators who primarily have a criminal intent from those who are mentally unbalanced and those who have political or ideological motivations. Hacker's breakdown implies that terrorist organizations may periodically engage in criminal activities and that among their ranks they can have some disturbed individuals. But it also suggests that, for the most part, terrorist organizations are concerned with achieving political or ideological goals (Hacker 1976). While this distinction gives us the big picture, we are most interested in the subset of politically motivated terrorism.

In order to understand terrorism, we need to use an interdisciplinary or multidisciplinary approach that integrates, at the very least, the fields of criminology, criminal justice, history, law, philosophy, political science, psychology, religion, and sociology.[1] It must also be appreciated that terrorism is a subset of political violence just like war, revolution, guerrilla warfare, coups d'état, low-intensity warfare, violent protests, and riots. It is also a type of criminal violence much like homicide and sexual assault. And finally, terrorism is a subset of political crime, like corruption, sedition, espionage, and human rights violations (Ross 2002a) (see exhibit box 2).

Exhibit Box 2
Multi-interdisciplinary nature of terrorism

Discipline: political science	Discipline: criminology
Types of political violence:	Types of criminal violence:
war	homicide
revolution	assault
guerrilla warfare	armed robbery
terrorism	terrorism
civil war	

Discipline: political crime

Types of oppositional political crime:

terrorism

sedition

treason

war crime

political corruption

The above discussion locates the phenomena, but it still does not provide a definition. Alternatively, we can examine what the experts, sometimes pejoratively referred to as "terrorologists," have to say (Herman and O'Sullivan 1989; Livingstone 1990). We all know, however, that if you speak to a hundred specialists, you may get a hundred different definitions.

Many researchers have suggested that in order to clarify what terrorism is, scholars and practitioners need to concentrate on terrorist incidents. Sederberg, for example, argues that "definitions should focus on the act and recognize that issues of actors and effects are areas for inquiry, not definitional attributes" (1991, 7). Hoffman and Claridge, in their work "The Rand–St. Andrews Chronology of International Terrorism and Noteworthy Domestic Incidents, 1996," expressed this same view as the basis of their definition, which stated in part that "terrorism is defined by the nature of the act not by the identity of the perpetrator or the nature of the cause . . ." (Hoffman and Claridge 1998,). Subsequent writers have also adopted this viewpoint (e.g., Shanty and Picquet 2000).

In the early 1980s, Schmid conducted an exhaustive analysis of fifty experts' definitions of terrorism. He concluded that there is no "true or correct definition" (1983, 110). Nevertheless, he developed a very helpful five-part consensus definition. According to Schmid:

> Terrorism is a method of combat in which random or symbolic victims [become] *target[s] of violence*. . . . Through [the] previous use of violence or the credible threat of violence other members of that group . . . are put in a *state of chronic fear (terror)*. . . . The victimization of the target . . . is considered extranormal by most observers . . . [which in turn] creates an . . . audience beyond the *target of terror*. . . . The purpose of [terrorism] . . . is either to immobilize the target of terror in order to produce disorientation and/or compliance, or to mobilize secondary *targets of demands* (e.g., a government) or *targets of attention* (e.g., public opinion). (Schmid 1983, 111, italics original)

Schmid's definition has earned a considerable amount of respect among scholars and policymakers. Although he subsequently proposed two revisions—one responding to difficulties critics had with the original 1983 consensus definition (Schmid and Jongman 1988) and another revised, short legal definition that equates a terrorist act as the peacetime equivalent of a war crime (Schmid 1992). Regardless of this extra work, many terrorism experts prefer the original formulation. With a few clarifications, the original definition meets the purposes of most researchers, policymakers, and practitioners (Ross 1988a; 1988b; 1991). The implication here is that if indeed a relatively acceptable definition has been constructed, statements like "One man's terrorist is another person's freedom fighter" should probably be interpreted as too relativistic, and thereby rejected.

For our purposes here, this conceptualization works with two qualifications. First, not all five elements must exist for an action or campaign to be labeled as terrorism, and second, violent attacks on nonhuman "symbolic" targets, having the other essential traits and objects, should also be considered as acts of terrorism.

We should also be careful in this context to distinguish illegal behaviors typically confused with terrorism, such as drug trafficking, as well as the illegal sales of arms, legal documents (such as passports), and currencies to finance terrorist groups. Although these criminal activities may be used to support terrorist organizations, they are "not by themselves a terrorist act without the inclusion of the element of premeditated violence. Taking a hostage for ransom in order to finance terrorist activity, on the other hand, is a terrorist act, because it involves violence" (Long 1990, 6) and the presumed political goals (to bring about some sort of political or social change) associated with or subsumed by the group's primary raison d'être.

September 11, 2001, and Beyond

In the aftermath of 9/11, American national security and law enforcement agencies are still struggling to find a proper definition of terrorism. This operational difficulty has not prevented them, however, from launching a massive counterterrorism offensive supported by enabling legislation in the form of the USA PATRIOT Act (which we will examine in a later chapter). The effects of these efforts will be felt in the immediate future.

Although some have suggested that the central act of 9/11 is a mass murder and that the perpetrators, if caught, should be charged with committing a war crime, the consensus of the world community's response to this tragedy has at least shown international acceptance for labeling acts of this level of violence as terrorism. Likewise, claims made by the perpetrators for "freedom fighter" status have been summarily rejected. A substantial segment of the international community has agreed that the perpetrators are terrorists. The horrible nature of their act, regardless of any arguments the alleged planners and supporters have articulated to justify their actions, has probably generated this global consensus.

Can the international community's response to the horrors of 9/11 assist the development of an internationally accepted definition of terrorism? At the very least, it should be clear that when the shock of an act passes any conceivable threshold of decency or humanity or when it reaches the level of violence of 9/11, must be condemned and punished as terrorism by the international community.

In fact, when we analyze the events of 9/11, they appear to have satisfied all five criteria of the Schmid definition of terrorism:

1. The World Trade Center and the Pentagon—both their personnel and facility—were highly *symbolic targets;*

2. This attack induced a *high state of fear* throughout the country and abroad, given the widespread media coverage, including the printing of victims' obituaries in the *New York Times* and other media;

3. By all accounts, the *victimization was extraordinary;*

4. The act created a *global audience;* and

5. The incident was *communicated repeatedly* to secondary audiences, such as the U. S. government, the American public, and the Arab and Muslim worlds.

Therefore, we can say that the act was indeed one of "terrorism"— and that our conceptual definition would meet with the consensus. The question now becomes, What has the 9/11 experience provided in the way of validating the definition and the common understanding of the phenomenon? Certainly, it must add to the public's sense of how terrorism is defined—even if it is merely akin to the U. S. Supreme Court Justice's famous comment about pornography: "I can't define it, but I know what it is when I see it." Is it not possible that 9/11 has sufficiently seared the public's conscience to stimulate unprecedented levels of pressure on both politicians and jurists, domestically and abroad, for the development of a more straightforward understanding of the issue— and thereby more focused and practical applications (i.e., international, trans-ethno-national, and cross-cultural counterterrorism programs) against the perpetrators? Perhaps, but in the wake of 9/11 it appears that a universally acceptable definition of terrorism, which is still an important international need, is unfortunately more the problem of some scholars and philosophers than of national security personnel.

Most fields of study progress from a concern with definitions to conceptual issues, and then on to classification and typology building (e.g., Denzin 1978; Mannheim and Rich 1986; Babbie 2001). We now move to a discussion of the types of terrorism.

Types of Terrorism

A typology makes distinctions among similar phenomena but also allows some sort of grading or ordering (Bill and Hardgrave 1981, 24). Much like definitions of terrorism, typologies of terrorism have proliferated over the past four decades. One of the earliest typologies of terrorism was developed by Walter (1969). Since then, several typologies have been developed to classify terrorist actions, groups, and individuals (Hacker 1976; Johnson 1982; Mickolus 1981; Mitchell 1985).

Schmid and Jongman (1988), for example, outline roughly ten bases for classifying terrorism. They list five different kinds of international terrorism put forward by various authors, then focus on actor-based, politically oriented, multidimensional, and purpose-based typologies. In terms of groups and individuals, generally, the distinguishing characteristics in typology building are ideology or their reasons for their motivation (see, for example, Hacker 1976; Post 1990).

Schmid and Jongman's first typology (actor based) distinguishes between state and nonstate actors. The second (politically oriented) differentiates between terrorism from above and below, and analyzes right-wing versus left-wing terrorism. The third (multidimensional) subsumes distinctions based on Thorton's (1964) and Bell's (1978) work. Not surprisingly, the authors conclude "one of the problems with typology building is the absence of a commonly agreed-upon definition of terrorism."

Flemming, Stohl, and Schmid (1988) have located fifty typologies, which they condense into four categories: terrorist groups, motivations, method of operation or their targets, and historical origins.

Finally, White, in a sobering tone, has suggested, "No matter how you decide to arrange the categories, you still cover the same ground" (2002, 209). However, he may be on shaky grounds when he concludes, "Therefore, it is probably best to consider a typology that helps provide a long-term criminological analysis" (White 2003, 210). There are a great number of problems with typologies. Some of the more important problems are: they can provide little connection to theory-building; they exclude exceptions; they can be conceptually confusing; they may be too general; and they're based on changing phenomena. If definitions are problematic, so then are typologies, which are context specific (bounded by time, culture, geography). Consequently, many typologies have minimum relevance. Nevertheless, one of the most relevant distinctions separates terrorist groups from guerrilla organizations.

What is the difference between a terrorist group and a guerrilla organization?

Members of guerrilla organizations typically reside in the countryside and work for many years to gain the trust of the people (typically peasants) living there. They have the support of the rural population and do not engage in indiscriminate attacks against citizens. This was the approach of Mao Tse-tung with the communist revolution in China, Che Guevara and Fidel Castro in the Cuban revolution, the Viet Cong in the Vietnamese revolution, and the Sandinistas in the Nicaraguan revolution. Although the aforementioned groups' tactics may resemble those of terrorists, it is not their intent to create fear among the local population (Ross and Gurr 1986). Guerrilla warfare or political insurgency may transfer to urban areas, thus the term "urban-guerrilla" warfare, but once again, the main approach is not to use terrorism against civilians.

What is the difference between terrorism and political assassination?

While the attempt to create fear lies at the core of terrorism, and terrorists certainly assassinate people, political or "pure" assassination is slightly different. It is usually "a politically motivated killing in which the victims are selected because of the expected political impact of their dying" (Turk 1982, 82). Although assassination is part of the arsenal of techniques used by terrorists, pure assassination is an attempt to eliminate a person and not necessarily an effort to strike fear into the citizens of a country (Ross 2003, 62–63).

Mickolus typology

The most popular, flexible, and useful typology is the one developed by Mickolus (1981), which is generally used by the State Department, Central Intelligence Agency (CIA), and numerous academics.

Mickolus distinguishes four types of political terrorism—interstate, domestic, state, and international/transnational—based on degrees of government control, direction or influence and whether nationals/citizens of more than one state are involved, as either perpetrators or victims (Mickolus 1981) (see exhibit box 3).

Exhibit Box 3
Typology of political terrorism

Nationals/citizens of one state or more involved?		
	Yes	No
No	international/ transnational	domestic
State controlled?		
Yes	interstate/ state sponsored	state

To begin with, *interstate terrorism*—also referred to as "state-sponsored" terrorism or "surrogate warfare"—is carried out by individuals or groups controlled or supported by a country, involving nationals of more than one state (for example, consider Libya's role in the downing of Pan Am Flight 103 over Lockerbie, Scotland, in December 1988).[2] What constitutes state support? This means that the government is giving resources, usually finances, sometimes safe haven, and at other times intelligence, to terrorists. Usually the help is a matter of degree; some groups receive a considerable amount of support, while others receive hardly any.

Domestic terrorism, on the other hand, is carried on by autonomous nonstate actors (i.e., they are not acting on behalf of a foreign government), takes place in their country of origin, is motivated by indigenous causes, and attacks domestic targets (the activities of the Irish Republican Army in Northern Ireland provide a good example). One of the deadliest spates of domestic terrorism in recent times has been in Algeria, where so-called Islamic extremists have been trying to overthrow the government. Since 1992, some 75,000 people have been killed, either by the terrorists or by the government (Hoffman 1998, 37).

State terrorism defines actions taken by a government against actual, suspected, or symbolic dissidents and/or opponents to the regime (as in death squads in Brazil or El Salvador). Usually this consists of the combined tactics of assassination, kidnapping, and death-squad activity (Ross 2000a; 2000b).[3]

International and transnational terrorism are carried out by autonomous non state actors and affect nationals of at least two states (when in 1972, for example, the Palestinian terrorist group Black September traveled to Munich, kidnapped, and then killed Israeli athletes).[4]

If we examine these distinctions closely, we notice that there are basically two types of terrorism: state and oppositional. The former refers to violent, fear-inducing actions by the government of a country and/or its bureaucracy, while the latter refers to similar activities targeted *against* the state or against interests allied with the state or existing government.

Why Does Terrorism Change?

None of the aforementioned types of terrorism are totally exclusive or static. There are three interdependent or complementary reasons to explain why terrorism changes: morphing, life cycles, and waves.

1. Morphing

Often a pattern develops, whereby state terrorism leads to domestic terrorism, which in turn leads to international terrorism. This pattern, which I call morphing, describes the status of groups and countries where terrorism has persisted. For example, shortly after the establishment of the state of Israel (1948), its army's violent actions against the Palestinian population led to Palestinian terrorism, which contributed to the internationalization of Palestinian political violence to gain publicity for their struggle (Chomsky 1983).[5] Similarly, in many Central American countries (such as Nicaragua and El Salvador), government oppression against workers and peasants led to the formation of guerrilla groups during the 1980s. These organizations, in turn, used terrorist tactics against the military (Chace 1984).

Terrorist groups often shift from committing domestic operations to orchestrating international incidents because the latter attracts more attention, publicity, recognition, and larger audiences. Moving its activities abroad may also help a terrorist organization minimize or avoid detection or capture, create additional fear beyond its traditional base of operations, garner more resources, obtain easier access to vulnerable targets, and ultimately could help the group achieve its objectives more quickly.

2. Life Cycles

We should also understand that many terrorist groups also have what we can conceptualize as a life cycle. This has implications for their actions, goals, activities, and changes in their membership. Terrorist organizations mature, becoming more sophisticated over time; unless their ranks have not been decimated by arrests, deaths, or disaffection. Terrorist groups typically get better at what they do particularly because they learn from their successes and failures. In sum, new members join the organization, commit violent actions, get arrested, burn out, settle down, and mature out of terrorism.

Both morphing and the cyclical nature of terrorism can occur not only at the group level, but also on a geographic level, incorporating both countries and regions alike. Naturally, these two concepts frustrate our attempts to understand and combat terrorism.

3. Waves

According to Rapoport (2003), over the past 120 years, there have been four waves of terrorism. Each has different causes, tactics, and reasons for decline. In his summary, he notes that "In the 1880s, an initial 'anarchist wave' appeared that continued for some 40 years. Its successor, the 'anti-colonial wave,' began in the 1920s and by the 1960s had largely disappeared. The late 1960s witnessed the birth of the 'new left wave,' which dissipated largely in the 1990s, leaving a few groups still active in Sri Lanka, Spain, France, Peru, and Colombia. The fourth, or 'religious wave' began in 1979, and if it follows the patterns of its predecessors, it still has twenty to twenty-five years to run" (Rapoport 2003, 37). He equates this with a "human lifecycle pattern, where dreams that inspire fathers lose their attractiveness for sons. Clearly, the life-cycle of the waves does not correspond to those of organizations. Organizations normally dissipate before the wave does, though sometimes an organization survives its associated wave. . . . By way of comparison, the average life of organizations in the third or new left wave is two years" (Rapoport 2003, 37).

On the surface, Rapoport's explanation makes sense, but not every time frame conforms to the description or criteria. For example, both the Irish and Palestinian struggles that have resorted to terrorism have lasted considerably longer than twenty-five years; the Irish movement has its origins in the 1800s, and the Palestinian in the partition of Palestine in 1948.

Hewitt's waves of terrorism in the United States

Hewitt (2000), in an attempt to test whether terrorism is fostered because politicians ignore their requests or because they pander to them, identifies four waves of terrorism in America: southern White Supremacists (1955–1972); Black militants (1965–1974); revolutionary/left-wing terrorism (1969–1977); and anti-abortionists (1977–1995). "Based on the American experience," Hewitt says, "sustained outbreaks of terrorism are associated with the existence of a substantial body of sympathizers and supporters. In all the four cases examined, a sizable number of people felt very strongly about some social/political issue—segregation, racial equality, the Vietnam war, abortion—and also felt that the political system ignored, or was hostile to, their concerns" (2000, 338–39).

Weinberg and Pedahzur's conditions for change

Finally, Weinberg and Pedahzur (2003) have outlined the conditions under which terrorist groups suspend violent activities and join or form political parties. Through an analysis of selected terrorist groups such as the Irish Republican Army (IRA), Euskadi Ta Askatasuna ([Basque Homeland and Liberty] ETA), and the African National Congress (ANC), they suggest that "transformation in the prevailing political order," "state repression," "the problems of clandestinely," and "government amnesty" are major factors that encourage this practice (21). Weinberg and Pedahzur demonstrate that political parties and terrorist organization share many similarities in their decision making and practices and that part of eradicating terrorism may be through helping terrorist organizations to engage in more political party type behaviors.

Now that we have explored the range of types of terrorism, we are going to delimit the subject matter of this text even further to focus on oppositional political terrorism, the subject of disproportionate media, governmental, and scholarly attention.[6]

Problems with Research on Terrorism[7]

Information on terrorism is located in a variety of sources (i.e., newspapers, popular magazines, private security trade journals, mercenary/soldier of fortune magazines, academic journals, private consultant reports, government documents and publications, chapters in edited books on terrorism, chapters in introductory texts on terrorism, and books about individuals and organizations that have engaged in terrorism). These mediums vary in the quality of analysis and breadth of coverage. Upon examining the scholarly literature, in particular, one is struck by the number of positive achievements as well as by the drawbacks of certain avenues of investigation in this area of research.

In general, the research on oppositional terrorism seems copious and equally balanced among the different ideological interpretations of terrorism; scholars have examined both left-wing and right-wing groups with relatively equal interest. These merits aside, upon closer examination, the work is also riddled with problems. Periodically, academics, activists, and informed observers have written critiques of the field of terrorism research (see, for example, Gurr 1988b; Herman 1982).

Many of these issues can be categorized as definitional and conceptual, ideological, theoretical, or methodological problems. Some of these difficulties were, at the time of their writing, fundamental stepping-stones in research. Others have become drawbacks over time simply because we have not transcended them.

Definitional and Conceptual Problems

The research on terrorism is plagued by a lack of consistent definition, by overinclusivity, and by the exclusion of state-sponsored incidents from case studies.

Often, the same (so-called) culprits are repeatedly referred to as "terrorists" by some scholars and commentators and their actions labeled as "terrorism" (Bell 1977). Some of these groups (such as the Industrial Workers of the World, skinheads, Jewish Defense League, etc.) are not necessarily terrorist organizations, but rather are political, racist, ethnic, nationalist, or religious groups in which a minority of their members—often without leadership or group approval—engage in acts of terrorism. Unfortunately, no evidence exists to suggest that the actions of such groups meet the definitional criteria of terrorism (see exhibit box 4).

Exhibit Box 4
Are all skinheads racist?
Skinheads are easy to identify because they typically shave their heads, wear padded army fatigue jackets, and black Doc Marten–style boots. Some are clearly racist, as evidenced by their speech, tattoos, and actions, while others are not. Suggesting that all skinheads are the same (that is, racist) does other individuals who choose this kind of dress a disservice. An examination of the origins of the skinhead phenomenon should put to rest the perception that all skinheads are racist. The founding devotees of this subculture are often referred to as "hardcore." When it became clear that racists numbered among their ranks, some skinheads formed an organization called Skinheads Against Racial Prejudice (SHARPS). The media and some scholars, however, appeared to focus disproportionately on the racist skinheads that frequented skinhead venues like concerts, thus contributing to a generalized perception that all skinheads are racist (Wood 1999).

This problem extends to confusing umbrella organizations and political parties with terrorist groups. For example, contrary to the popular belief, the Palestinian Liberation Organization (PLO) is not a terrorist organization. It is better understood as a governing body of various Palestinian factions, ranging from educational and health-related bodies to the more military wings like al-Fatah, the Popular Front for the Liberation of Palestine, and General Command. Likewise, the IRA organization refers both to a political division and a military wing: the military/terrorist wing is the Provisional Irish Republican Army (PIRA).

Also problematic is the tendency to equate nationalities with terrorism. While nationality is a relevant factor, other important background characteristics may be more important in determining the identities of terrorists. Granted, a considerable amount of terrorism has been conducted by nationalist-inspired groups. For example, the Armenian struggle to avenge the genocide of over a million Armenians at the hands of the Turkish Army during World War I has been one of the primary motives of the terrorist organization known as the Armenian Secret Army for the Liberation of Armenia (ASALA) and the Justice Commandos for Armenian Genocide (JCAG). Similarly, Sikh terrorism has historically been conducted by Dal Khalsa.[8]

However, if we identify specific nationalities as terrorists, we run into a problem of unnecessarily fueling prejudices (subtle or overt), including profiling, stereotyping, or infusing racism and bias into our identification and decision making. Not every person from Latin America, for example, is a narco-terrorist, nor is each Muslim or Palestinian a terrorist (Shaheen 1984). Unfortunately, there have been many recent examples of such loose categories being used in counterterrorist security programs. Poorly constructed and ineptly applied, these classifications are often little better than stereotypes or, worse, profiling—particularly in the wake of 9/11 with the use of large-scale security screening at airports and border crossings.

Moreover, many terrorist organizations include members from diverse nationalities. Thus, focusing on one nationality to the exclusion of others may prevent antiterrorist agencies from properly scrutinizing appropriate suspects. Finally, categorically linking a nation to terrorist organizations may tend to imply, for some, that citizens of certain countries condone terrorist actions. Similarly, some researchers, not to mention the mass media, call many actions "terrorism" and groups that are simply nationalist in origin "terrorists."

Further, some authors (Johnpoll 1976; Gurr 1989) tend to lump diverse events, individuals, and groups who engaged in alleged and actual criminal activity with terrorism. Many of the actions that these individuals and organizations committed were distasteful, yet permissible under the existing laws of the day.

Additionally, sensationalistic and emotional language often undermines the objectivity of some research and literature. Writing like this can produce unnecessary and misdirected fears. Furthermore, there is an abundance of research on counterterrorism measures against international terrorism and a lack of research on domestic terrorism (e.g., Clawson 1989). The fact that the public believes the number of international acts of terrorism is greater than domestic incidents is most likely due to heightened publicity, fear of strangers, particularly since the media often fails to make these complex distinctions.

Finally, some researchers appear to be fixated with classifying the types of terrorist groups, but with little consensus among the different typologies. For example, Homer (1983) suggests classification of nationalist, international, and intimidating groups. Harris (1987) proposes white leftists, Puerto Rican leftists, black militants, right-wing extremists, and Jewish extremists. Gurr (1988b) advocates vigilante, insurgent, transnational, and state divisions. Alternatively, White (1991) outlines foreign, revolutionary nationalist, ideological left, ideological right, and criminal groups using terrorist tactics (167).

The usefulness of any of these typologies becomes questionable when we recognize that many of the terrorist groups can and do fit into more than one category. Many analysts also neglect to mention that group membership or claims of responsibility for an action may very well be posturing on the part of the alleged culprits. Similarly, individuals and groups unconnected with terrorist organizations may conduct acts of violence and claim responsibility in the name of the terrorist group, thus convincing the public, media, and authorities that a "legitimate" terrorist group committed the act and adding to the impression that a particular terrorist group is larger, more sophisticated, or better organized than it truly is. Most importantly, the majority of this typology building or classification is not related to theory building, which is generally the most common reason for typology construction.

In response to these problems, there should be a conscious attempt to minimize over- and underinclusivity as well as mere repetition of broadly acknowledged information. A consensus definition of terrorism (e.g., Schmid 1983) would be part of the solution. This definition would have to be amenable to academics, criminal justice and national security practitioners, and legislators and would help in the accurate identification of acts of terrorism and terrorists. So, too, would an effort by researchers to conduct proper literature searches and reviews. Rehashing information that has already been disseminated does not adequately further the development of terrorism studies. Researchers should make a concerted attempt to understand that typology building is not an end in itself, but rather a beginning of theoretical development.

Ideological biases

Some of the research in the field of terrorism suffers from an overly liberal or conservative bias and from a neglect of radical or critical perspectives (Ross 1998). As a result, the research ignores state or corporate complicity in terrorist acts.

First, while trying to appear balanced, some liberal-minded authors misrepresent the actions of certain groups. For example, Vetter and Perlstein (1991, 63) outline "Pro-Life and Pro-Choice Activists" in one of their terrorist categories, but describe only the former's bombing activities while neglecting to mention any actions taken by the latter. Moreover, to date, there has been no evidence of pro-choice activists engaging in terrorist acts as defined here.

Second, most current research reflects a narrow conservative perspective. In many instances the research is done by individuals who work for government organizations or who thrive in private consulting firms working on contract for government agencies. This material is published in either academic journals (e.g., Monroe 1982; Tierney 1977), larger compendiums on terrorism (Stohl 1990), or government reports. This type of research serves a variety of purposes ranging from public education to public relations and propaganda. For example, in October 1987, the FBI's entire *Law Enforcement Bulletin* was devoted to terrorism. Much of the content, however, simply justified the organization's policy decisions and targeting practices. Citing the agency's success in thwarting terrorist actions is too often self-serving instead of illuminating.

Third, much of the liberal and conservative literature rarely mentions corporate or government complicity in facilitating acts of terrorism (through state-sponsored terrorism). As far back as the nineteenth century, abundant evidence suggests that the Molly Maguires (an Irish group that practiced terrorism in the United States) were aided by Pinkerton agent provocateurs (Johnpoll 1976, 31). During the late 1950s and early 1960s, anti-Castro Cubans were trained by the CIA (Marchetti and Marks 1974, 108–17). Similarly, the activities of the FBI, the lead agency responsible for gathering data on and for combating domestic terrorism, contributed to Ku Klux Klan terrorist actions against the civil rights movement (Churchill and Vander Wall 1988).

We must be cautious about simplistic analysis, both by experts and activists, including arguments that beat to death the clearly understood fact that states commit the majority of terrorism (Barak 1991; Ross 2000a; 2000b).

Theoretical problems

Research on terrorism does not rigorously deal with the problem of causes and effects, the stock and trade of empirical research. Initially, causes of terrorism in general or with respect to certain groups are marshaled, but do not build upon the work done by other theorists (such as the work by Crenshaw 1981). Much like the work on typologies, this disconnected theorizing about the causes of terrorism creates the perception that research in this area is noncumulative and exists in a theoretical vacuum. At the same time, much of the literature is divorced from the broader work on political violence and crime research.[9] Most theories are monocausal ventures and overly simplistic.

Additionally, declines in the number of terrorist acts are attributed almost solely to counterterrorist initiatives and/or intelligence agency efforts and "special techniques" (Monroe 1982), rather than to decisions made by the terrorists themselves. Like the literature on the causes of terrorism, the work on the decline of terrorism is often not tied to previous research or theories (Ross and Gurr 1989; Crenshaw 1991).

Moreover, and closely related to research on the decline of terrorism, there is a paucity of work on the responses, effects, and outcomes of terrorism. Most analysis done on countering the terrorist threat deals with international terrorist acts and neglects domestic terrorism. Another type of response to terrorism concerns itself with policymaking (for example, Celmer 1987; Farrell 1982). Again, the analysis of policymaking issues is mainly concentrated on international terrorism and rarely on domestic terrorism. With the exceptions of Flynn (1978) and Zwerman (1988), few pieces address the ways in which the "correctional system" responds to terrorists (von Tangen 1988). White, for example, provides an excellent critique of the problems that the FBI counterterrorist establishment faces. He writes:

> The lack of a common approach is complemented by the lack of routinized counterterrorist policies. Although the FBI is officially the lead agency in responding to domestic terrorism, in reality a whole host of law enforcement, national defense, and civilian security bureaucracies have some responsibility. Although many of these agencies have exchanged official rules and procedures for joint operations, the line-level workers usually have no idea what the joint responsibilities are. The FBI has a solid internal management system, but counterterrorism demands multiagency management structures. (White 1991, 163)

Finally, and most importantly, many of the hypotheses advanced are based on questionable or insufficient evidence. Others have not been subjected to testing or secondary analysis, hence perpetuating the noncumulative nature of this type of research. Consider, for example, Johnpoll's (1976) six "lessons . . . drawn" from his review of the history of terrorism in the United States. He suggests that "confrontations of the Weathermen had little effect on the social order" and that "the Weathermen died in a Greenwich Village blast" (42). Unfortunately, he simultaneously overgeneralizes and does not provide evidence to support his claims, nor does he explain nearly a decade's worth of activities carried on by this group under a slightly different name.

Only when theories are developed and tested can the social scientific understanding of terrorism be improved. A better method of analysis might start with the application of common theories and models of political action, political violence, and criminal violence to the process of terrorism.

Methodological problems

Beyond theoretical problems, there are numerous methodological shortcomings to the existing research. The literature is primarily descriptive; there is an overreliance on secondary and state-produced source information; studies suffer from questionable rigor; and there is minimal use of statistical and comparative analysis.

First, the majority of the literature (regardless of the source) is descriptive, content to simply list the various terrorist groups and provide a brief history of the organizations (for example, Bell and Gurr 1979; Gurr 1988a; White 1991, 22–30), rather than analyze and explain data. Similarly, some authors have published only the manifestos of these groups (such as Pearsall 1974) or important documents related to terrorism, and have not provided any interpretation or analysis of the content. The end result is that there is little systematic analysis of the internal dynamics of terrorist organizations, their causes, and the effects of these actions upon their targets.

Such investigation is necessary in order to place terrorism in its proper political, social, economic, and historical contexts, as well as to institute better methods of prevention and response. Researchers need to go beyond the descriptive data currently assembled and engage in theory development and testing. When the research and policymaking community reaches a point where it discovers that we do not have the available data, then and only then should we return to collect descriptive data.

Second, with the exception of a limited number of case studies, most of the research uses secondary source material (e.g., media accounts and government documents). Moreover, those efforts that do involve primary data are questionable in terms of their validity and reliability. Presently the research and policymaking community does not have an abundance of "thick descriptive" primary source information, such as Bell's (1997) and Chaliand's (1983) work on terrorist organizations, which rely upon observation and interviews with terrorists. This, of course, presupposes that terrorists themselves would grant access or that law enforcement would allow contact (other than prosecutors and defense counsel) to terrorists once caught. Additionally, we have very few insider accounts (such as autobiographies) of terrorists.

Third, there is a shortage of rigorously performed and publicly available case studies of individuals and organizations that have engaged in terrorist activities and terrorist acts. By underutilizing the case-study method, the research and policymaking community limits discussion of firsthand accounts of terrorists. Many well-known groups such as the New World Liberation Front, May 19 Communist Organization, United Freedom Front/Unit, Armed Resistance Unit, American Nazi Party, and anti-Castro Cuban groups have been ignored for case-study analysis. Even less work has been done on individual terrorists. Although the external validity (i.e., ability to generalize or experimenter bias) of case studies has often been criticized (most case studies have been done only on those terrorists who have been caught, hence biasing the representativeness of the sample—only "unsuccessful" terrorists are included) these shortcomings can be overcome by developing several case studies or by using "analytic induction" to deal with the problem of generalizability (Denzin 1978).

Fourth, with the exception of organizations such as Risk's International and the RAND Corporation, most of the marshaled statistics are derived from government-sponsored databases (or data sets) such as annual reports like the *FBI's Uniform Crime Reports Bomb Summary* or *FBI Analysis of Terrorist Incidents and Terrorist Related Activities in the United States* (started in 1977). This problem persists despite the fact that, in addition to the Department of Homeland Security and big-city police departments with their own intelligence sections, there are several federal agencies with an interest in monitoring terrorism in the United States: the FBI, the CIA, Customs, the Department of State, and the Defense Department.

FBI statistics are problematic. In this vein, Stinson (1984) argues:

> Local police agencies almost always constitute the first force responding to a terrorist incident. In addition, local police agencies often must confront criminals who are using terrorist tactics, even though these incidents are not classified as terrorism by the FBI. Despite the Bureau's mandate, confusion seems to exist about the roles of the various law enforcement agencies with regard to terrorism. Policymakers need to define the functions of local, state, and federal agencies in responses to terrorism. (quoted in White 1991, 168–69)

Another problem is that the FBI's reports have "failed to account for many terrorist incidents because the classification system was skewed" (White 1991, 170). This led, for example, to data on abortion-clinic bombings, which occurred primarily during the 1980s and 1990s, being picked up by the Alcohol, Tobacco, and Firearms (ATF) division of statistics rather than by the FBI. Although in 1986 "the FBI formalized and limited its definition of terrorism" (White 1991, 170), "local and state law enforcement agencies are not required to abide by that definition . . . [and] there are no clear criteria for categorizing criminal actions under the terrorist rubric. Even the FBI classifies some terrorist actions as common crimes" (White 1991, 163).

Fifth, we lack nonpartisan data sets assembled from nongovernmental agencies and nonpartisan organizations (for example, the media). While the RAND Corporation has established its own terrorism events database (see Hoffman 1987), little has progressed since Karber's observation that "we lack . . . the accepted statistical base . . . necessary for identification" (1971, 521). He notes differences between the National Bomb Data Center's statistics "and those compiled earlier by the Permanent Subcommittee on Investigations of the Senate Committee on Government Operations" and the ATF. The differences lie in "distinguishing explosive . . . from incendiaries" (that is, between bombs and something that is flammable) and the "means of data collection" (522). According to Karber, "The development and refinement of consistent coding criteria would not only facilitate the study of terrorism in varying urban environments but would also permit cross-national comparison" (533).

Sixth, regardless of the data source, much of the research avoids statistical analysis. Those investigators who do cite statistics often do so with little interpretation (for example, Monroe 1982). Almost all authors who present data use descriptive rather than inferential statistics. Thus, theory testing is kept to a minimum.

Seventh, there is a lack of comparative (geographical and historical) approaches to the study of terrorism, whether at the national, regional, state, group, or individual level. And most authors who conduct comparative studies do so only at the descriptive level. Intra- and inter-country comparisons of terrorist groups, if theory-driven, would help us refine causal theories as well as contribute to effects-based theories.

Techniques that could mitigate some of these difficulties include the use of rigorously developed questionnaires administered to snow-ball samples (using available subjects for initial study) of terrorists. The data are then analyzed to determine the relative explanatory potential of commonly held theories on terrorism and crime activity (Hamm 1992). Additional techniques include the development of biographies of terrorists through newspaper accounts, autobiographies, and historical accounts of individuals supplemented by governmental-agency data provided on request (e.g., Handler, 1990), and the assembly of data from nontraditional sources, such as the National Abortion Foundation (e.g., Wilson and Lynxwiler 1988). Only when a conscious attempt to analyze terrorism in a systematic social-scientific fashion is approached will the research and policymaking community better understand terrorism and encourage its decline or fashion effective risk-management to address its occurrence.

Finally, the study of terrorism has become profitable for a number of entities, including many of our cultural industries (Schiller 1989). Both Herman and O'Sullivan (1989) and Livingstone (1990) have written books that are critical of this phenomenon. Herman and O'Sullivan (1989) criticize the agendas of individuals who conduct research on terrorism; not only do Herman and O'Sullivan focus on the industry that this form of political violence has spawned, but they also try to look at the "ideology and ideological management . . . because the industry is designed to develop, refine, and disseminate" the terrorist threat. Similarly, Livingstone (1990) criticizes the motivations of individuals who conduct research on terrorism and those organizations that provide consulting advice. In particular, he has difficulties with well-known counterterrorist (C-T) organizations, popular responses, and renegade operators in the fight against international terrorism; people running their own counterterrorist schools and services; and the popular reaction to terrorism and the hype surrounding these facets.

Conclusion

This chapter has outlined the different definitional and conceptual issues confronting individuals who wish to understand terrorism. It also reviewed the various typologies of terrorism and settled on an analytic schema for later use to easily distinguish among the different types (see Mickolus 1981).

Some of the pitfalls of the early literature on terrorism were inevitable since it was produced when few studies of this form of political violence and crime had been published. When researchers became interested in the phenomenon of terrorism as an area of research, there was little understanding of its nature, incidence, causes, method of study, or utility. Consequently, there was a certain confusion as to where terrorism belonged in academic research. These early studies reflected the embryonic state of the field.

However, some of the problems prevalent in the early studies are still very much present in much of the literature of today. To increase the coherence of the study of terrorism—both as a field and as a part of the broader disciplines of political violence, behavior, and crime—we need to deal systematically with the problems discussed in this chapter.

Questions, Chapter 1

PART ONE: MULTIPLE CHOICE

Circle the letter of the most appropriate answer.

1. What are two basic types of terrorism?
   a. state
   b. congressional
   c. b and d
   d. oppositional
   e. a and d

2. What is a synonym for interstate terrorism?
   a. state-sponsored
   b. domestic
   c. international
   d. transnational
   e. genocide

3. Who suggested that terrorists can be divided into three types of perpetrators?
   a. Ross
   b. Hacker
   c. Schmid
   d. Mickolus
   e. Hoffman

4. The terrorist bombing of the Federal Building in Oklahoma is an example of
   a. state terrorism
   b. transnational terrorism
   c. domestic terrorism
   d. international terrorism
   e. revolutionary terrorism

5. Which of the following is an example of state terrorism?
   a. death squads in Brazil
   b. the beating of Rodney King
   c. an attack by al-Fatah against the state of Israel
   d. all of the above
   e. none of the above

6. Who developed the distinction among terrorists as either being criminals, crazies, or crusaders?
   a. Hacker
   b. Mickolus
   c. Ross
   d. Schmid
   e. Tenent

7. In order to have a complete understanding of terrorism, researchers should adopt what kind of approach?
   a. dynamic
   b. policy-based
   c. normative
   d. multidisciplinary
   e. all the above

8. Which ideological group of terrorists would like to restore things, society, and politics to the way they were in the past?
   a. right-wing
   b. separatist
   c. left-wing
   d. extremist
   e. none of the above

9. Which ideological group of terrorists would like to abolish private property?
   a. right-wing
   b. separatist
   c. left-wing
   d. extremist
   e. none of the above

10. Among the following, what type of political crime has been most popularly studied since the 1970s?
    a. assassination
    b. internal war
    c. revolution
    d. state violence
    e. terrorism

11. Who developed a consensus definition of terrorism?
    a. Ross
    b. Tilly
    c. Schmid
    d. Taylor
    e. Mickolus

12. What year was the Palestinian Liberation Organization formed?
    a. 1934
    b. 1945
    c. 1964
    d. 1970
    e. 1980

13. Terrorism is a subset of
    a. political violence
    b. political crime
    c. criminal violence
    d. all of the above
    e. some of the above

14. What is Mickolus credited with?
    a. developing the first causal model of terrorism
    b. outlining a useful typology of terrorism
    c. analyzing the effects of terrorism
    d. calling into question gray-area phenomena
    e. none of the above

15. Why is labeling groups "terrorists" problematic?
    a. it could be a subtle form of racism
    b. rarely do labels stick
    c. because not all parts of the organization may engage in political violence
    d. no research has been done on this subject
    e. all of the above

PART TWO: SHORT ANSWER

1. In the context of terrorism, what are the differences between criminals, crazies, and crusaders?

2. Provide a detailed outline of Mickolus's typology.

3. Why would a terrorist organization shift from committing domestic terrorism to international terrorism?

4. How did Schmid develop his definition of terrorism?

5. List three different types of terrorism groups identified by Post.

6. What are three problems identified by Sederberg with creating a definition of terrorism?

7. List four characteristics of domestic terrorism.

8. Explain the concept of morphing in the context of terrorism.

9. What are two ways that terrorism has changed since the 1990s?

10. What is a terrorologist?

11. What are four different types of terrorism?

12. Are all skinheads racist?

PART THREE: ESSAY

Present a logical argument with supporting facts that takes into consideration multiple interpretations. Answer in paragraph form. Be as specific and detailed as possible; avoid generalizations.

1. What do you consider to be the most important problem in defining terrorism and why?

2. What is wrong with identifying terrorists simply by their nationality?

3. What things have changed over the past decade that may have a bearing on any explanation of terrorism?

4. Why would a terrorist organization shift from committing domestic terrorism to international terrorism?

5. How can a left-wing terrorist organization also be a nationalist-separatist group at the same time?

6. Given what you have learned already, what is the best way to counter terrorism?

7. Is there a relationship among the different types of terrorism and why?

CHAPTER TWO

Tracing the Historical Trajectory and Contemporary Trends

Terrorism is not a new phenomenon. This chapter outlines three dominant periods in the history of terrorism, then subdivides the last time frame into four further blocks. We'll then discuss how researchers (government or academic) go about studying terrorism, breaking down their work into qualitative and quantitative research. We'll conclude with a review of trends in terrorism, covering changes that have occurred over the past four decades in terms of number of incidents, types of actions, kinds of targets, regional dispersion, and groups that have evolved.

Oppositional political terrorism has occurred since the dawn of human history. But the nature of this type of political violence and crime has changed over time, evolving from localized and domestic activities to regional and international events (Weinberg and Davis 1989, chapter 2). Consequently, terrorism has become an experience shared by many individuals, organizations, and states.

Before continuing, however, why is studying the history of terrorism important? We can identify nine interrelated reasons:

1. We can observe trends in terrorist groups, tactics, and strategies over time.

2. It provides a context in which we can understand the phenomenon.

3. It might help the majority population of a country better understand the minority.

4. It makes citizens, governments, and researchers more sensitive to the needs of their constituencies and groups beyond national borders.

5. We can see what types of people and organizations commit terrorism, which allows us to understand why they feel the need to engage in terrorism.

6. If the past predicts or somehow acts as a guide to the future, then the study of history provides a basis from which to develop and test theories of cause and of appropriate levels of response or prevention.

7. It could help us determine, to a limited extent, the scope, nature, and intensity of terrorism.

8. We might be better able to respond in a rational fashion and perhaps implement more effective policies and practices.

9. It demonstrates that terrorism is not a new phenomenon.

In short, studying the history of terrorism will guard against the well-used expression: "Those who forget the past are destined to repeat it." By the same token, we must be cautious about thinking that, in an absolute sense, history repeats itself.

Nevertheless, historical analyses must be treated cautiously. Most historical explanations are a summary of lots of names, dates, and places; facts that have been assembled elsewhere. This perhaps explains why many historical analyses are often perceived by many students to be unnecessarily boring or overwhelming. Additionally, the history of terrorism can become confusing because many of the names of individuals and groups—particularly if the organization goes by an acronym—sound similar. In short, there are three basic periods of terrorism: ancient, modern, and contemporary.

Ancient Terrorism

The earliest time frame, the ancient one, encompasses the period covering 66–1870 AD. Two major groups were active in the ancient period:

the Sicarri and the Assassins. Some of the more notable features of these groups, when compared to contemporary terrorist organizations, includes that these "lasted longer," they were "responsible for much greater destruction," and they were "more religious in character" (Taylor 1988, 38).

1. The Sicarri

Originating in 66 AD, the Sicarri were a religious sect active in the Jewish zealots' struggle in Palestine (modern-day Israel) against the Roman occupation. The group took its name from the word "sica, the short sword that was the favorite weapon of the sect members" (Vetter and Perlstein 1991, 30). The Sicarri were extremist, nationalist, and anti-Roman: "Their victims, both in Palestine and outside, were moderates, the Jewish peace party" (Laqueur 1977, 7–8). They destroyed the house of Anaias, the high priest, the palaces of the Herodian dynasts, and the public archives (Laqueur 1977, 7–8). The Sicarri ceased activity in 73 AD (Rapoport and Alexander 1983; Rapoport 1988).

2. The Assassins

The Assassins began to use terrorist tactics in 1090. They were a relatively small Islamic sect, originally based in Persia (modern-day Iran and Iraq), later spreading to Syria. The Assassins "defended their religious autonomy (and way of life) against the Seljuqus [essentially a Turkish dynasty] who wanted to suppress them" (Laqueur 1977, 8–9). They killed "prefects, governors, caliphs" (Laqueur 1977, 8) and one of the kings of Jerusalem. In the thirteenth century they were suppressed by the Mongols.

Their name derived from *Hashashim*, the Arabic word for hashish eaters. The Assassins used to smoke hashish, the resin from marijuana plants, to get high before committing acts of terrorism (Vetter and Perlstein 1991, 30), which is not too different from many contemporary criminals who are high or intoxicated while committing a murder or robbery. The Assassins ceased their activities in 1275 AD.

Modern Terrorism

The second historical stage in terrorism took place roughly between 1871 and 1960. Several organizations—the majority of which had leftist sentiments and fleeting existences—began their activities in this period (See Exhibit Box 5 for a distinction among socialism, communism and anarchism). Groups that operated in this era include, but are not limited to: the Narodnaya Volya, anarchist groups, the Social Revolutionary Party, and radical nationalist-separatist groups in Ireland and Armenia.

1. Narodnaya Volya

The Narodnaya Volya ("People's Will") operated in Russia between 1878 and 1881. They assassinated government, political, and military officials. However, most of the members (former university students frustrated with autocratic political leadership) were eventually arrested, and consequently this group faded as a potent force in Russian politics (Wardlaw 1982; Laqueur 1977, 11–12).

2. Anarchists

These individuals and groups are opposed to organized government and private property. Some of them engaged in political terrorism and other kinds of political violence and crime between the 1880s and 1930s in France, Spain, Italy, and the United States. They attempted several assassinations and, in some cases, were successful in taking the lives of kings, presidents, prime ministers, leading statesmen, judges, and chiefs of police. An attack was mainly the work of a single individual often referred to as a "lone wolf." Anarchists generated considerable attention and "helped to create an impression of an international conspiracy which in fact did not exist" (Wardlaw 1982, 21–22).

In the United States, one of the earliest anarchist incidents was in connection with the May 1886 Haymarket Square Riot in Chicago, in which a bomb was detonated during a labor demonstration, killing eight police officers and four protesters, and injuring one hundred other individuals present (Avrich 1986). More dramatic, however, was the 1901 assassination of then-president William McKinley. This incident "marked the end of anarchist political murder in the western democracies. Anarchism survived as a movement in Russia until World War I, and in Spain until the beginning of World War II" (Vetter and Perlstein 1991, 36), but internationally it became more associated with the trade union movement. In 1905, American anarchists were able to form the International Workers of the World (also known as the Wobblies), which pressed for labor reforms. The common image of an anarchist terrorist was that of an individual dressed in black with short black hair, beady eyes, and a beard.

3. The Social Revolutionary Party

The Social Revolutionary Party, another Russian terrorist organization, was formed in 1902. This group wanted to overthrow the czar (the Russian equivalent to a king) and was responsible for assassinating a large number of prominent individuals. In October 1905, when the czar announced the creation of the Duma (the legislative assembly), the Social Revolutionaries suspended terrorist activities. However, the group resumed its attacks in January 1906, when the Duma officially opened, and once more renewed their violent actions when the Duma was dissolved in July 1906. The Social Revolutionary Party finally stopped activities in 1911 (Laqueur 1977, 12, 41; Wardlaw 1982, 19).

Exhibit Box 5
The differences between socialism, communism, and anarchism
In general, socialism advocates greater state (government) control of the economy. This includes state-run businesses, which run the gamut from airlines to factories to agricultural production. Under socialism, citizens have universal access to health care and education. Political leadership positions are elected and/or appointed. Socialism, as envisioned by Karl Marx, was seen as a step along the road to communism.
Communism, originally conceived by Marx and later modified by Lenin, involves almost complete state control of the economy and of most facets of life. A small elite group often referred to as "the politburo" runs the affairs of state. Leadership positions are generally appointed.
Anarchism is a condition whereby no state exists, and decisions are typically made on an ad-hoc basis through the process of consensus. Few societies currently operate in this manner. Exceptions include Mondragon Cooperative (Spain) and Quaker society (also known as the Society of Friends) which make decisions using collectivist principles. In the United States, it is legal to be a socialist or communist, but in some jurisdictions it is illegal to be an anarchist. Additionally, if you are a foreigner entering the United States and consider yourself an anarchist or a member of an anarchist organization, you must declare yourself as such to the Immigration and Naturalization Service. Failure to do so could result in a criminal charge.

4. Nationalist-Separatist Groups

Several nationalist-separatist organizations used terrorism during the modern period. Three dominant groups resorted to this type of political crime: the Chinese, the Irish, and the Armenians. Other nationalist or separatist organizations using terrorism after World War I were sometimes successful in assuming power and leadership of their respective states, and ceased operations afterward.

A small, but noteworthy group is the Boxers. At the end of the nineteenth century (after 1895) the colonial powers of Austria, France, Great Britain, Italy, Japan, and Russia were dominating China both economically and militarily. Both the Chinese peasantry and monarchy felt demoralized by this situation. In time a group of peasants skilled in the martial arts organized the "Society of Righteous Fists" (more popularly known as the Boxers). This secret group (or triad) thought they had magical powers that would allow them to stop "foreign" bullets. Not only did they want to drive the foreigners out of China, but they also wanted to overthrow the imperial dynasty. The Chinese Empress Dowager Tsu His skillfully manipulated the Boxers to attack the foreigners. Starting in 1900, Boxers in the countryside terrorized Christian missionaries, converts, and other foreigners. As they gained strength and thousands of followers, they moved to urban areas. When they got to Peking (now known as Beijing), the capital where many foreigners lived, they were in a standoff. Although the foreigners were eventually saved, the movement continued and later contributed to the Boxer Rebellion in 1905 (Preston 2001). The Boxers "contributed substantially to the nationalist movement headed by Sun Yat-sen" (Vetter and Perlstein 1991, 31).[1]

In 1172 King Henry II of England gained control of Irish lands, and over the next five centuries increased British control over the Irish territory. *Irish nationalist terrorism* began as early as 1791, partly due to agrarian unrest. The Irish have since then been struggling to make Great Britain leave the island of Ireland. In 1791, both "Catholics and Protestants joined in the rebellion. The rebellion failed, but this uprising set the stage for the formation of the Irish Republican Brotherhood, also known by the Gaelic name Fenians, in 1858 . . . the Brotherhood, committed to a violent overthrow of British rule, engaged in various acts of violence and terrorism" (Vetter and Perlstein 1991, 11).

In the 1870s and 1880s an offshoot called "the Dynamiters" bombed selected targets in English cities, while another group known as the Irish National Invincibles (or Invincibles for short) assassinated two leading British politicians in Phoenix Park, Dublin, in 1882. After that incident, "several decades of calm" followed "with new upsurges in 1916, 1919–21, before the Second World War and then again in the 1970s" with the birth of the Irish Republican Army (Laqueur 1977, 13). Although the history is complicated, largely as a result of what is called the Easter Rising on April 24, 1916, Northern Ireland remained occupied by the British: "although the Rising was put down by force, in 1921, the Irish agreed to a treaty that declared independent sovereignty for an Irish Republic composed of twenty-six of the thirty-two counties" (Vetter and Perlstein 1991, 37).[2] (See Exhibit 6)

Armenian nationalist terrorism has mainly been directed toward Turks. After a series of genocides by Turks during World War I—during which about 1.5 million Armenians perished—several groups have engaged in retaliatory terrorism, primarily Armenians in the Baltic states and later in other places around the world. The first actions commenced in the 1890s, but this upsurge was short-lived. Further actions by Armenian terrorists took place "in the 1890s, and again after 1918 in the form of assassinations of individual Turkish leaders who had been prominently involved in the massacres of Armenians" during World War I; this kind of activity has "continued sporadically to the present day. In 1975 there was an upsurge of [Armenian] terrorism" (Laqueur 1977, 13).

After World War I, terrorist operations "were mainly conducted by right-wing and nationalist-separatist groups. Sometimes these groups were both right-wing and separatist, as in the case of the Croatian Ustacha, which received most of its support from Fascist Italy and Hungary" (Laqueur 1977, 17). During the 1920s, terrorism was a tactic employed by nascent fascist groups that were emerging throughout Europe in Germany, France, Hungary and Romania (Laqueur 1977, 17). There are several notable examples of nationalist-separatist terrorist groups that operated during this time that later disbanded because they eventually assumed power and leadership of the states they fought to liberate. Some of these groups include the Irgun and Stern Gang during the British occupation of Palestine (1937–1948), EOKA (the National Organization of Cypriot Fighters) in Cyprus (1954–1978), and the National Liberation Front (FLN) in Algeria (1954–1962).

Map of United Kingdom

Exhibit 6

Contemporary Terrorism

The period between 1960 and the present can be called contemporary terrorism. Since 1968, there has been a sustained increase in the number of both terrorist incidents and groups formed in advanced industrialized democracies.[3] Terrorism in this period has been more violent (as measured by number of individuals injured and killed). Many new groups are better organized and more sophisticated than those in previous historical eras. Terrorism after the early 1960s is also better documented and studied. Moreover, there is more public, political, and national security awareness of terrorism.

In general, there are four important differences between the terrorism of the contemporary period and previous terrorist waves:

1. Most of the terrorist groups of the 1960s were left-wing in orientation or used left-wing phraseology in their appeals and manifestos.

2. Foreign powers, directly or discreetly, provided help to terrorist movements.

3. Operations in foreign countries became far more frequent.

4. The ability of authorities to counteract terrorism was more restricted than in the past (Laqueur 1977, 176–77). They were obliged to abide by the rule of law. Now many advanced industrialized countries have special legislation that allows authorities greater powers in cases of suspected terrorism.

Consequently, terrorist movements and acts of international terrorism have sprung up almost all over the world.

In general, we can divide the history of terrorism during the past four-and-a-half decades even further, into three overlapping time periods. Groups are more or less revolutionary/nationalist-separatist, left-wing, or right-wing in terms of their ideologies.

1960s–1970s: Revolutionary and nationalist-separatist

During the 1960s, many groups with strong nationalist sentiments that were part of larger countries became increasingly outspoken. Some among their ranks resorted to violent political actions, including terrorism. Among the nationalist-separatist groups, there are both right- and left-wing terrorist organizations.

In Canada, the *Front de Liberation du Québéc* (FLQ) operated between 1962 and 1972. This was primarily a nationalist-separatist organization, with left-wing sympathies, that wanted the predominantly francophone province to break off from Canada and establish a fully autonomous socialist state. This group was responsible for numerous bombings, as well as the much-publicized kidnapping in October 1970 of James Cross, the British Trade Commissioner to Canada and the murder of Pierre Laporte, a member of the Quebec (Provincial) National Assembly (Fournier 1984; Ross 1995).

In 1964, the *Palestinian Liberation Organization* (PLO) was formed. Under this umbrella structure, a number of terrorist groups took action in Israel (including the Popular Front for the Liberation of Palestine [PFLP], discussed below). Later the PLO included as many as eight terrorist organizations. In 1969, Yasser Arafat's al-Fatah gained control. In 1972, Black September, a Palestinian terrorist organization that formed in Jordan, began to launch attacks against both Israelis and Jordanian political leaders. This group was responsible for the massacre of nine Israeli athletes at the Munich Olympics in September 1972.

In the aftermath of the 1967 Six Days' War (during which the countries of Egypt, Lebanon, Syria and Jordan simultaneously attacked Israel), George Habash and Wadi Haddadd, both trained as medical doctors, founded the *Popular Front for the Liberation of Palestine* (PFLP), "based on a number of political groups which had been in existence since the late 1940s" (Laqueur 2003, 101). The PFLP had a Marxist-Leninist orientation similar to that espoused by "Cuba, Vietnam, North Korea, and the left-wing terrorist forces in Western Europe with which it cooperated. It also regarded the Arab bourgeoisie an 'objective ally of Zionism' against which war should be waged" (Laqueur 2003, 101). This group received support from the Soviet Union and from other communist countries; this also meant that it was distrustful of Yasser Arafat, the head of the PLO as he was perceived as a concessionist.

The Basques, who live in the northwestern part of Spain, have their own language and culture. Since the 1950s, Basques have struggled for independence. *Euzkadi Ta Askatasuna* (ETA) ("Basque Homeland and Security") was formed by Basques in 1966, and by 1968 started terrorist activities: "A more militant group, the ETA-M, broke away from the ETA in 1974. ETA-M describes itself as the military wing of the ETA and . . . was responsible for the worst atrocities of the 1970s and 1980s. Both groups have waged a campaign under the name ETA. The campaign reached its zenith between 1977 and 1980 and declined steadily throughout the 1980s. The ETA was responsible for more than 600 deaths between 1968 and 1996" (White 2003, 189). Some members sought refuge in southern France, and initially, the French government was accommodating in giving them temporary safe haven. In the 1980s, however, the French arrested and convicted about eighty

Basques under terrorism-related charges. Although most Basques are very nationalistic and want more autonomy, they do not support terrorism: "In these circumstances, one of the prime tasks of the Spanish government has been opening up the political system to the Basques, while allowing them to maintain their cultural heritage. This strategy has served to delegitimize terrorism" (White 2003, 190).

Some of the groups discussed early under the modern period of terrorism continued their activities into the contemporary period. During the 1960s and to this day, the *Provisional Irish Republican Army* (PIRA) in Northern Ireland has carried out attacks against Protestants living there and against Great Britain. In 1975, the *Armenian Secret Army for the Liberation of Armenia* (ASALA), having a Marxist orientation, formed with the goal of striving for the independence of Armenians in Turkey. ASALA was responsible for a number of embassy seizures and plane hijackings, and was most active in the United States, Canada, and Europe.

Left-wing/anarchist terrorism

Leftists typically integrate a distrust of government, concern for social class, desire to abolish or strictly control private property, want to alleviate oppression and discrimination, and the belief that governments support an elite group (especially capitalists) who benefit from the labor of the working class. Starting in the early 1960s, there were vibrant student movements in Europe, Latin America, and North America. They coalesced around opposition to American participation in Vietnam and distrust of the excesses of capitalism. Among their ranks were individuals and offshoot groups that engaged in terrorism (Hoffman 1998, 26). Most drew their membership from white middle-class and upper-class individuals of the new left.

In 1962, for example, the *Tupamaros* formed in Uruguay, and with an anti-imperialism and U.S. intervention into its country's affairs platform, proceeded to bomb, kidnap, and assassinate military officers and other government officials. The group consisted of young professionals such as teachers, lawyers, and doctors, and its activities led to the fall of the democratically elected government of Uruguay. The Tupamaros are best remembered for the 1970 murder of Dan Mitrione, an American adviser to the Uruguayan police force, as documented in the Costa Gravas movie *State of Siege* (1973) and the book *Hidden Terrors* by Langguth (1978). By 1971, the Tupamaros held the all-time record for multiple and cumulative diplomatic hijackings; "in response, the country's military seized power and proceeded to use torture and various other coercive means to destroy the Tupamaros. During the military crackdown, most members of the Tupamaros who could, fled into exile. . . . In 1983 the military became willing to return to the barracks and permit the restoration of Uruguay's democracy. New parliamentary elections were held. The Tupamaros re-surfaced as a peaceful political party and won a handful of seats in the new legislative body" (Weinberg and Pedahzur 2003, 26).

During the late 1960s, the *Weathermen/Weather Underground* was established in the United States. Radical elements of the Students for a Democratic Society (SDS) formed this group to commit terrorist actions against the United States government. They were opposed to capitalism and U.S. involvement in Southeast Asia (particularly the war in Vietnam). They attacked offices of the Reserve Officers' Training Corps (ROTC) on university campuses and in cities. Originally called the Weathermen, they later changed their name to the Weather Underground in order to minimize any sexist connotations.

In 1969, the *Red Brigades*—also known as *Brigatte Rose*—formed in Italy. Documented in the movie *Year of the Gun*, its original members were drawn from the sociology department at the University of Trento. The group terrorized the judiciary, police, and big business and was responsible for the assassination of former premier and Christian Democratic Party leader Aldo Moro in 1978 (Weinberg and Eubank 1987b).

Contemporaneously, the Japanese Red Army (JRA) was formed. The group began operations in its home country and then engaged in terrorism in different locations around the world. Responsible for the Lod airport massacre in 1972, JRA also carried out a number of spectacular hijackings (Farrell 1990).

In the 1970s, the left-wing Peronist *Montoneros* in Argentina killed ex-president Pedro Aramburu. This group stepped up its attacks in 1975 and 1976, and this violent activity was partially responsible for ushering in a military dictatorship.

The Baader-Meinhoff gang, which later reconstituted itself as the *Red Army Faction* (RAF), formed in 1977. This West German terrorist group was largely influenced by anarchist principles. Featured in much of the German New Wave cinema, this organization was named after its two founders—Andreas Baader and Ulrike Meinhoff—and was responsible for bombing corporations and American military installations and for kidnapping German businessmen (Becker 1978).

And in 1979, the group *Action Directe* formed in Belgium and France. It engaged in a widespread campaign of bombing and assassinations against government figures, "Zionists," or businesses with Jewish connections. Later, the group was part of the European-wide, anti-North Atlantic Treaty Organization (NATO terrorist alliance that emerged in the 1980s (Dartnell 2001).

Most of the left-wing/revolutionary groups present in North and South America and in western Europe no longer exist, in part because authorities defeated them, or because they alienated their supporters by the targets they selected and tactics they utilized, or by continuous doctrinal debates that appeared overly complicated and contradictory (Weinberg and Pedahzur 2003, 84–85). (See Exhibit Box 7)

Right-wing terrorists

There is a long tradition of right-wing violence in America and elsewhere. Some of the more dominant groups that have engaged in terrorist acts include the Ku Klux Klan and the Aryan Nations. In Western Europe during the 1980s, however, a number of terrorist groups with right-wing leanings formed. On the Italian right, for example, three main groups operated: the New Order, the National Vanguard, and the National Front. They were "radically opposed to the revolutionary aims of Marxist-Leninist organizations. . . . In none of the other democracies did this kind of right-wing terrorism achieve the virulence it took on in Italy" (Eubank and Weinberg 1987b, 3).

After World War II, few neo-fascist groups existed in Italy. The most prominent was the Italian Social Movement (MSI) formed in 1946. During the 1950s, doctrinal disputes resulted in the formation of a splinter group called the New Order. This new organization attacked left-wing groups and targets in an effort to discredit them, and attempted to forge alliances with the national police, military, and other sympathetic groups throughout Europe (Weinberg and Eubank 1987b, 35–37). Eventually, in 1969, this group turned to terrorism and committed some of the more sensational acts of terrorism in recent Italian history, including the now-famous bombing of the National Agricultural Bank at the Piazza Fontana in Milan (December 1969), in which 17 people were killed, and the Bologna Train station bombing (August 1980), in which 84 people were killed and 180 injured. The Right was upset with the slow pace of the government's dealing with the left-wing terrorists, and was also disgruntled with the communist and socialist parties they considered too powerful.

Exhibit Box 7
A comparison between left- and right-wing objectives and parties

Left-wing	Right-wing
more government intervention, particularly in the economy (e.g., more taxes)	less government intervention less taxes
more equality/social justice	protection of individual liberties
pro-choice	anti-choice
pro–affirmative action	no racial quotas
more gun control	no gun control
pro–environmental protectionism	nostalgic vision (e.g., restore things to the way they were in the past)
pro–social services, increased public funding	pro–free market
anti-death penalty	pro–death penalty

Most political ideologies and political organizations and parties want change (or progress), but they vary on the methods on how to achieve it and the pace at which it is achieved (i.e., incremental, radical, or extreme).

Political Parties

Anarchists	Conservative Party
Communist Party	Christian Coalition
Green Party	Reform Party
Progressive Party	Libertarian Party
Socialist Party	Republican Party
Liberal Party	
Democratic Party	

Three principal reasons account for the demise of right-wing terrorism in Italy. First, new laws were instituted that created longer sentences for convicted terrorists. Second, national security organizations were improved. Third, during the 1980s, Italy as whole became less polarized (Weinberg and Eubank 1987b).

The 1980s: State-sponsored, religious fundamentalist, and single-issue terrorism

By the mid-1980s—initially through the work of conspiracy theories perpetrated in books like Claire Sterling's *The Terror Network*—the notion of state-sponsored terrorism came to public attention. Conspiracy theories suggest that "seemingly isolated terrorist incidents perpetrated by disparate groups scattered across the globe were in fact linked elements of a massive clandestine plot, orchestrated by the Kremlin and implemented by its Warsaw Pact client states to destroy the Free World" (Hoffman 1998, 27). Although there may be some truth to the theory, Sterling's book made more of it than clearly existed. Nevertheless, this book and the policy furor surrounding it led to an increased focus by then-U.S. president Ronald Reagan and national security agencies on state-sponsored terrorism, through which not only the Soviet Union, but countries such as Cuba, Iran, Iraq, Libya, and North Korea were helping terrorist groups or exercising their foreign policy objectives through them.

In 1979, two significant events occurred that have had a bearing on terrorism over the next two decades: the fall of President Anastasio Somoza in Nicaragua by the leftist guerrilla organization called the Sandinistas, and the overthrow of the shah in Iran by a group of people that included Islamic fundamentalists. The Ayatollah Khomeini became the leader of Iran and led the first modern theocracy (government rule based on religion). At the same time, the American embassy in Tehran was occupied by so-called student activists and the remaining embassy staff held hostage.[4]

By the mid-1980s, a number of Islamic fundamentalist and Middle Eastern terrorist groups formed. Three of the most prominent Islamic fundamentalist groups are Hezbollah, Islamic Jihad, and Hamas. In addition to their fiery rhetoric, they have carried out numerous suicide bombings. This usually involves a car or truck, laden with explosives, driven into a military vehicle, barracks, or compound. When the bomb exploded, not only would it kill the driver or courier, but it would also cause considerable death and injuries among citizens and soldiers who were present. Alternatively, an individual carrying explosives concealed on his or her body would walk into a crowded market or bus station and detonate it.

Hezbollah, "Party of God," a Shiite Muslim fundamentalist group, emerged in Lebanon during the 1980s. Originally established to kick the Israelis out of their country, with military backing from Iran and financial support from Syria, it now aids the Palestinians in their historical struggle against Israel. Motivated by the success of the Iranian Revolution, this organization originally wanted to start a theocratic state in Lebanon; it has since abandoned this approach and now has elected members who serve in the Lebanese parliament. It gained international prominence through a series of high-profile kidnappings of prominent Americans and was also responsible for the April 13, 1983, suicide bombing of the U. S. marine barracks in Beirut in which 263 Americans were killed. Its members are counted in the thousands (Westcott 2002).

The *Islamic Jihad,* another Shiite fundamentalist organization, is based in Damascus (Syria) and has financial support from both Syria and Iran. It has concentrated its suicide bombings in Israel against soldiers and civilians. It wants to create an Islamic Palestinian state and is against pro-Western Arab states; this is why it has committed actions in Jordan and Lebanon.[5]

Started in 1987 after the Intifada (which included street protests by Palestinian youths), originally as a charitable and social service organization, *Hamas* does not recognize Israel's right to exist and wants Palestinians to rule the land granted to the Israelis before the 1949 United Nations (U.N.) partition mandate. Although the actual number of members is unknown, it has thousands of supporters, as well as both military and political wings. It has been responsible for several suicide bombings on Israel citizens. Hamas has been antagonistic to the Palestinian National Authority (PNA). This led to the 1996 PNA arrest of one thousand Hamas members. Its base of support is primarily in Gaza and it has operated at times with the assistance of the Jordanian government.[6]

During the 1980s, analysts also noted the presence and increase in the number of individuals and groups in Western countries that resorted to terrorism in furtherance of narrow political goals or *single-issue terrorism* (Smith 1998). Three issues attracted radicals who resorted to terrorism: animal rights (e.g., Animal Liberation Front), pro-life/anti-abortion, and protection of the environment (e.g., Earth First). Individuals and groups wedded to these causes have engaged in violence ranging from property damage to assault, bombings, and murder. In these cases there is a fine line between direct action (typically confined to property damage) and political terrorism. Apparently, evidence exists of cooperation among these diverse groups, all of which is aided by access to the Internet.

1990s: Narco-terrorism, gray-area phenomena, and dark networks

In the early 1990s, the terms "narco-terrorism" and "gray-area phenomenon" were introduced into the terrorism lexicon. The first term referred to the "use of drug trafficking to advance the objectives of certain governments and terrorist organizations"—identified as the "Marxist-Leninist regimes" of the Soviet Union, Cuba, Bulgaria, and Nicaragua, among others" (Hoffman 1998, 27). Powerful illegal drug cultivators and traffickers formed alliances with terrorist groups for mutual benefit. Regions that have generated interest by politicians, practitioners, and scholars in the narco-terrorism phenomenon are South America, Middle East, Africa, and Asia, all of which contain countries that are major cultivators, distributors, and processors of drugs. However, the majority of interest focused on Latin America and on Colombia in particular, where the cocaine cartel needed protection and rebel forces wanted resources (primarily money, in this case). This relationship, sometimes labeled "convergence theory," combined the essential elements of not only terrorism, but also organized crime and state sponsorship, especially when the state (or those in positions of power) was corrupt. In many respects, ideological concerns were placed on hold and access to money prevailed (Hoffman 1998, 28; Picarelli and Shelly 2002; Schmid 1996).

Much of the Colombian terrorist activity has centered on Medellin, the epicenter of cocaine trafficking and the alleged home of the drug cartel, in response to the government's anti-drug campaign. Car bombs explode and people are kidnapped or assassinated there on a routine basis. In August 1989, stories emerged about British and Israeli mercenaries who were training and advising the Colombian drug lords and gangs who have a tenuous relationship with the terrorist organizations (Killyane 1990). Apparently, Pablo Escobar, the cartel's leader, allied himself with the April 19 Movement (M–19) and with the Revolutionary Armed Forces of Colombia (FARC).

In addition to narco-terrorism, gray-area phenomena—places and situations in which local and regional politics are run by a criminal organization that uses terrorism to assert its authority—are also on the rise. These locations are particularly unstable and security is maintained not only by the military, but also by irregular forces/private armies (Hoffman 1998, 28). Examples of gray-area phenomena would include Afghanistan during the 1990s under the rule of the Taliban, or Somalia under the control of the warlords, prior to the failed American peacekeeping effort in 1993 (as documented in the movie *Black Hawk Down*).

Finally, a relatively new term, "dark networks," is being used to describe alliances made between terrorist groups, criminal organizations, and regional warlord factions (Arquilla and Ronfeldt 2001).

Contemporary Trends in Terrorism

We tend to get caught up in the spectacular terrorist events and ignore the long-term trajectories. In order to have a better understanding of the contemporary patterns of terrorism, the following section provides a description of a number of trends, including the frequency of terrorism, geographic spread, targets, tactics, and terrorist groups. However, before analyzing this, we need to understand how these data are derived.[7] Specifically, it is important to examine the sources for the information we have on terrorism.

Data sources

Prior to the mid-1970s, the majority of information on terrorism was presented in case studies of particular movements, groups, and individuals that used terrorism and in case studies of countries that experienced terrorism. This material—developed by scholars, journalists, and government agencies—was generally descriptive, atheoretical, and primarily normative.

In the mid-1970s, however, we saw an attempt among some scholars, private research companies, and governmental departments to systematically collect data on the actions and characteristics of terrorism. The majority of these efforts were rudimentary quantitative studies, which unlike the descriptive studies, allow us to speak with greater precision about terrorist phenomena. The most basic statistics for the study of terrorism are *events data,* important information gathered on each incident over a specified period of time.

This approach to the study of terrorism helps us to spot trends, predict future events, understand how the tactics and targets of terrorism have changed over time, develop and test hypotheses, and approach terrorism in a scientific fashion. It has allowed researchers and policymakers to understand the frequency of terrorism and, occasionally, to test hypotheses. There are several advantages to events databases. They give us a better idea of the scope, nature, and intensity of terrorism over time; they provide us with a context.

An events-data disposition focuses on the discrete incident as its unit of analysis. This method has been used in the creation of numerous large-scale studies of political conflict (e.g., Gurr 1966). Most of these projects did not, however, have a separate variable for terrorism, but instead included terrorist acts under other types of violence. During the early 1970s, however, events-data methodology was eventually applied to international terrorism.

Since the mid-1970s, there has been an increase in attempts to collect quantitative data on terrorism. Nevertheless, these data sets suffer from a number of problems, including too-broad definitions of terrorism; limited public availability; a focus on regional tallies rather than on country totals; a lack of distinction between domestic and international events; inclusion of acts of violence that are not terrorism; and a readiness to include events that are not confirmed as terrorist motivated.

Similar to what happens in the business world, many of the incident-level data sets on terrorism have either integrated with others, are unavailable to the public, or no longer exist. Meanwhile, new data sets have entered the academic, corporate, and state marketplace (Ross 1991). Nevertheless, three data sets have managed to withstand the resource-intensive demands of maintaining a data collection enterprise. When a data source is cited, it is commonly based on data from the Control Risks Group Data Base, RAND Corporation Data Base, or the State Department/Central Intelligence Agency/International Terrorism: Attributes of Terrorism Events (ITERATE) I, II, and III data sets.

The economic obstacles to creating and maintaining a data set are most evident when one observes that the first two have been created by private research organizations, and the latter—at least ITERATE I and II—by Mickolus with funding from the CIA. While all of these data sets have been criticized on several accounts, they also have practical advantages.

First, the London-based Control Risks Group (http://www.crg.com) maintains a data set on domestic and international terrorism. Formed in 1975, this business (with more than four hundred employees and sixteen offices worldwide) serves the security requests of businesses and corporations. The company specializes in four areas: "political and security risk analysis," "confidential investigations," "security responses," and "crisis response." Not only do its country files contain data on terrorist actions, but they also include information on criminal behavior. Updated monthly, the "Data Solve" information system from Control Risks Information Services is available in several formats. While publicly available, the cost to use this service is high, thus limiting its accessibility. To remedy this situation, the company has a policy of giving free information to students conducting research on terrorism, but only in the form of aggregate totals.

Second, the RAND Corporation (http://www.rand.org), headquartered in Santa Monica, California, is an independent, nonprofit think tank that performs contract and grants-funded research for various sponsors; mainly the government and large businesses. It has gained a reputation for conducting wide-ranging studies on subnational, low-intensity conflict and on domestic and international terrorism. Not only has RAND published a number of chronologies and developed some groundbreaking research on terrorism—primarily through its two principle terrorist experts, Brian Jenkins and Bruce Hoffman—it has also constructed a number of databases on various areas pertaining to terrorism.[8] Although their data sets are not publicly available for others to analyze, some of the reports generated with these data make it into the public domain.

Finally, up until the last few years the State Department/CIA/ITERATE (http://www.state.gov) data sets were the best-known and most widely used public sources for researchers studying international terrorism. Numerous variables per case are coded. Originally, this database was developed from two RAND chronologies and from press accounts in the *New York Times,* the *Washington Post,* and other prominent media sources. By 1980, it listed more than two hundred sources. ITERATE has three major advantages: it is publicly available for a nominal cost; ITERATE I and II are accessible for free from member institutions of the Inter-university Consortium of Political and Social Research, located at the University of Michigan; and it has a readily accessible chronology and a code book so that researchers can use it to check the validity of coding or create their own data sets. For the past decade the State Department, through its Office of the Coordinator for Counter-Terrorism issued an annual "Patterns of Global Terrorism" report.[9] On the downside, the State Department data set is limited to international terrorism, and data for most charts is limited to the years between 1981 and 2003. Unfortunately, only the most recent statistics 1996–2003 are available to the public. Finally, the State Department's data set includes hoaxes and threats which tends to over count the number of actual incidents.

In April 2005, the U.S. State Department formally announced that it would no longer disseminate global reports on terrorism.[10] Instead this function would be handed over the National Counter-Terrorism Centre, which is part of the Central Intelligence Agency. The data are in fact managed by the National Memorial Institute for the Prevention of Terrorism (MIPT) located in Oklahoma City. According to the web site the new database (www.tkb.org) is made up of data from the RAND Terrorism Chronology 1968–1997; RAND-MIPT Terrorism Incident database (1998–present); Terrorism Indictment database (University of Arkansas); and DFI International's research on terrorist organizations.

In the meantime, new data sets on international terrorism have been started by a number of academics, but information on these projects is scant. Some of the more widely discussed collections are those initiated by Paul Wilkinson at the University of Fyfe (Scotland), Ariel Merari at the Jaffee Center for Strategic Studies in Tel Aviv (Israel), John B. Wolf at the John Jay College of Criminal Justice (New York), Alex P. Schmid at the University of Leiden (Netherlands), and A. J. Jongman at the Polemical Institute of Groningen State University (Netherlands).

Despite the previously mentioned drawbacks with most data sets, the majority show the same general patterns. However, not all data bases answer the basic questions of who, what, when, where, and why in a comprehensive manner. Thus, for the purposes of this chapter, statistics are based on a variety of sources, including information from the State Department's "Patterns of Global Terrorism" reports. Where appropriate State Department information was not available, then our discussion must rely on RAND reports, or MIPT (terrorism knowledge base) data. Readers must be made aware that data for 1968–1997 covers only international incidents whereas the statistics for 1998–June 30, 2004, covers both domestic and international incidents.

Another caveat is also in order. Though many acts of terrorism are successfully thwarted by the combined efforts of law enforcement and

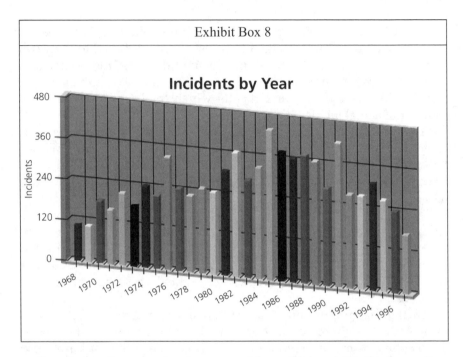

Exhibit Box 8

Incidents by Year

national security agencies, because of fears that sensitive information will be leaked, thus jeopardizing ongoing investigations or the likelihood of conviction, these successes are rarely made publicly available (P. Jenkins 2003, 126–27). This information should help us better contextualize the empirical data on real or actual terrorist acts. In other words, the available databases may underestimate the actual terrorism that is perpetrated or in the process of being organized. Unlike previous databases, this one selectively integrates domestic terrorism.

Annual statistics

From 1968–June 30, 2005, there have been approximately 9,718 international political terrorist events, ranging from a low of 103 incidents in 1969 and 2000 to a high of 440 in 1985. This breaks down to an average of about 259 incidents each year (www.tkb.org). The prevailing impression given by the media, public officials, and some experts concerned with international terrorism, however, is that terrorism is on the increase. For the most part, increases are relative to the time period under investigation; increases are not linear, as media accounts might imply. As far back as the 1960s, the frequency of terrorism has been cyclical, with several peaks and valleys. This is not surprising, as terrorism fluctuates due to general factors involved in causation and decline (as we shall see in chapters 3, 4 and 5). In 2004, the most recent complete year for which statistics are available, the total number of international terrorist incidents was 330—56 events more than in 2003. However, not all events are of the same magnitude and intensity. For example, the magnitude of the September 11, 2001, attacks on the World Trade Center and the Pentagon might lead to the conclusion that there has been a steep increase in the number of terrorist events overall, which is not actually the case (Exhibit Box 8).

Geographic spread

The number of countries experiencing some sort of terrorist activity each year has gradually increased. In the late 1960s, international terrorist incidents occurred in an average of 29 countries each year. This average climbed to 39 countries in the early 1970s and 43 in the late 1970s. For the first three years of the 1980s, the average number of countries experiencing international terrorist incidents was 51, and for the period from 1983 to 1985, the average was 65 incidents.[11]

Although terrorism is experienced throughout the world, some regions currently suffer a disproportionate amount of the world's terrorism. Regions experiencing the largest number of terrorist activities change almost every year. Between 1968 and 2005 (June 30), for example, the Middle East received the brunt of terrorist attacks (6,743), and East and Central Asia incurred the lowest number of incidents (198) (www.tkb.org). About twenty countries account for between 75 and 90 percent of all reported incidents. The top three countries that experience the largest amount of terrorism (approximately 75 percent) are, in descending order of frequency, Israel (including the Gaza strip and the West Bank), Pakistan, and Colombia.

Targets

Since the 1960s, the range of terrorist targets has expanded. At the beginning of the 1970s, terrorists concentrated their attacks mainly on property and institutions, whereas in the 1980s, they increasingly targeted people. Almost every conceivable structure has been hit, including embassies, factories, airliners, airline offices, tourist agencies,

Exhibit Box 9
International Terrorist Incidents 1968–June 30, 2005

Year	Incidents
1968	106
1969	103
1970	180
1971	157
1972	210
1973	175
1974	237
1975	213
1976	330
1977	240
1978	224
1979	227
1980	240
1981	305
1982	366
1983	287
1984	328
1985	440
1986	378
1987	364
1988	375
1989	362
1990	286
1991	421
1992	273
1993	273
1994	312
1995	267
1996	240
1997	171
1998	161
1999	125
2000	103
2001	205
2002	297
2003	274
2004	330
2005	134

Data from www.tkb.org

hotels, airports, bridges, trains, train stations, reactors, refineries, schools, restaurants, pubs, churches, temples, synagogues, mainframe computers for large businesses and organizations, data-processing centers, and office towers.

A considerable amount of public and media attention has been directed toward the possibility of terrorist attacks on nuclear facilities and the potential resulting fallout. Indeed, there have been breaches of security at these places; however, most of the incidents were carried out by anti-nuclear protestors trying to halt or delay the construction of new nuclear facilities rather than destroy existing ones.

Americans, the British, the French, Israelis, and Turks account for approximately half of all the nationalities victimized by terrorists.[12] The individuals attacked include diplomats, military personnel, tourists, businesspeople, students, journalists, children, nuns, priests, and the Pope. According to MIPT/tkb statistics, since 1968, the majority of targets private citizens and property (3,821).

From 1968 to June 30, 2005, out of the 22,457 incidents, there were a total of 75,245 injuries and 29,642 fatalities (www.tkb.org). Based on 2004 State Department figures, about 16 percent (2,998 individuals) were American citizens.

By the end of 2001, largely because of the events of September 11, the number of deaths rose to approximately 3,000. Typically, only 15 to 20 percent of all terrorist incidents involve fatalities; of those, 66 percent involve only one death. Less than one percent of the thousands of terrorist incidents that have occurred in the past two decades involve ten or more fatalities. Incidents of mass murder, sometimes achieved through suicide bombings, are truly rare. This has led some experts, like Brian Jenkins, to repeatedly suggest that "terrorists want a lot of people watching rather than a lot of people dead" (B. Jenkins 1979, 169).

Tactics

Terrorists operate with a fairly limited repertoire of attacks. Seven basic tactics have accounted for 97 percent of all terrorist incidents: bombings (13,217), assassinations (2,182), armed assaults (3,657), kidnappings (1,652), arson (868), hijackings (232), and barricade and hostage incidents (201) (www.tkb.org). In short, terrorists blow things up, kill people, or seize hostages. Every incident is essentially a variation on these activities. Bombings appear to be the most deadly.

Exhibit Box 10			
Terrorist Incidents, by Region		**Range:** 01/01/1968–07/30/2005	
Region	**Incidents**	**Injuries**	**Fatalities**
Africa	989	8742	3352
East & Central Asia	198	5344	223
Eastern Europe	1215	4901	1873
Latin America	3398	3514	2175
Middle East / Persian Gulf	6743	24468	9840
North America	582	1845	3574
South Asia	3349	17374	5968
Southeast Asia & Oceania	736	3685	1248
Western Europe	52444	5372	1389

Although the use of weapons of mass destruction (WMD), such as biological, chemical, nuclear, or toxic weapons, is a topic of constant concern, bombings of all types continue to be the most popular terrorist method of attack. Approximately 50 percent of all international events are bombings. This is followed, in terms of numbers, by armed attacks, arsons, and kidnappings. In addition, the number of arson incidents, bombings, attacks on and assassinations of diplomats has increased in the past few years.

While the majority of bombs are simple incendiary devices, terrorists have made and often use more sophisticated explosive weapons. Rudimentary bombs in particular are easy to construct. Bombings also typically involve the least amount of group coordination and thus are one of the easiest terrorist tactics to employ. Additionally, they are relatively cheap; the group can get a considerable amount of "bang for its buck" through using bombs.

Terrorist groups

Some terrorist organizations show considerable endurance, operating for a lengthy period of time, replacing their losses, preparing for new

Exhibit Box 11			
Terrorist Incidents, by Target		**Range:** 01/01/1968–07/30/2005	
Target	**Incidents**	**Injuries**	**Fatalities**
Abortion Related	5	2	2
Airport & Airlines	805	2375	2359
Business	3258	9734	4933
Diplomatic	2620	8413	1273
Educational Institutions	416	1349	475
Food or Water Supply	9	5	0
Government	3312	7301	3456
Journalists & Media	483	221	181
Maritime	134	263	130
Military	798	4362	1450
NGO	286	256	264
Other	1446	2181	1450
Police	1457	4963	2822
Private Citizens & Property	3831	13885	5714
Religious Figures/Institutions	762	4927	1662
Telecommunication	121	73	35
Terrorists	216	513	402
Tourists	244	1495	585
Transportation	896	11688	1936
Unknown	659	903	317
Utilities	699	336	196
TOTAL	**22457**	**75245**	**29642**

attacks, and turning into semipermanent subcultures. Other groups have fleeting existences.

In 1991, for example, Crenshaw examined the longevity of seventy-six terrorist organizations. According to her study, many groups have

Exhibit Box 12			
Terrorist Incidents, by Tactic	Range: 01/01/1968–07/30/2005		
Tactic	**Incidents**	**Injuries**	**Fatalities**
Armed Attack	3657	10318	5604
Arson	868	297	367
Assassination	2182	955	2763
Barricade/Hostage	201	2198	896
Bombing	13217	60274	15293
Hijacking	232	377	475
Kidnapping	1652	135	736
Other	152	385	231
Police	1	6	4
Unconventional Attack	56	103	3004
Unknown	239	197	270
TOTAL	**22457**	**75245**	**29642**

exhibited remarkable stability and tenacity, but almost half of the organizations either no longer exist or no longer commit acts of terrorism. However, at least ten groups—including al-Fatah, the Popular Front for the Liberation of Palestine–General Command (PFLP–GC), and Euzkadi Ta Askatasuna (ETA)—have been in operation for twenty years (Crenshaw 1991). The MIPT/tkb database (7/30/2005) lists 792 terrorist organizations. Probably no more that two hundred are active in any given year.

Over the past 37 years most terrorist incidents are attributed to "Other Group" or "Unknown Group." This means that the organizational affiliation could not be positively identified. In situations where the organization was positively identified, Hamas (446), ETA (387), and the National Liberation Army (in Colombia) (282) have committed the greatest number of incidents. Those groups that are responsible for the highest number of fatalities are al Qaeda (3521), Hezbollah (821), Tanzim Qa'idat al-Jihad fi Bilad al-Rafidayn (a Palestinian group) (615), and Hamas (577).

Exhibit Box 13			
Incidents of Major Terrorist Groups, 01/01/1968—07/30/2005			
Group	**Incidents**	**Injuries**	**Fatalities**
Abu Nidal Organization (ANO)	82	654	210
Abu Sayaf Group (ASG)	52	491	197
al-Fatah	198	1322	417
al Qaeda	27	6476	3521
Amal	69	65	67
Anti-Castro Cubans	213	55	86
Armed Islamic Group	64	359	506
Armenian Army for the Liberation of Armenia (ASALA)	78	269	46
Basque Fatherland and Freedom (ETA)	387	538	61
Black September	92	132	30
Communist Party of Nepal-Maoists	261	292	133
DHKP-C (Devrimci Sol)	73	90	20
Earth Liberation Front	50	0	0
Front di Liberazione Naziunale di a Corsica (FLNC)	116	27	0
Hamas	446	2787	577
Hezbollah	176	1475	821
Irish Republican Army (IRA)	83	139	28
Jewish Defense League (JDL)	72	37	5
Kurdistan Worker's Party	83	211	38
Liberation Tigers of Tamil Eelam (LTTE)	72	2431	514
Manuel Rodriguez Patriotic Front	51	15	1
National Liberation Army (Colombia)	282	202	124
New People's Army (NPA)	78	48	67
Other Group	2028	7935	3483
Palestine Liberation Organization	62	588	39
Palestinian Islamic Jihad (PIJ)	66	663	134
People's War Group (PWG) (India)	75	122	112
Popular Front for the Liberation of Palestine	103	646	163
Red Army Faction	41	62	3
Revolutionary Armed Forces of Colombia	455	1000	450
Shining Path	136	265	130
Taliban	118	205	213
Tanzim Qa'idat al-Jihad fi Bilad al-Rafidayn	117	1302	615
Tupac Amaru Revolutionary Movement	105	21	20
Unkown Group	13068	25172	10648

Research and Analysis Methods

A variety of techniques are used by journalists, practitioners, experts, consultants, and scholars in conducting research on terrorism. This information appears in the context of journal articles, chapters in scholarly books, academic monographs, newspaper and magazine articles, and books for popular audiences. In general, this work can be divided into qualitative and quantitative approaches. The former deals primarily with description, while the later focuses on the collection and analysis of statistics.

A subtle but necessary distinction should also be made between research produced for popular audiences and that conducted for the academic or scholarly community. Work for the academic audience is more rigorous but may lack the excitement and sensational appeal to sustain a wider interest. Nevertheless, a symbiotic relationship exists between popular and academic writers. At various times they depend upon or use research from each other.

Periodically, researchers conduct comprehensive reviews of the research on terrorism and the methods used by investigators. Since the examples from which they draw are illustrative, these writings are not meant to be comprehensive, but rather illustrative as well. Building on similar work by Schmid (1983) and Gurr (1988b), we will review salient contributions in both qualitative and quantitative approaches to terrorism studies.

Qualitative research on terrorism

The bulk of research on oppositional political terrorism uses qualitative methods. This approach primarily consists of descriptive accounts of terrorists, their actions, and measures to combat these actions. Often this work is assembled into case studies that later appear in articles and books. Some of the better information is gathered through participant observation (doing those things under investigation and watching subjects engaged in a particular activity of interest to the researcher) and can be divided into two tiers of literature, separated by the degree to which they use primary versus secondary data or sources of information. Qualitative research helps us to understand the psychology of participants and the social setting in which they operate. It also aids in contextualizing the material that is developed in quantitative studies (Mannheim and Rich 1996 or Babbie 2001).

1. First-tier research

There are four basic types of primary source information on terrorism: autobiographies, "incident reports," hostage experiences, and firsthand accounts of implementing policies. In general, the closer researchers are to sources, the greater the potential for validity.

When terrorists write about their experiences, it is either in the form of *autobiographies* (for example, Vallieres 1972a; 1972b; Iyad 1981; de Vault 1982; Hansen 2002; Ayers 2003) or handbooks on techniques (Marighela 1971). The memoirs may be produced while they are on the run, incarcerated, or after their release. Other books are written once they have renounced terrorism and assumed political office. In general, autobiographies try to rationalize the violence they engaged in or encouraged others to perform. Often they are ideological writings or tactical suggestions.

"Incident reports" may be a bad term, but occasionally individuals (soldiers, commanders, etc.) who were participants in rescue efforts or antiterrorist campaigns will give an account of their actions (e.g., Loomis 1984; Netanyahu 2001). These reports often portray the writers as heroes operating in a crazy or complicated situation or environment.

A handful of *hostage accounts* were written in the 1980s. For example, Terry Waite and Terry Anderson, both held captive by Middle Eastern terrorists in southern Lebanon during the late 1980s, published firsthand accounts of their time in captivity (Anderson 1993; Waite 1993).

Some statesmen have written *firsthand accounts of implementing policies* that describe their countries' experiences with terrorism and how they have developed policy to combat it (such as Netanyahu 1986). Otherwise high-ranking government officials have also discussed terrorism. Former senior CIA officer Robert Baer (2003) wrote a book on his experiences dealing with terrorism, as did Richard Clarke (2004), the former White House national coordinator for security, infrastructure protection, and counterterrorism on President George W. Bush's National Security Council.

While all four types of the above-mentioned writing are rich in detail, they are often too biased in the authors' perspective; a little more distance would have improved this kind of research. Primary source data tend to be more accurate than secondary source information; in many respects there is no substitute for firsthand experience or observation. But eyewitness accounts can suffer from bias. The copious research about the fallibility of eyewitness testimony (see Loftus 1996) casts a sobering shadow on the benefits of qualitative research methods. As in the childhood game of broken telephone, each new person receiving the information consciously or unconsciously interprets, shapes, and distorts it.

2. Second-tier research

In general, there are five types of second-tier qualitative studies on terrorism: biographies of terrorists, case studies of terrorist organizations, case studies on types of terrorism, case studies on particular terrorist incidents, and case studies of terrorism in selected regions and countries. This methodology focuses on analysis of primary research (i.e., firsthand accounts like those discussed above), occasional interviews, and the integration of other secondary research (other analyses of primary research). This kind of qualitative research involves the intense examination of terrorists' autobiographies and biographies, terrorist propaganda (Cordes 1987), case studies of groups, and some comparative case studies of groups.

A number of individuals have compiled *biographies* of well-known terrorists or individuals who have engaged in terrorist actions such as Yasser Arafat (Hart 1984), Menachim Begen (Seidman 1990), Osama bin Laden (Bodansky 2001), Carlos "the Jackal" (C. Smith 1976; Dobson 1977), and Abu Nidal (Melman 1986). Once again, the emphasis is on description with some analysis, but theories are rarely articulated or tested.

Some reporters and scholars have spent a great deal of their careers researching and writing *case studies of terrorist organizations* (e.g., Burke 2003). Some, like Bell (1997), an American academic, have accompanied members of the Provisional Irish Republican Army on raids and bombing missions. Chaliand (1983), a French reporter, conducted research on both guerrilla organizations and on terrorist groups. Case studies on the Front de Liberation du Québéc (FLQ) have been produced by Fournier (1984) and Stewart (1970). And a number of case studies have been produced on such groups as the Baader-Meinhof gang (Becker 1978); ETA Basque separatists (Clark 1984); Black September (Dobson 1974); and the Western European group Action-Directe (Dartnell 2001).

In the past decade, many edited books have been published with separate chapters on particular groups. This kind of effort is often preceded by a conference at which the papers are presented, discussed, and then later assembled (Ross 1991). Crenshaw, for example, has edited a series of case studies on terrorist groups (1994). In the past three years, we have seen an increase in the publication of case studies of al Qaeda done by reporters (Reeve 1999) and scholars (Gunaratna 2002).

Some researchers have focused disproportionately on *case studies on specific types of terrorism*. Most dominant are the research on hijackings (Joyner 1974), hostage taking (Aston 1986; Sandler and Scott 1987), narco-terrorism (Ehrenfeld 1992), eco-terrorism (Nilson and Burke 2002), biological threats (Miller, Engelberg, and Broad 2001), and nuclear terrorism (Allison 2004; Allison et. al 1996). Much of this research is the work of reporters and/or comes out of conference presentations.

Although many writers examine terrorist events in passing, researchers periodically focus on *case studies of particular terrorist incidents* that have attracted considerable attention. Case studies that fit in this genre include those on the September 1972 Munich massacre (R. Miller 1990b), the June 1985 Air India tragedy (Blaise and Mukherjee 1987), the December 1988 Pan Am Flight 103/Lockerbie incident (Emerson and Duffy 1990; Cohen and Cohen 2001), and the August 1998 bombing in Omagh by the IRA (Dingley 2001). Most recently, the 9/11 attacks have led to considerable scholarly attention. This latest incident has led to the production of a great number of case studies ranging from works done by reporters (Posner 2003), to scholars (Pysczynski, Solomon, and Greenberg 2002; Dudziak 2003), to government reports (United States 2004).

Finally, many researchers have developed *case studies concerning the pattern of terrorism in a specific region or country*. In particular, this line of inquiry looks at the causes and effects of terrorism and reviews government documents in each country's war against terrorism. Some of this work includes a focus on Western Europe (Corrado 1983), sub-Saharan Africa (Denemark and Welfling 1983), and Latin America (Sloan 1983). This research tends to focus on advanced industrialized countries like the United States (Bell and Gurr 1979; Bodansky 1993; Smith 1994), West Germany (Kellen 1990), Canada (Ross 1988b), and Italy (Weinberg and Eubank 1987b; Ferracuti 1990; della Porta 1992). Edited books with separate chapters devoted to terrorism in each country are among the popular results of this approach (Buckley and Fawn 2003).

Most secondary source research depends on open source work (interviews done by others). Typically, investigators depend on this information to create their own studies. The majority of the "data" is thus in fact secondary source material, with little research depending on primary information. The analysis of this secondary source information is problematic, because the further an investigator is from the primary source, the more distorted the information may be. Again, each new person may put his or her spin on the analysis and findings. This approach also lacks the intimacy one might achieve by getting information from the field or—preferably—directly from the source. A considerable amount of case-study research has been the work of reporters, rather than scholars. Perhaps journalists' flexible schedules and audience needs better allow them to engage in this kind of research.

Quantitative research on terrorism

The amount of quantitative studies on oppositional political terrorism pales in comparison to the number of those that depend upon qualitative methods. The majority of research on terrorism has been marked by theoretical generalizations based upon a lack of hard data (Mickolus 1981, 1–3). Statistical information, specifically that on political terrorism, is generally unavailable to the public, inaccurate, dated, or limited to international or transnational events. Nevertheless, when examining quantitative research on terrorism, it becomes clear that the bulk of work has been done through the statistical analysis of information collected through content analyses of newspaper reports on terrorism and information contained in incident-level databases.[13]

The most prevalent and relevant quantitative data for the study of terrorism is events data. The main change in terrorist research over the past thirty-five years has been an increase in attempts to conduct quantitative studies using sophisticated statistical modeling (e.g., Midlarsky, Crenshaw, and Yoshida 1980; Sandler, Tschirhart, and Cauley 1983; Atkinson, Sandler, and Tschirhart 1987; Im, Cauley, and Sandler 1987; Laplan and Sandler 1988; O'Brien 1996; Smith and Damphouse 1996; Smith and Orvis 1994). This shift, aided by the development of more portable and economically priced computers and statistical programs that could do quick computations, has improved database research. As research on terrorism became more sophisticated and useful, more people became interested in and properly trained to conduct more advanced research.

Databases can help us determine trends, give us a better idea of who is committing terrorist acts, compile the types of terrorism that occur, and analyze how terrorism has changed over time. A data set will also allow researchers to test hypotheses in a quantitative manner and to develop models. This work has been used primarily to aid descriptive research, contagion studies, and recommendations for policy changes and practitioner responses. This kind of information, it is believed, will ultimately help us predict future incidents.

Surveying the major databases

One of the best descriptions of data available was conducted by Schmid (1983, chapter 3). An alternative data-gathering exercise was a survey performed by Fowler (1981). Unfortunately, both Schmid and Fowler's listings are outdated, and many of the compilers cannot be tracked down to confirm the current status of their databases nor their data collection methods (Ross 1991, 21–26). Regardless, data sets can be categorized based on whether they were constructed by scholars, government agencies, or research corporations, as well as by the degree to which they focus on domestic versus international/transnational terrorism.

To begin, the majority of databases have focused on international and transnational terrorist events, whereas other types of terrorism (e.g., domestic) have been seriously underrepresented (Mitchell 1985; Gurr 1988a; Ross 1988a; 1988b). Three data sources we've already discussed that specialize in international/transnational terrorism and are routinely identified by analysts are: the Control Risks Group Data Base, RAND Corporation Data Base, and the State Department/Central Intelligence Agency/International Terrorism: Attributes of Terrorism Events (ITERATE) I, II, and III data sets (that is, Mickolus 1981).

More recently, after 9/11, the United Nations Office for Drug Control and Crime Prevention (now the Office for Drugs and Crime) has created a database through its Terrorism Prevention Branch. Although details are sketchy, this organization claims that its database has been used in the capability building (developing the research know-how) of countries throughout the world.

The RAND–St. Andrews (University) Database on Terrorism and Low-Intensity Conflict (Hoffman and Claridge 1988) was built from articles that appeared in newspapers and magazines from around the world. This research effort has since been renamed the Centre for the Study of Political Violence Data Base Project.[14]

The International Policy Institute for Counter-Terrorism in Herzlia, Israel (http://www.ict.org.il) has also established a database on terrorism. Although this database is available online, the details on how these data are gathered are not publicly available, and it lacks the capability of statistical analysis that most terrorism researchers would need.

Over the past six years, a cooperative effort has taken place between the Oklahoma City National Memorial Institute for the Prevention of Terrorism (MIPT) and RAND. Their database provides information on incidents of both domestic and international terrorism. Built on open-source information and at a cost of $700,000, this is one of several projects the MIPT (http://www.mipt.org) is pursuing.

Most of the databases on domestic terrorism have been constructed by academics (Ross 1991; 1994b; Smith 1994; Smith and Damphouse 1998; Sloan 1983; Weinberg and Eubank 1987a; 1987b). The majority of this work is limited to terrorism that occurred in a single country (see, for example, Clark 1983; Ross 1988b; 1994b; Weinberg and Eubank 1987b) or to campaigns perpetrated by a single group or motivated by a particular issue. Some researchers restrict their data collection efforts to a handful of campaigns (e.g., Hewitt 1984; Hewitt 1990). Rarely, however, are cross-national quantitative studies of terrorism performed (such as Engene and Skjolberg 2002; Bueno de Mesquita 2005a). Few projects that are statistical in nature involve cross-national statistical research.

There are four primary reasons why just a small amount of cross-national quantitative studies of terrorism exists:

1. The cost of compiling and acquiring data is prohibitive.

2. There is limited methodological sophistication of scholars to do complex quantitative research.

3. Investigators are reluctant to share data.

4. The various data sets are different (they have unique selection criteria, alternative formats, and so on), thus making comparison between data sets difficult.

These problems can be attributed to several causes. One is the limited methodological sophistication of scholars. There are two basic types of statistics: descriptive and inferential. For most general inquiries, all one really needs to know are descriptive statistics—frequencies, mediums (averages), modes, ranges, and other elementary statistical measurements—and, for the most part, this is what the State

Department provides to the public. However, when more complex questions are asked, one needs not only inferential statistics—regression analysis, factor analysis, path analysis—but also the ability to interpret them. Many individuals who work in this area of research, while having some basic understanding of elementary statistics, do not know how to do more complex quantitative studies.

Another reason why cross-national quantitative studies are limited involves the unwillingness of governments to share intelligence with academics and the lack of cooperation among scholars. Government agencies are frequently distrustful of outsiders who may scrutinize their work, and most scholar-researchers will try to exhaust the utility of their data sets (euphemistically called "mining") and publish as much of their own analysis as possible before releasing the data sets to the public or other academics—if they do so at all. Researchers also tend to reify their data sets and the methods they use to collect and analyze the materials. Furthermore, the fact that many data sets are dispersed in a variety of different formats often makes comparison difficult. Finally, the cost of compiling and acquiring data is perhaps the biggest roadblock.

The development of cross-national and longitudinally comparative measures of political terrorism is an extremely complex task. Over the last decade, however, some significant gains have been made with this research. This includes work by Bueno de Mesquita (2005a; 2005b), which looks at the types of individuals who join terrorist organizations and government reactions to terrorism.

There remain several potential problems with the events-database approach. First, there is no guarantee that the same stringent collection standards were used to develop each project. Second, there is no assurance that all the same variables were coded. Third, rarely is the reliability of the source material (e.g., newspapers) questioned or verified. Finally, there is no guarantee that data sets exist for all of the countries under investigation. This kind of research is typically devoid of emotion; it may unnecessarily distance researchers so they will be less attuned to the subtleties of the situation.

Other cautions are in order. It is important that each step be carefully carried out to ensure the quality of the entire project; this will improve the overall accuracy and meaningfulness. Coders must be careful about what sort of actions they include in the data set. For example, can we justifiably say that a terrorist action has occurred if we do not know the perpetrators' intent? What qualifies as an act of terrorism thus depends to a certain extent on the perception of the audience, including, in this instance, the perception of the coder.

Additionally, most databases intentionally include hoaxes and threats. This is problematic because almost anyone can make a phone call and threaten to commit a terrorist act or build something that resembles a bomb. Another issue is that of ecological fallacy: what may seem to make sense in the general case may not be easily translatable to a single incident.

Conclusion

The best starting point to maximize the utility of data-collection efforts and minimize errors might be to create separate data sets for each country using indigenous (local) sources (such as *Le Monde* for France, *La Prensa* for Spain, etc.) and to then link them with the international databases. Then perhaps a reliable master or comprehensive database could be created, one that integrates the MIPT data set with those that are linked to country-specific collection efforts. If the Canadian case is illustrative (Ross 1988; 1994b), then as much as 75 percent of terrorist acts that occur in any given country do not show up in a data set that focuses exclusively on international/transnational terrorism. This would, of course, necessitate a team of researchers who are fluent in the languages of the countries whose news media are to be screened. There is no question that creating a database to quantify domestic political terrorism would be time consuming, costly, difficult, and may reify bias.

Until a sufficient number of data sets are combined or until a master one is created, the empirical study of terrorism is hampered. The results of a comparative analysis achieved through crossnational studies would permit us to test for system-wide characteristics. While this type of approach would be ideal, it would also tend to be very costly in terms of time and financial resources.[15] We must also be mindful of the problem of diminishing returns; specifically, researchers should gauge the benefit that will be achieved by combining more and more databases to minimize the possibility that no event was ignored, against the additional resources that projects of this nature will cost and the predicted additional reliability and validity that will be afforded.

A satisficing strategy (doing something so it is passable) might reduce the costs of such an endeavor. There are several possible cases or countries to study. It would be ideal to examine all of these options, but because the data are very limited or costly to collect, a smaller sample would be preferable. Three frameworks to choose from make for natural comparisons: advanced industrialized democracies, Western nations, and Anglo-American democracies.

The first option is to look at all advanced industrialized democracies where significant campaigns of domestic political terrorism have taken place. Advanced industrialized democracies share general political, economical, and social similarities but are culturally diverse. Terrorism is also particularly unexpected and disruptive of the normal political process in advanced industrialized democracies. Unfortunately there are a considerable number of countries that fit this criteria, thus the cost of assembling appropriate research material would be high.

The second strategy would be to examine terrorism in Western nations. This term, however, is a bit ambiguous. According to *Webster's*, a Western nation is one that is based on "Greco-Roman traditions" (Webster's 1980, 1321). This type of definition would thus preclude nations such as Japan, which does not derive from Greco-Roman traditions, but has had a substantial amount of terrorism.

The final and preferred option would be to look at Anglo-American democracies (i.e., the United States, Canada, the United Kingdom, Australia, and New Zealand). The Anglo-American democracies are particularly appropriate for a comparative case study. Despite differing political institutions, all four share a common set of underlying political values that emphasize liberalism, individualism, and a willingness to compromise (Alford 1967, 71). The governmental and electoral systems in each country generally encourage the persistence of a two-party system at the national level, despite frequent electoral interventions from minor or third parties. The style of political leadership tends to be pragmatic, compromise seeking, and nonideological (Graetz and McAllister 1987, 45). But most importantly, all have distinctive communal minorities. Despite the similarities between these countries, there have not been any sustained campaigns of terrorism in either Australia or New Zealand.

In sum, it is difficult to suggest that either qualitative or quantitative research is more important or more effective. Each serves a specific purpose that is often dependent on what sort of research has been conducted to date, available resources, and the types of questions that are asked. Additionally, mechanisms and protocols should be established, and organizations like Europol, Interpol, and the United Nations should be encouraged to share data with terrorism researchers. This could even be coupled with the creation of a well-funded international center on terrorism to facilitate data collection and dissemination. Minimizing the concerns listed above and incorporating these suggestions may prove a step in the right direction of providing more comprehensive and rigorous research on terrorism as well as more informed policy decisions.

Questions, Chapter 2

PART ONE: MULTIPLE CHOICE

1. What type of political terrorism do most events databases on this subject examine?
   a. domestic
   b. state-sponsored
   c. ideological
   d. transnational
   e. corporate

2. Who stated that terrorists would rather have a lot of people watching than dying?
   a. Arno
   b. Hoffman
   c. Jenkins
   d. Rosen
   e. Schmid

3. What were two major terrorist groups operating between 66 to 1870 AD?
   a. crazies and crusaders
   b. the Sicarri and the Assassins
   c. anarchists and communists
   d. Macedonians and Armenians
   e. none of the above

4. What were three major terrorist groups operating between 1871 and 1960?
   a. the Sicarri, the Assassins, and the Thugs
   b. crazies, criminals, and crusaders
   c. Macedonians, Serbians, and Armenians
   d. anarchists, socialists, and communists
   e. none of the above

5. What is the use of drug trafficking to advance the objectives of certain terrorist organizations called?
   a. coup d'état
   b. oppositional terrorism
   c. narco-terrorism
   d. conspiracy-based terrorism
   e. morphing

6. Since databases on terrorism were first created, the spectrum of terrorist targets has:
   a. increased
   b. decreased
   c. decompressed
   d. strengthened
   e. minimized

7. During which decade did terrorists disproportionately begin shifting their attacks toward people?
   a. 1960s
   b. 1970s
   c. 1980s
   d. 1990s
   e. 2000s

8. Three major groups that were active in the ancient period are:
   a. the Boxers, the Sicarri, and the Assassins
   b. criminals, crazies and crusader
   c. Macedonians, Serbians, Armenians
   d. Social Revolutionary Party, Narodnaya Volya, and Anarchists
   e. none of the above

9. Who were the Sicarri?
   a. Praetorians
   b. people who used hashish in their ceremonies
   c. Jewish zealots
   d. theorists who integrated case studies and cross-national research
   e. Russian terrorists

10. In 1902, which terrorist group attacked political figures in Russia with the intention of overthrowing the czar?
    a. anarchists
    b. the Assassins
    c. the Boxers
    d. Social Revolutionary Party
    e. Narodnaya Volya

11. In the second tier of qualitative research, analysts look at:
    a. autobiographies
    b. primary sources
    c. biographies
    d. all of the above
    e. none of the above

12. The terrorist group called the Assassins derived their name from the Arabic name for
    a. meat-eater
    b. hashish-eater
    c. lazy man
    d. tomb raider
    e. none of the above

13. The majority of research on terrorism is:
    a. historical
    b. quantitative
    c. qualitative
    d. causal
    e. victims' accounts

14. Since the 1960s, terrorism has:
    a. increased
    b. decreased
    c. stopped
    d. increased and decreased in a cyclical fashion
    e. none of the above

15. Who developed a database on terrorist groups?
    a. Ross
    b. Crenshaw
    c. Gurr
    d. Schmid
    e. all of the above

16. What is an advantage of an events database on terrorism?
    a. publicly available
    b. minimal cost
    c. allows us to track trends
    d. precise
    e. available to share with other countries

17. In which time period did Irish terrorism start?
    a. ancient
    b. modern
    c. contemporary
    d. historical
    e. none of the above

18. In what country were the Boxers a militant sect?
    a. China
    b. Japan
    c. Korea
    d. Palestine
    e. Syria

19. A *sica* is
    a. robe
    b. gun
    c. bomb
    d. dagger
    e. manual for terrorists

20. The most well-known and utilized events data set for terrorism has been compiled by
    a. RAND Corporation
    b. Risks International
    c. CIA/State Department
    d. BDM
    e. Ross

21. What is the name of an independent "nonprofit" organization that performs contract and grant work for state and federal governments, some of which focuses on terrorism?
    a. Control Risks
    b. Booz Hamilton
    c. IBM
    d. RAND Corporation
    e. none of the above

22. In which country did the Red Brigades originate?
    a. Austria
    b. Canada
    c. France
    d. Italy
    e. United States

PART TWO: SHORT ANSWER

1. What are six basic tactics of terrorist?

2. What is the significance of Sterling's research on terrorism?

3. What are three advantages of ITERATE?

4. What is the difference between qualitative and quantitative research on terrorism?

5. According to State Department statistics, what is the most popular method of terrorist attack?

6. According to State Department statistics, over the past ten years what region of the world had the most amount of international attacks?

7. What is the modern-day name of the country or countries that the terrorist group called the Assassins operated in?

8. What are two problems with including threats and hoaxes in databases on terrorism?

9. What is the difference between terrorism that took place before and after the 1960s?

PART THREE: ESSAY

1. How has terrorism changed since the 1960s?

2. What are three advantages of events databases on terrorism?

3. Why is it important to study the history of terrorism?

4. Is there a connection between religion and terrorism?

CHAPTER THREE

Exploring the Causes[1]

There are few studies on the causes of terrorism. Nevertheless, when causation is examined, most explanations fall into three categories: structural, psychological, and rational choice. This chapter will construct a model that integrates structural and psychological causes of terrorism to help researchers test the relative importance of previously identified factors and their interactions,[2] as well as to help us better understand who commits terrorism and why an event or terrorist movement occurs. A good model might allow practitioners (such as analysts, policymakers, and those working in the field) to better allocate resources. It could also aid practitioners in their development of more informed and effective counterterrorist responses, thus enabling us to be more prepared to combat or even, ideally, to prevent terrorism.

Ultimately, terrorism is a synergistic phenomenon with causes that interact with its effects. As an ironic result, some of the factors that explain the effects of terrorism are intimately connected to its decline (see Ross and Gurr 1989; Crenshaw 1991; Ross 1995). A heart attack provides good analogy of how cause and effect are intertwined. Most reasonably health-conscious people know that in order to prevent a heart attack, you need to eliminate fat in your diet, and you need to exercise. There may also be a genetic disposition, over which you have no control. However, simply knowing all of this information without acting on it won't help you; after you experience your first heart attack, however, you might re-examine its causes and take steps to prevent a second heart attack. Thus, the causes (poor diet and exercise) that led to the effect (the heart attack) forced you to readdress the causes, thus changing the future effect. Causation is linked to effect, and effect, in turn, influences causation.

Our model treats the five processes it explains as interconnected. Those processes are joining, forming, staying in, and/or leading a terrorist organization, and engaging in terrorist actions. It is generally recognized that an individual does not need to be part of a terrorist group in order to commit violent, politically motivated actions. Take for example, Theodore Kaczynski, the Unabomber: over a decade, on his own, he sent letter and parcel bombs, with devastating effects, to individuals he believed were harming the environment and contributing to the alienation created by technology. However, the process of engaging in terrorism is usually aided by serving as a member of or leading a terrorist group, and the number of acts committed by a single person is likely to increase if these acts are conducted in a group setting (Oots 1986; Crenshaw 1985).

Literature Review

Few researchers have developed a general causal model or theory of the causes of terrorism. More common are studies that list several possible factors but fail to specify the interactions among them (Gross 1972; Hamilton 1978; Targ 1979; Crenshaw 1981; Johnson 1982, chapter 8; Hudson 1999). These analysts have nonetheless produced an important and necessary knowledge base from which to conduct further study. Among their accomplishments are:

- identification of important causal variables;

- elaboration of factors which are important in the stages of terrorism (Crenshaw; Johnson);

- description of individual factors in a historical context (Targ);

- partial development of a typology of causes (Crenshaw, Johnson);

- deduction of factors from more general theories of conflict (Hamilton);

- identification of processes which are contributing and sufficient (Gross);

- specification and empirical testing of relationships among some of the variables (Hamilton); and

- the construction of models on the causes and sequences of terrorism (Gross; Hamilton).

Merits aside, these works suffer from a series of problems that include, but are not limited to, the absence of a comprehensive theory or a model of terrorism. Three standard social science steps must be taken if this current enterprise is to succeed: we must define our terms, assemble our factors, and specify our relationships.

Methodology

When we address the usual causation factors—structural and psychological (which includes rational-choice factors, for our purposes)—it is easier to study structural factors first, mainly because this is less resource intensive than a psychological approach. In general, structural theories posit that the causes of terrorism can be found in the environment and the political, cultural, social, and economic fabric of societies. Psychological theories, on the other hand, try to specify and explain the mental processes of individuals and groups. For the latter, it is usually necessary to interview participants—in the field, in prison, and in other places where access is difficult or dangerous.

Terrorism—the dependent variable (understood to be the factor or process which is affected by all the contributing variables)—can be interpreted in terms of three levels: its scope, intensity, and amount. This is based on the assumption that certain types of independent variables lead only to low levels of terrorist violence (such as embassy takeovers), while other types of independent variables lead to higher levels of terrorism (such as bombings). It is also usually hypothesized that the greater the number and intensity of the causes of terrorism (the independent variables) are, the more terrorist acts will perpetrated by any particular terrorist or their organization (the dependent variable). If these factors are causally related, then the systematic elimination or lessening of these elements should lead to a decrease in terrorism.

Each type of terrorism has a different pattern of causation. In the main, terrorism is a response to a variety of subtle, interacting, ongoing, and changing psychological and structural factors manifested by perpetrators and audiences (victims, the public, the business community, government).[3] Thus, the relative importance of each independent variable depends on the context, which includes the type of perpetrator,[4] terrorist act,[5] target,[6] country, and time period. We'll avoid this kind of micro-level theorizing, however, in an effort to increase the parsimony of the proposed model. Though considerable diversity exists among terrorists, their organizations, and the context in which they operate, if analysts are to move beyond case studies (with the subjects often chosen at random), it is imperative that generalizations be made. The model proposed here is general enough to accommodate a variety of different individuals, groups, and contexts. It will outline variables and hypotheses that are logically connected and amenable to empirical testing.

To develop the model, nine types of studies on terrorism and terrorists were reviewed: 1) attempts to construct inclusive theories of causes; 2) studies that comment on causes; 3) case studies on causes for the development of terrorism in various countries; 4) case studies of individual terrorists; 5) case studies on particular organizations and movements that committed a substantial amount of terrorism; 6) case studies of terrorism in various countries; 7) analyses of individual causal factors; 8) work primarily concerned with critiquing other research; and 9) literature reviews on terrorism.

The Model

Those processes that theorists consider important in explaining the causes of terrorism were identified. All appropriate information was integrated into easily understandable categories, propositions specified, and developed into a comprehensive causal model.

By consolidating ten principal structural factors and five main psychological causes, the model summarizes a complex array of processes. Since structural processes precondition the psychological ones, we begin with a discussion of structural causes and then move to psychological ones. The proposed relationships among the previously outlined variables are diagrammed in exhibit box 14.

Structural causes

Ten structural causes of terrorism are delineated in our model. In general, most of these factors act as independent variables, but at other

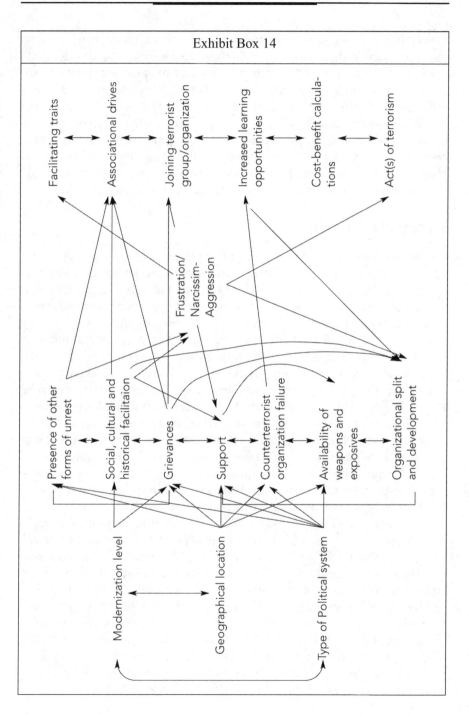

Exhibit Box 14

times, they can behave as dependent ones, in causal ordering. Following Crenshaw's distinction (1981), these causes may be divided into permissive factors (which create the conditions) and precipitant variables (things that immediately trigger) factors. Three permissive causes are predicted, from least to most important, as *geographical location, type of political system,* and *amount of modernization.* And the seven precipitants are hypothesized, from least to most important, as *social, cultural, and historical facilitation; organizational split and development; presence of other forms of unrest; support; counterterrorist organization failure; availability of weapons, explosives, and composite materials;* and *grievances.*

1. Permissive causes

Permissive factors are endemic to all societies. Geographical location, the type of political system, and the amount of modernization are ideal conditions that are necessary but not sufficient interacting predecessors that create the conditions for terrorism. They are deeper systemic conditions that prestructure the presence of the precipitants.

As a *geographical location,* cities are more likely than rural environments to facilitate terrorism. Urban environments allow terrorists several benefits over rural locations (Wilkinson 1977, 61–62; Grabosky 1979; Crenshaw 1981, 382). Cities offer three major advantages to terrorists: logistical superiority, support, and resources (urban locations usually have a closer proximity to resources). Sympathizers may offer assistance (material and technological) in an urban setting, and new recruits can be found in sites such as impoverished neighborhoods and institutions of higher learning. Finally, urban centers are usually closer to resources and offer more of them—including audiences and targets—in addition to access to weapons, explosives, and composite materials.

The *type of political system* in place in a country is another permissive factor. Terrorism is facilitated in prosperous democracies (Hamilton 1978; Gurr 1979; Turk 1982; Eubank and Weinberg 1994). A number of reasons may account for this phenomenon: the accessibility of victims by foreign terrorists (for example, al-Fatah attacks in France, September 5, 1973); guarantees of fundamental civil liberties promoting movement, access to the media, and the free expression of dissent, all of which accommodate diverse political values and demands (Gurr 1979, 43); the proliferation of narrow-based social issues; and the existence of police forces that are generally law abiding. These factors are rarely found in or safeguarded in other types of political systems.

Modernization of a society, the most important of the permissive factors, produces several factors that encourage terrorism (Crenshaw 1981, 381; Johnson 1982, 163–66). Six of these variables include 1) a variety of better, more sophisticated, vulnerable targets; 2) destructive weapons and technology; 3) mass media; 4) populations with increased literacy; 5) conflicts with traditional ways of life; and 6) improved networks of transportation. Modern societies encompass urban environments and create pressures that frequently encourage the establishment of democratic political systems. In the main, modern societies are causally prior to democracy because they press for democratic changes (Huntington 1968).

2. Precipitant causes

The precipitant causes are the motivating or triggering factors that are necessary to move an individual or group to begin or continue terrorist actions. These are social, cultural, and historical facilitation; organizational split and development; presence of other forms of unrest; support; counterterrorist organization failure; availability of weapons, explosives, and composite materials; and grievances. They typically work in concert with each other.

Social, cultural, and historical facilitation consists of shared attitudes, beliefs, customs, habits, myths, opinions, traditions, and values that permit the development of nationalism, fanaticism, violence, and terrorism in a subgroup of a population (Wilkinson 1974, 96; Crenshaw 1981, 382). This facilitation may reinforce terrorists' perception that the risks of committing violence are relatively small; have an inspirational effect which leads to imitation; increase a member's commitment to the group; disseminate information that will inspire and justify an individual's or group's use of violence; supply discontented individuals or organizations with enough technological knowledge and ideological justification to support their use of terrorism; provide the inspiration needed to cause a contagion of similar events elsewhere in the world (Redlick 1979; Midlarsky, Crenshaw, and Yoshida 1980); or mitigate such phenomena as doctrinal debates and factionalization, defections, fear, and growing resistance to leaders' demands and political strictures. Thus, if an organization has an ideology advocating violence, then there should be a higher motivation to act upon these dictates. Social, cultural, and historical facilitation leads to support, organizational development or split, and may contribute to the failure of counterterrorist practices.

Most terrorist groups develop as "result of a split between the moderate and the more extreme wings of an already-existing organization" (such as a political party) (Laqueur 1977, 103; Weinberg and Pedahzur 2003), that is, *organizational development or split*. Sometimes divisions create a rivalry within and among terrorist groups that can lead to clashes among the various groups which, in turn, reduces their effective power (Laqueur 1977, 104). At other times, an organizational split that leads to the creation of a terrorist group may bring about more violence. Both established and offspring organizations are motivated to demonstrate their willingness to engage in terrorism by competing for resources and proving to their presumed, actual, or potential constituency that they are serious about their goals. Organizational development or split usually leads to new venues that support terrorism and channel a population's grievances.

The existence of *other forms of unrest* (political, economic, social) among populations—violent or nonviolent—may act as a catalyst for terrorism. These forms of unrest can include war, revolution, guerrilla warfare, strikes, protests, demonstrations, riots, or other groups' terrorist actions (Monti 1980). Unrest can serve as a motivator for terrorist organizations, provide learning opportunities, increase the legitimacy of violent actions, and heighten grievances. Unrest both inside and outside state boundaries may influence individuals and groups to commit terrorism. Generally, the closer the proximity of unrest, the higher the likelihood that it will act as a catalyst (Midlarsky, Crenshaw, and Yoshida 1980). Presence of other forms of unrest is promoted when there is a communication mechanism that relays this information to disgruntled populations. Other forms of unrest can also heighten grievances and lead to organizational splits and development. This process, generally referred to as "contagion," is a form of imitation and is present in various forms of political violence and crime.

Support from a variety of actors facilitates terrorism (Laqueur 1977, 110–16; Sterling 1981; Cline and Alexander 1984; Clutterbuck 1986). Help may be in the form of finances, training, intelligence, false documents, donations or sales of weapons, explosives, composite materials, provision of sanctuary or safe housing, propaganda campaigns, ideological justification, public opinion, legal services, or a constant supply of recruits. Some of the sources from whom terrorist organizations receive support either directly or indirectly are other members of the aggrieved population (i.e., sympathizers),[7] states, national security organizations,[8] individual terrorists, terrorist and guerrilla organizations, organized crime groups, the media,[9] emigrant populations, philanthropists, academics, and professionals. These constituencies help terrorists to further the terrorists' goals, to promote their own objectives, or to obtain financial gain. Their support can lead to the failure of counterterrorist organizations, greater availability of weapons, explosives, and composite materials, and grievances.

The *failure of counterterrorist organizations*—police, military, national security and intelligence services, prisons, private security companies, and the government in general—to detect, prevent, combat, and control terrorism may provoke, maintain, and encourage terrorism.[10] Problems common to most organizations are found in antiterrorist agencies, but more specifically, antiterrorist or counterterrorist organizations' inability to control terrorism is related to a number of failures in their responsibilities or aims. They are unable to strengthen agencies charged with antiterrorist functions; increase the risks for terrorists and people who might join or support them (thus deterring terrorists); maintain the semblance of democracy; detect terrorists; preempt terrorist actions; and make appropriate organizational changes. In short, the failures of counterterrorist organizations—which vary over time—enable terrorist groups to acquire weapons, explosives, and composite materials. They may also increase oppositional grievances and encourage the support of terrorist organizations by aggrieved populations.

The *availability of weapons, explosives, and composite materials*[11]—as well as the knowledge needed to build them—is an important result of the failure of antiterrorist organizations and of a society with relatively permissive weapons, explosives, and composite materials–related legislation, policies and practices. Terrorists have had few problems obtaining weapons, explosives, and composite materials (Hippchen and Yim 1982), which can be acquired in four ways: purchases, gifts, theft, or construction. The availability of weapons, explosives, and composite materials leads directly to support of such activities; no one wants to back a powerless organization. Counterterrorist organization failures, on the other hand, can affect the tactics that terrorists choose. Other factors include liberal gun-possession laws (as in the United States) or recent civil wars involving numerous kinds of weapons and explosives (as in Afghanistan or Lebanon), which are more accessible afterwards.

Grievances—actual and perceived, putative and general—are probably the most important structural variable. This is not to say that mobilization, leadership, and entrepreneurship are not important, but grievances are central to all terrorism. Grievances, commonly manifested as coercion, discrimination, oppression, and repression—often against an identifiable subgroup of a larger population (minorities or elites, for example)—can lead to terrorism (Hamilton 1978; Crenshaw 1981, 383; Gurr 1990). Grievances leading to terrorism can be divided into seven categories: economic, ethnic, racial, legal, political, religious, and social. Grievances are directed against a variety of individuals, groups, organizations, classes, races, and ethnicities, both public and private (such as the government, businesses, unions, the military, police, religious organizations, political parties, and so on). Unheeded grievances can lead to the development of a social movement, interest group, or political party, or, in extreme cases, an individual, cell, group, or organization that engages in terrorist actions. Alternatively, in a nonviolent organization, the intensification of grievances or lack of success in obtaining the groups' objectives may lead to organizational splits and the development of different subunits that *do* engage in terrorism (e.g., component parts of the PLO). Finally, grievances can lead to the support of terrorism. A third party aware of the grievances may seize an opportunity for influence by giving support to candidates likely to engage in terrorism. The presence of other forms of unrest, social, cultural, and historical facilitation, or organizational split and development heightens the intensity of already felt grievances.

In summary, structural factors interact with each other to create an environment that permits terrorism. In general, the permissive causes structure the type and amount of precursors to a group's choice of terrorism, which is facilitated by precipitant causes that interact with each other. While all of the seven precipitants may motivate individuals or groups to choose terrorism as a means by which to obtain their goals, typically the pattern is more complex. For example, grievances can lead to support; support may reinforce grievances or the availability of weapons, explosives, and composite materials; counterterrorist organization failure can lead to support; and organizational split and development may lead to grievances.

Psychological causes

The second part of our model concerns the psychological causes of terrorism, developed by consolidating five principal factors and a series of interrelated hypotheses. Psychology has different schools, areas of research, and theories that offer some insight into the causes of terrorism. Seven psychological theories that explain terrorists' behavior are most prominent in the scholarly literature: 1) psychoanalytical (Morf 1970); 2) learning (Pitcher and Hamblin, 1982); 3) frustration-aggression (Gurr 1970); 4) narcissism-aggression (Perlstein 1991); 5) trait (Russell and Miller 1983); 6) developmental (Sayari 1985); and 7) motivational/rational choice (Crenshaw 1990). These theories are partial explanations, as none are in and of themselves sufficient to explain the psychological causes of terrorism. The alternative strategy proposed here *integrates* these approaches.[12]

According to this integrated view (which incorporates both permissive and precipitant causes), childhood and adolescent experiences condition individuals to develop personality traits that predispose them to engage in acts of terrorism. The development of these traits can be explained by biological, psychoanalytic, learning, and frustration- or narcissism-aggression theories. These attributes motivate individuals to commit terrorism alone, form bonds with other people who are predisposed to engage in terrorism, or develop, join, remain in, or lead terrorist organizations (terrorists experience the most important learning opportunities within the context of a group, as we have discussed). These processes, in turn, shape the cost-benefit calculus of individual terrorists.

The psychological part of the model consists of five etiological factors of terrorism listed in increasing order of importance: *the development of facilitating traits, frustration or narcissism-aggression, associational drives, learning opportunities,* and *cost-benefit calculations.* These processes are present in each individual, but their importance and unique combination varies among terrorists, groups, and contexts.

A considerable effort has been directed at identifying basic personality traits of terrorists (for example, Gutmann 1979), to learn *the development of facilitating traits.* The underlying assumption of this work is that specific characteristics predispose people to individually engage in terrorism, join terrorist organizations, and/or commit this type of political violence on behalf of a group. Although a generalized personality profile of terrorists has been criticized and largely discounted (Crenshaw 1986, 385; Wilkinson 1977, 193), the results from profiling studies (Russell and Miller 1983; Jager, Schmidtchen, and Süllwold 1981) have provided investigators some insights on the personality traits of terrorists. A few of the more prominent characteristics are, from least to most reported: fear, hostility, depression, guilt, anti-authoritarianism, a perceived lack of manliness, self-centeredness, extreme extroversion, a need for high risks or stress, and alienation (see Ross 1994a, 20–24).[13]

Despite being periodically discredited (Friedland 1992, 86), some analysts have argued that terrorism is caused by frustration manifested in aggression, that is, *frustration-aggression* (see Dollard et al. 1939; Gurr 1970).[14] Even though it is recognized that not all frustration experienced by individuals results in aggression (Merton 1938), under some conditions, a proportion of it does. In the main, frustration may be caused by the accumulation of unresolved grievances. Even though frustration-aggression may cause individuals to lash out at the targets of their frustration on their own, they may also perceive that it would be better to join others who share the same beliefs (Sutherland 1947).

Some terrorists are individuals who have previously received blows to their ego. This psychological injury, it is argued, leads to aggression if an individual encounters an appropriate target. This is what is meant by *narcissism-aggression* (Pearlstein 1991). Narcissistic injury and rage may be present, but they are generally not sufficient as an explanation, because those experiencing this reaction may engage in something other than an act of terrorism to placate their anger. Instead, many terrorists experience frustration, a need to consolidate or make up for the lack of meaning in their previous careers (such as criminals who turn to terrorism), or want to redress grievances held by others.[15]

Although some terrorist events are committed by individuals acting alone, the majority of violent political acts of this nature are performed by groups or organizations through what are called *associational drives* (Oots 1986; Friedland 1992, 82). Joining a terrorist group can be a conscious attempt (or unconscious reaction) to affiliate with others who share similar personalities, can provide benefits, and further their individual goals.[16] There is a tendency for some marginal, isolated, and lonely individuals with troubled family backgrounds to be attracted to particular terrorist organizations. For these individuals, belonging to the terrorist group is the first time they feel a sense of belonging (Post 1984). In fact, Weinberg and Davis (1989) identify a "push/pull dynamic": recruits may experience a "push provided by internal psychological attributes and . . . [a] pull offered by the organizations to which these individuals become attached" (97).

Belonging to a terrorist organization, then, serves a series of purposes: it educates and socializes individual members (Post 1984, 251); legitimizes the collective grievances of individual members; satisfies the need of its members to belong; expresses members' individual traits; and develops a shared identity and commitment to a cause

(Hacker 1976, 295). The group "diminishes or eliminates conflicts among the followers through group identification in the service of a cause, [and] cements the group into a coherent whole" (Hacker 1976, 43); it "permits precise role definitions in relation to and in the service of the cause" (43) and protects individual members (295).

Terrorist groups also provide *learning opportunities.* The groups and the commission of terrorism itself satisfy a number of psychological needs of those predisposed to use this form of political behavior. Although terrorists bring some knowledge and skills, members of an organization are exposed to many varied learning experiences, allowing them to adopt different roles that shape their orientations and behavior.[17] Terrorism is thus a learned behavior that can be explained by general principles of learning theory. Certainly learning in other conflict situations has been identified (Pitcher and Hamblin 1982), and the two most important learning theories applicable to terrorism are operant conditioning (Skinner 1938), and social learning/modeling (Bandura 1973).[18] The first recognizes that in order to get some sort of benefit or achieve a goal or reward, a person continuously modifies his or her behavior in an active fashion through a sequence of steps. The second suggests that individuals learn through a process of observing and/or interacting with others, then modeling or imitating that behavior.

Ultimately, the choice to engage in a terrorist action is a conscious or unconscious *cost-benefit calculation,* sometimes referred to as an expression of political strategy (Crenshaw 1990), in which expected utility is calculated individually by each terrorist and collectively by the terrorist group.[19] In other words, terrorists do what they do not because they are crazy or suffer from psychological maladjustments, but because they are relatively rational human beings (Corrado 1981), and examinations of their motivations will show a well–thought out logic for their behavior (Kaplan 1978). Most terrorists (Baader-Meinhoff gang, Shining Path, Tupamaros, etc.) see their actions as cost-effective means to achieve individual, collective, tangible, or symbolic recognition, attention, or publicity for their cause; disrupt and discredit appropriate targets; create fear and/or hostility in an audience identified as the "enemy"; provoke overreaction by the government and its coercive agencies; create sympathy amongst potential supporters; and increase control, discipline, and morale within the terrorist group (Hacker 1976). In this light, terrorist choices are rational, based on the purposes and goals of terrorism. It has been argued that the greater the sophistication—as measured in terms of planning, selection of target, and risk involved—the greater the amount of rational choice involved in the process.

In summary, the psychological causes are affected by the structural ones. The organization of society, including the type of political and economic system as well as historical factors, present options that affect the decisions and choices of individuals and organizations to engage in terrorism.

Conclusion

Although this chapter reviewed the structural and psychological causes of terrorism and outlined a number of individual, group, and structural level processes, the utility of the model will be best determined when these propositions are tested. Testing of each hypothesis (or many) would require operationalization of these processes, deciding the type of methodology to use (for example, comparative case study versus events-database analysis), and collecting data in a systematic fashion. Unfortunately, no comprehensive, publicly available data set exists that can be used to test these hypotheses.[20]

Testing and subsequent modification of this proposed model should lead to a comprehensive theory of terrorism. Researchers who work in this area should be encouraged to gather appropriate data that would allow them to empirically test the propositions. A better understanding of the complex underpinnings of terrorism would enable analysts to better link the causes of this type of political violence and crime and consequently develop more comprehensive explanations.

Causal modeling of the type developed here should be regarded as an iterative process. First-generation causal models in a field of inquiry such as terrorism, which is descriptively rich but analytically barren, will provide the foundation for future and more complex models. Testing should also include all types of oppositional terrorism (domestic, international/transnational, and state sponsored). More sophisticated generations of the model would be placed in the larger context of the literature about the causes of political violence and crime research. Additionally, factors would be better outlined, operationalized, and tested quantitatively to determine the strength of these relationships. Case studies of countries and groups could be based on foreign-language reports for greatest accuracy. Finally, more refined models may be constructed and tested as more evidence accrues on the subject of terrorism. Terrorism has not disappeared. Increasing separatism and ethnic conflict in the former communist states and satellites of the Soviet Union and elsewhere, and the proclivity of some religious fundamentalists (Muslim, Christian, Catholic, Protestant, Sikh, etc.) to incorporate acts of terrorism will provide an up-to-date laboratory in which to study and combat terrorism well into the twenty-first century.

Questions, Chapter 3

PART ONE: MULTIPLE CHOICE

1. Is there a relationship between causation and effects explanations of terrorism?
   a. yes
   b. no
   c. depends on the statistical technique used
   d. none of the above
   e. some of the above

2. In explaining the structural causes of terrorism, which of the following is a permissive factor?
   a. ideology
   b. type of political system
   c. early childhood experiences
   d. none of the above
   e. all of the above

3. What is the most important structural cause of oppositional political terrorism?
   a. type of political system
   b. location
   c. availability of weapons
   d. grievances
   e. support

4. Who developed explanations for the structural causes of oppositional political terrorism?
   a. Crenshaw
   b. Gurr
   c. Kellett
   d. Mickolus
   e. Turk

5. According to the scholarly literature, are most terrorists suffering from some form of psychopathology?
   a. yes
   b. no
   c. depends on the sophistication of the evaluation technique
   d. only those who get captured
   e. only the anarchists

6. Which of the following is NOT one of the psychological theories that explain terrorist behavior?
   a. learning
   b. grievances
   c. psychoanalytical
   d. developmental
   e. motivational

7. In explaining the psychological causes of terrorism, which of the following is a permissive factor?
   a. availability of weapons and explosives
   b. early childhood experiences
   c. ideology
   d. type of political system
   e. counterterrorist organization failure

8. What type of casual theory on oppositional political terrorism is most amenable to empirical testing?
   a. individual
   b. psychological
   c. structural
   d. a and b
   e. none of the above

PART TWO: SHORT ANSWER

1. What is the difference between a permissive and precipitant cause of terrorism?

2. What are seven structural causes of oppositional political terrorism?

3. What are five psychological theories that have contributed to the understanding of oppositional political terrorism?

4. In the context of the causes of terrorism, what is a cost-benefit calculation?

5. What are four kinds of support a terrorist organization may get?

6. List six grievances leading a group to resort to terrorism.

7. List five steps and/or parts in the psychological causal model of oppositional political terrorism outlined in this chapters.

PART THREE: ESSAY

1. Why should we have a theory or model on the causes of political terrorism?

2. How would you test the causal model or selected aspects of it?

3. Is the mafia a terrorist organization?

4. Why is it important to study the psychological causes of terrorism? And what inherent problems plague this kind of research?

CHAPTER FOUR

Understanding the Effects[1]

This chapter integrates five actor-based models that outline the effects of terrorism. The "process of effects" encompasses the consequences, outcomes, reactions and responses to terrorism. It begins by analyzing two conflict theories in order to sketch the responses of terrorists, victims and victims' families, victims' friends, the general public, and the government. An examination of both causal and effects models will help us understand the rise and fall of terrorist groups. Although much has been written on the effects of terrorism (Wardlaw 1982; Hewitt 1984; Weinberg and Davis 1989, chapters 5–7; Sederberg 1989, chapter 6), particularly counterterrorism efforts (Livingstone and Arnold 1986), a comprehensive model of the responses has not been developed.[2] The purpose of this chapter is to create a series of relatively comprehensive actor-based models that outline the responses to (effects of) terrorism. In order to accomplish this task, a currently existing conflict model will serve as a framework to sketch these responses and to specify some of the more important hypotheses. This work provides a tool to explore and test the responses, and ultimately, cycles of terrorist-target interaction.[3]

Models of Conflict Processes

Different models of conflict processes have been developed to explain the effects of terrorism. "Conflict processes" and "conflict theory" are the broad terms used to describe the scholarly explanations for violent interactions between and among individuals, groups, nations, and countries. It draws its material from fields of inquiry such as criminology, political science, psychology, and sociology.

The action-reaction model

One of the more popular conflict theories is Lichbach's (1987) action-reaction (A-R) model. Although sophisticated in its own context, the A-R model is both over- and underinclusive in its explanation of the process of terrorism. The model is overinclusive because it incorporates many types of political protest with dynamics not often found in terrorism (such as demonstrations, sit-ins, peaceful marches, protests, and civil disobedience). On the other hand, the A-R model is not inclusive enough to accommodate some of the more important variables found in terrorism (such as ideology, motivational level, criminal histories, etc.). Moreover, Lichbach's model leads to a finite outcome; processes are rarely so precise in the political arena. Finally, the model and conclusion are not applicable to the particular symbiotic relationship between terrorists and audiences.

The stimulus-response model

The stimulus-response (S-R) model (Holsti, Brody, and North 1964), though criticized as being insufficient (Lichbach 1987, 260, 288), is more appropriate to explain the dynamic interaction between terrorist group(s) and other actors.[4] This model is interactive because while the opposition group (i.e., a terrorist organization) engages in violent activities against victims, the general public, the business community, and the government, these targets or the authorities may retaliate in turn or respond in other ways that affect the opposition group.

In the S-R model, terrorist attacks are considered to be inputs to the target country and its constituency. The state and its constituency respond; their response is their output. This output is then received as an input to the terrorist or terrorist group. Thus, the cycle of stimulus and response is perpetuated almost indefinitely. Although the S-R model is loose and lacks the predictive features of the A-R model, it better captures the actors and interactions of terrorism. Before continuing, however, the characteristics of the S-R model, the stimulus, and the response must be examined separately and more closely.

1. Characteristics of S-R models

We must remember that individuals and groups using and responding to terrorism make rational choices in advancing their objectives: in other words, they are free to choose those weapons, techniques, and targets that would serve their purpose best. Part of this decision-making process depends upon experience. Terrorists and audiences generally learn from their successes and failures, however they define those terms, and modify their behavior with the goal of enhancing their chances of achieving their objectives in subsequent attacks. It is also true that the type of effect depends on the context—the kind of society, political system, and terrorism exercised in these domains. Thus, making generalizations is difficult. However, we can identify some characteristics of the stimulus-response model.

- S-R activities occur in two basic environments: domestic/national and regional/international (Weinberg and Davis 1989, 139).

- S-R activities impact individuals and organizations both directly and indirectly.

- S-R actions taken by the actors are also dependent on timing. In this respect, the responses are proactive (anticipatory) or reactive (responsive). Hardening targets, developing antiterrorist technology, signing separate treaties among states, introducing new laws, and collecting intelligence are all examples of proactive measures. Retaliatory military strikes and negotiations during hostage situations, on the other hand, are reactive measures.[5]

- Actors in the political arena continuously scrutinize, criticize, and assess each other's performance.[6] Consequently, any reaction is bounded by the perception of the situation (as in Iran under the shah in 1978 and early 1979); the rhetoric of the actors (as in the 1993 Reagan administration's tough talk in the case of Lebanon and terrorism); or impression management (as in the South African government under Botha in 1985 and 1986).

- Responses can be both psychological and structural, with the understanding that some actors' reactions cluster more at one level than at another. For example, the majority of victims and/or their immediate family and friends respond psychologically, as they experience terrorism primarily at the individual level of analysis. Opportunism and lobbying, on the other hand, can be considered structural processes that come into play if victims are released or escape.

2. The stimulus

A close examination of the S-R model reveals that there are several dimensions and levels of interaction that condition the process. Terrorism is a form of communication (Schmid and de Graff 1982): terrorists "deliver" their communiqués to the authorities and to the general public both directly and indirectly. Attacking state targets (such as governmental officials or properties) is considered a direct channel to the authorities, while attacking non-state targets (such as bystanders) is considered indirect (i.e., through a third party) (Thorton 1964, 77–79). The target audience may believe that these events are important enough to warrant a response, and their reactions can cover a host of possibilities. These responses are interpreted by the terrorists as stimuli and motivate similar, modified, or new actions. Therefore, the first cycle is complete, and the next phase of S-R interaction begins, albeit changed by the utilization of various methods and targets of attack, and countermeasures or responses (see exhibit box 15).

3. The response: An actor-based typology

Academic literature occasionally advances typologies of different kinds of terrorism (Schmid with Stohl and Flemming 1988, chapter 2). Yet a typology of *responses* to terrorism has not been developed. Not all actors respond or are capable of reacting the same way. In general, S-R actions affect five types of actors: terrorists, victims and their friends and family, the general public, businesses, and the government (what we can conceive as the audience, and terrorists themselves, the initial catalysts).[7] Each of the five actors' behavior may resemble another's (i.e., stimuli may look like responses), but there are subtle differences in the methods, intensity, and duration of each type of action among the participants.[8] Finally, in the aftermath of a terrorist event, there are what may be classified as short- and long-term effects. The first include fear and anger, the second passage of antiterrorism legislation.

In summary, terrorism is a form of communication, decisions are made in a rational-choice framework, and responses are conditioned by learned behavior (previous responses to stimuli), behavior that is sensitive to context. Typing response—by who has exercised it, where it

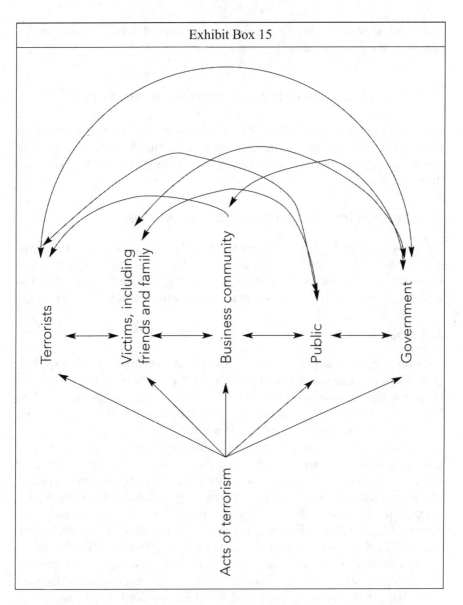

Exhibit Box 15

takes place, or when—is a double-edged sword. It may weaken or strengthen the perception of legitimacy and credibility of each actor in relation to other. Even though the environment, type of event, and timing are important, typing response by actor is easiest to operationalize (i.e., to measure and or convert into something that is meaningful to test) and serves as the principle organizational tool to analyze the effects of terrorism in this chapter.

Five actor-based response models

Five basic actors are involved in any terrorist incident: the terrorists themselves, their victims, the general public, businesses, and government. Going forward, we will discuss the effects of terrorism on each of these actors.

The effects of terrorism on perpetrators (terrorists)

Terrorists and their groups[9] show essentially seven responses to terrorism. These interrelated actions are, from those least enacted to those most often used, resource procurement, negotiation, group identity-building exercises, training, innovation, planning, and tactical violence.

1. Resource procurement

Groups acquire resources (money, expertise, recruits) to achieve their objectives. If these are not obtained through donations from supporters (in the wider population or foreign governments) or legal means, then terrorist groups may get them through illegal channels such as drug trafficking, protection rackets, bank robberies, hostage takings, and so on (Adams 1986). Terrorists engage in intelligence activities, including gathering, sharing, and evaluating information. This may also lead them to test the vulnerability of targets. In order to obtain necessary resources, and as a response to government crackdowns, terrorists may engage in alliance building. The Japanese Red Army, for example, formed bonds with al-Fatah; the Front de Liberation du Québéc partnered with the Black Panthers; and during the 1980s, several European groups formed an alliance to attack NATO targets. Not only have terrorist organizations formed agreements with other similar groups, some (e.g., Palestinian groups and the Japanese Red Army) have also found support from so-called rogue states (e.g., North Korea, etc.)

Terrorist groups may engage in criminal activities that produce income in order to finance their actions. This activity can include actions such as kidnapping, protection rackets, and illegal control of certain labor markets (Adams 1986). Illegal means of raising funds can also include the sale and/or cultivation of illicit drugs. Terrorist groups need to acquire new and more sophisticated weapons and explosives and communications technology in order to better threaten or engage in violence (Jenkins 1992, 19). If they cannot buy, steal, or receive these items from supporters, then terrorists will construct them with guidance from readily available sources (Powell 1971).

2. Negotiation

Due to government crackdowns or because of burnout (Ross and Gurr 1989) terrorists may also resort to negotiation with state actors (particularly when general amnesties are offered), supporters, or allies. These processes are evident in the repeated attempts by the Israeli government to negotiate with the Palestinian Liberation Organization (PLO) and the British government's efforts to deal with the Irish Republican Army Provisionals (PIRA).

3. Group identity-building exercises

Terrorist organizations engage in group identity-building exercises as well (Crenshaw 1981; Weinberg and Davis 1989, 151). Many terrorist activities are committed in order to improve solidarity in the group. For example, many of the efforts of Palestinian terrorist organizations during the 1970s and 1980s were an attempt to build esprit du corps.

4. Training

Organizations wanting to improve their success train their members both in techniques and ideology. This can include establishing training camps or fighting guerrilla campaigns in other countries. This is a prime example of the learning processes which were discussed in the last chapter.

5. Innovation

If governments crack down, or terrorist groups feel as if they are not meeting their objectives, then they may be motivated to innovate by acquiring or developing new technologies, hardware, and explosive materials; utilizing different tactics; and/or getting more or better training. For instance, during the 1970s, when governments improved their ability to prevent or resolve hijackings, terrorist groups depended on other attention-getting tactics, such as suicide bombings (Jenkins 1992, 18; Pape 2003). Terrorists may resort to innovation in response to various factors. Demographic shifts may force them to change their zone of operations. The response of their audience—the psychological and behavioral reactions of victims, their families, supporters, and the general public; public desensitization and anger; media propagation; increased security by businesses; hardening of targets; and greater surveillance—may force them to innovate in the cause-and-effect cycle discussed in the previous chapter.

6. Planning

Carrying out a successful terrorist attack usually requires a considerable amount of advanced planning and preparation. This may include conducting surveillance, intercepting communications, and understanding the routines of public security agencies. It also means that resources need to be acquired and mobilized in order to carry out the incident. The 9/11 incident is a case in point. Subsequent investigations into the attack have determined the plans were in the works since Ramzi Yousef's 1993 failed attempt to blow up the twin towers.

7. Threat and use of tactical violence

Finally, it goes without saying that the raison d'être of terrorist groups is to create fear. They do this through the threat and use of tactical violence.

In summary, terrorist effects are partly a result of their objectives and partly a result of the reactions of other actors in their environment. The most immediate actor(s) terrorists have to deal with, of course, are victims.

The effects of terrorism on victims and their families and friends

Identifying the actual victims of terrorism is difficult. According to Taylor (1988, 17), with some exceptions, "There is relatively little literature analyzing the 'victimology' of terrorism." Vetter and Perlstein (1991) suggest that a terrorist act "may affect a number of people: the immediate victims of the terrorist assault; their families and close friends; those in authority, who are often forced to make life or death decisions concerning the fate of hostages; the fellow countrymen of the initial victims;

and, eventually, everyone in the world community of law abiding nations" (68).

Despite who else may be broadly affected, some analysts, like Vetter and Perlstein, restrict the label of victim for "those who suffer direct assault from terrorists" (1991, 68). Other analysts believe this is too narrow and extend the term to families and friends.

In general, if victims survive a terrorist action, they may develop a variety of conscious and unconscious psychological and behavioral reactions as a result of the trauma (Ochberg and Soskis 1982; Long 1990, 133). There are eight interrelated psychological processes that victims may experience, some as a result of so-called defense mechanisms. These factors are listed in the chronological, temporal order that they are experienced: fear; shock; grief; guilt; identifying with the terrorists; if they are released or escape, isolation, alienation, or withdrawal; opportunism; and lobbying the government. These reactions vary based on the type of terrorist action, the victim's personality, the duration of the event, and the timing of the incident. All of these responses are reactive; none are proactive, unless one considers survival or hostage training that potential victims might receive.

1. Fear

Terrorism creates fear in individuals attacked, those who survive, witnesses, and the family and friends of the victims. That is why it so effective. The suddenness and unpredictability of it all helps contribute to this strong emotion.

2. Shock

Shock, also known as trauma (which can lead to denial and disbelief), might be present in victims during the initial event (Long 1990, 133). Shock may be caused "when they are faced with the reality of forcible detention and maybe abduction" and is "perhaps associated with psychological arousal and hypersensitivity" (Taylor 1988, 19). Taylor also suggests that denial of the event may be a "means of adjusting to it" (1988, 19).

3. Grief

Additionally, victims can experience grief, sometimes expressed as rage, bereavement, or anger. These emotions are "the psychological reaction to the loss of a loved one, of a cherished goal, or a cherished aspect of one's life" (Vetter and Perlstein 1991, 69). More concretely, the victims may have been "badly beaten or injured, possibly maimed" or "feel impotent in retaliating against their terrorist aggressors" (Vetter and Perlstein 1991, 70). They "can also grieve, however, for the loss of an image of themselves. . . . This grieving may be accompanied by the depressed feelings that accompany other grief reactions and may also precipitate depressive illnesses in persons who are predisposed" (Vetter and Perlstein 1991, 70).

4. Guilt

Moreover, victims often feel guilty. Guilt "can arise over why the victim allowed himself or herself to get caught, why s/he was spared when others were tortured or executed, . . . was released or escaped when the others were not, or how difficult it was for family members to cope without him or her" (Long 1990, 133).

5. Identification with captors

Additionally, victims may identify with their terrorist captors. This process is generally referred to as "hostage-identification" or "Stockholm" syndrome, in which feelings of camaraderie, closeness, empathy, sympathy, friendship, and even love may develop among hostages and terrorists (Hacker 1976, 107–10). In this situation, "physical proximity and exclusive interdependence between captors and captive promote budding emotions of belonging. Antagonists forcibly thrown together turn into co-victims and easily find the common enemy that victimizes them both" (Hacker 1976, 114–15). Patty Hearst, who was allegedly transformed from a victim to a soldier of the Symbionese Liberation Army (SLA), is the textbook example of this phenomenon.[10] (See Exhibit Box 10)

6. Isolation, withdrawal, and alienation

If they are released by or escape from their captors, or are freed by security forces, victims may isolate themselves. This reaction may be a product "of guilt that they did not do everything possible to escape, and shame at being humiliated and defiled. . . . When defense mechanisms . . . fail to relieve anxiety during the incident, a trauma-related anxiety syndrome develops that can last for several years" (Long 1990,

Exhibit Box 16
Stockholm syndrome

This term was coined after it was discovered—through the use of a listening device—that during a bank robbery in 1973 in Stockholm, Sweden, and throughout protracted hostage negotiations, two of the women held captive had what appeared to be consensual sexual relations with the bank robbers. In 1974 a similar incident, after Patty Hearst, granddaughter of William Randolph Hearst, the famous newspaper magnate, was allegedly kidnapped by the Symbionese Liberation Army (SLA), she appeared to join their cause. After capture, she was kept in a closet (and suffered sensory deprivation). Shortly after this, she was caught on bank security cameras assisting the SLA in bank robberies around Oakland, California. When she was later released by the SLA and charged with the bank robberies, her defense team argued that she was suffering from Stockholm syndrome.

According to advocates of Stockholm syndrome, captives can have positive feelings—physical or emotional—for their captors, though they cannot necessarily explain why. Nevertheless, Stockholm syndrome is not without its skeptics. We assume in these cases that hostages have been brainwashed or somehow psychologically transformed, but there is a fine line between sympathizing with your captors and actively committing crimes on their behalf. It appears that Stockholm syndrome may simply be a convenient excuse used by skilled defense lawyers. Since her jail term, and in an ironic twist, Hearst married her police bodyguard who supervised her, and she is a periodic guest on CNN's *Larry King Live* talk show.

136). Isolation may also result from the victims "dealing with the initial shock of imprisonment and perhaps the stress of exposure to degrading or frightening conditions" and actually "may be an important element in coping with" the terrorist event (Taylor 1988, 20). The stress caused by the situation may lead to what has been identified as the "General Adaptation Syndrome" (Taylor 1988, 20). This isolation may be coterminous with "depression and recrimination, associated with feelings of helplessness" (Taylor 1988, 19).

7. Opportunism

Release can also lead victims into opportunism. They may suddenly have their status elevated or may use their stigma to build a career

(Goffman 1963). The mass media, security forces, private security businesses, and academics sometimes interview victims in hopes of gaining insights from victims' experiences; by the same token, victims may, on their own initiative, capitalize on their "expertise" by contacting the same types of actors in an effort to derive income, feed their ego, or change policies and practices.

8. Lobbying

Finally, release may result in victims lobbying private foundations, the business community, and the government to improve conditions for groups that terrorists represent, or to improve physical security to prevent or minimize the possibility of death, injury, and destruction as a result of future terrorist attacks. Some have argued the families and friends of 9/11 victims were instrumental in lobbying the White House and U. S. government for the creation of the 9/11 Commission (United States 2004) which pressed for intelligence reforms.

In the main, the family and friends of victims have reactions that are similar to those experienced by the victims and themselves (Long 1990, 136).[11] Unlike victims, however, their families or friends may *blame* the victim (Ryan 1971); later, "if captivity is prolonged, blame, anger, and hostility later shift to authority figures" (Long 1990, 137). Long notes, "Usually this [process] begins with lessening confidence in the foreign government authorities at the scene, but generally it soon spreads to the embassy at the scene and ultimately to one's own government at home" (1990, 137–38). Additionally, significant others may try to *affiliate* with people in the same situation or those who have experienced similar tragedies and stresses. They may feel isolated from news concerning their loved ones, possibly look to derive some psychological support, or may attempt to collectively make their demands heard by the government (Long 1990, 138).

But aside from these issues, victims' reactions are similar to those of their friends and family members. Victims, however, are a narrow category of people affected. Perhaps more important is the general public.

The effects of terrorism on the general public

The general public responds to terrorism in different ways. The various "publics" (e.g., ethnic, racial, religious, domestic, regional, and international communities) are all affected differently. Nevertheless, eleven dominant responses can be discerned among the general public. These interrelated reactions are, listed from least to most prevalent: popular culture co-optation,[12] nationalism, desensitization, physical and psychological problems, demographic shifts, the sharpening of group differences, loss of legitimacy for the state, lobbying of the government, media propagation, anger, and fear. Many of these responses are similar to those of victims and their families and have been termed the "disaster" syndrome (Taylor 1988, 24).

1. Popular culture co-optation

Concurrent in many societies with the growing acceptance of terrorism as a part of life is the glorification of this type of political violence, that is, the integration or co-optation of terrorist images into popular culture. This is sometimes referred to as "terrorist chic" or the "commodification of culture." Terrorist images and themes have been utilized in mainstream, popular, and underground culture (Selzer 1979). According to Weinberg and Davis, "Acts of terrorism offer the possibility of commercial spin-offs. Films, television series, and popular novels have all been done in order to exploit the popular fascination with the subject" (1989, 127). Several works of fiction, some of which have been produced as motion pictures (*Black Sunday, Little Drummer Girl, Invasion U. S. A.*, etc.), have exploited terrorist themes to attract large thrill-seeking audiences (Livingstone 1990; Williams 2002). Terrorist images have also permeated areas such as fashion (for example, the Kaffiyeh, the traditional red and white checked Arab headdress, worn as a scarf by some American college and university students during the 1980s, and to this day at peace rallies as symbol of solidarity with the people of Palestine), and the fine arts (such as painting and sculpture) for increased attention and shock value.

2. Nationalism

Citizens of countries that fall victim to terrorism tend to look inward for support and are likely to bolster their group identities, and as a result nationalism related to terrorism has increased. This nationalism is fueled by the media through articles with provocative headlines like "We bombed Libya" and through broadcast television polls asking leading questions such as, "Should we bomb Iran?" The nationalism that terrorism engenders has also become a way of rallying popular support for aggressive foreign policy (Herman 1982). According to

Weinberg and Davis (1989), "citizens of democratic countries often endorse the use of extraordinary means when the elimination of terrorism is the end" (136). These unusual means can lead to racism, including unwarranted aggression toward immigrants, refugees, and guest workers, particularly visible minority populations suspected of being terrorist sympathizers. Consequently, increases in nationalism fuel ethnocentricism. In the United States in 1979–80, for example, anti-Iranian feelings followed the Iranian seizure of the American embassy in Tehran. Similar effects were noticed in the wake of 9/11 toward Muslims and individuals of Middle Eastern descent (or believed to be from these ethnic groups or parts of the world). Much of this nationalism is thought to foster a county's esprit de corps (Hewitt 1990).

3. Desensitization

Although fear is a nearly universal reaction among the general public, desensitization has also been prominent. The growth of terrorism has socialized some normally complacent individuals to the realities of the seriousness of terrorism.[13] However, if people in countries such as Israel, Lebanon, and Northern Ireland were totally paralyzed by fear created by their long history of dealing with terrorism, they would not be able to function. Thus they must engage in some psychological blocking to cope with environments in which a considerable amount of terrorism occurs.

4. Physical and psychological problems

Closely connected to anger, fear, and outrage are physical and psychological difficulties that individuals living under conditions of high terrorism develop. It has been reported that terrorism in Northern Ireland has led to "an 81 percent increase in alcohol-related problems leading to [hospital] admissions in that region" (Weinberg and Davis 1989, 137). This phenomenon may be an attempt to desensitize oneself to the realities of terrorism. Alternatively, these problems may force individuals to immigrate to other countries.

5. Demographic changes

Demographic changes occur as individuals who feel threatened because of terrorist violence leave areas where this form of political behavior is prevalent (Poland 1987, 240). As people flee, the economy suffers, which leads to a series of corollary problems. As Poland points out, "Eventually businesses and industry will move to safer locations since increased terrorism prohibits people from daily shopping or attending their jobs. The result is chronic, high unemployment and economic chaos" (1987, 240).

6. Sharpening of group differences

In countries that experience terrorism by particular ethnic, racial, or religious group, differences in societies will become more salient. In these contexts, "All members of the opposing . . . group [may] . . . be seen as belonging to the enemy camp" (Weinberg and Davis 1989, 132). This has led to racial profiling. In this case not against African Americans as terrorists but individuals from the Middle East, India, and Pakistan. In some cases, the public hysteria in the wake of 9/11 led some uninformed people to confuse Sikhs, many of whom wear turbans, as Muslim terrorists.

7. Loss of state legitimacy

A protracted and successful terrorist campaign provides terrorists with a strong weapon: discrediting the central authority and its legitimacy (Wilkinson 1986, 33). The general public's loss of confidence in the government will increase instability in the country. Distrust of state information and actions grow, as in the example of the U.S. government's widely mocked and ignored color-coded warning system rating the imminence of the threat of terrorism.

8. Lobbying

The lobbying of government (and businesses) to introduce stiffer penalties for terrorist activities, increase target hardening, and generate support for public security is an important general public response. If the government, private foundations, and some businesses want to maintain their legitimacy in the face of terrorist incidents, they will often respond to lobbying in some manner.

9. Media propagation

In some countries, the media has propagated terrorist intentions and actions (see Miller 1982; Schmid and de Graaf 1982; Weimann 1987).[14]

Because of the media's hunger for instant news and sensationalism, the media, some argue, becomes a tool terrorists manipulate to spread their message. For example, media coverage of the Black September hostage-taking of Israeli athletes during the 1972 Munich Massacre, when Munich Olympic Games probably gained more publicity than any other political activity conducted by any faction of the PLO or by any other terrorist group of the times.

10. Anger

Obviously, the general public often experiences anger and outrage due to terrorists' actions. Sometimes such reactions are aimed at the government, at actual or failed efforts to retaliate (Friedland and Merari 1985; Taylor 1988, 28–31; Weinberg and Davis 1989, 136). Some individuals have protested government slowness in negotiating with terrorists.

11. Fear

Finally, fear is a perennial reaction, and after terrorist incidents, there is a notable increase in the public's level of fear (see Friedland and Merari 1985; Poland 1987; Taylor 1988, 26). For example, many Americans cancelled plans to travel to Europe during the summer of 1986 (primarily in response to the hostage-taking incidents in Beirut and the La Belle discotheque bombing in West Berlin). The same pattern occurred during the Gulf War (1990—91), and shortly after 9/11, because tourists were afraid of being caught in a terrorist event.

In summary, the general public's responses vary based on the type of terrorist action, experience with terrorism and the victims' reactions.

The effects of terrorism on the business community

The business or corporate community has responded to terrorism with three basic types of outcomes: entrepreneurial, tactical, and political.[15] In general, seven principal business community responses are embedded in these three outcomes. These effects are, from least to most important, increased security, compliance with terrorist demands, development and expansion of security-related businesses, increased development and sales of antiterrorist technology, proliferation of ter-rorologists, government lobbying, and disruption.

1. Increased security

To begin with, businesses may decide to increase their security by hard-ening their premises, hiring security personnel to improve threat detec-tion (both inside and outside their organizations), or by making payoffs (paying protection) to terrorist groups so they will not attack.

2. Compliance

Compliance, also known as cooperation, with terrorist demands (which may include giving money to terrorists and their organizations), is one option that businesses wanting to minimize the costs of disruption may pursue. Another kind of compliance is doing business with only certain types of ethnic or racial groups.

3. Development and expansion of security-related businesses

Combating terrorism is profitable for certain segments of the business and corporate community. Since the 1960s, there has been an increase in the number of new businesses and on the expansion of existing businesses specializing in antiterrorist services for other corporations, the general public, and the government.[16] In the main, their activities fall under four areas: education (this may include training), consult-ing (providing information or threat assessments), products (insur-ance, antiterrorist technology), and security provision (executive protection, architectural design and construction). Consequently, pro-viding antiterrorism services and supplies has now become a big business. Tactical responses have led to a large amount of money and physical and personnel resources being diverted into security func-tions (Schiller 1987). This process may contribute to inflation (Poland 1987, 238).

4. Increased development and sales of antiterrorist technology

The number of businesses specializing in antiterrorist services, the development and sale of *antiterrorist technology* has also grown. A number of new products have entered the market in an effort to combat terrorism. Some of these items include portable vapor detectors, x-ray units, metal detectors, and improved alarm systems. Businesses encourage the government and other companies to install these products at vulnerable targets.

5. Proliferation of terrorologists

Terrorism has also spawned the growth of media and academic experts, personalities, or (to use Herman and O'Sullivan's pejorative term) "terrorologists" who enjoy "linkages" (such as free office space, access to seminars, an institutional credibility, etc.) and share their opinions and perspectives with research institutes, think tanks, political parties, private businesses, and government departments. The distinctions between terrorologists and their host institutions are often blurred. Accordingly, as Herman and O'Sullivan point out, "They have a vested interest in 'threat inflation,' as their business is contingent on adequate volume of terrorism against which to protect their clients. Security business also ties the participants more closely to the government security establishment in exchange of information and a revolving door relationship" (1989, 187).

6. Lobbying

Like some victims, friends and family of victims, and the general public, the business community also partakes in lobbying of elected and appointed officials. This can include corporate representation at government hearings or on committees and the distribution of reports and other public relations measures to the citizenry to help create sympathetic constituencies.

7. Disruption

Finally, disruption to business can occur in areas where terrorist activity occurs as a result of property damage, relocation, loss of sales and income, inflation, and the cancellation of business plans.

In short, the business community is an important actor whose responses to terrorism impact the tools, personnel, and systems developed to combat terrorism, the economic health of the overall community, and ultimately, the longevity of the existing political system. In areas where terrorism occurs, the effects of terrorism on business must be considered, particularly by governments that want to preserve their legitimacy and power.

The effect of terrorism on the government

As we've seen above, the concerns of victims and their friends and family, the general public, and the business community about terrorism are generally channeled to the government—or the authorities or the state—through the implications of terrorism and lobbying. The problem of how to provide security without losing legitimacy is a major dilemma to the target state(s). In the main, government responses fall into three dimensions: judicial/legal initiatives; tactical approaches; and policy formation and implementation. The government's responses are dictated by several factors beyond the terrorist attack itself.[17] Every government has an obligation to react and respond in some manner (even symbolically), in order to indicate concern and interest to its citizens.[18] The issue of response is wider than that of combating terrorism (see Chapter 9). And combating terrorism is particularly complicated when two or more governments are involved (Aston 1986, 66–77).

1. Judicial/legal initiatives

In the main, there are five major judicial/legal responses to terrorism by governments. These reactions are, in increasing order of frequency, the development of specialized correctional facilities, special-enactment legislation, new developments in international laws, international collective agreements, and regional and bilateral agreements.

Some countries have constructed *specialized jail facilities* (similar to Supermax prisons in the United States) for terrorists on or awaiting trial. For example, in 1981, after the capture of what they considered to be leftist terrorists, New Jersey authorities constructed a separate unit within the main jail for the defendants. The state specially trained the correctional staff assigned to work exclusively with these defendants, hired 170 extra security personnel, and paid overtime to support additional court personnel, surveillance equipment, and daily bomb sweeps in and around the courthouse (Zwerman 1988). Similar situations existed in West Germany during the 1970s with the Baader-Meinhoff gang and the construction of the Mannheim prison. Currently, we are housing suspected or actual members of al Qaeda in Guantánamo Bay, Cuba.

Occasionally, governments will implement new laws against the use of terrorism. This is generally termed *special enactment legislation* or exception or antiterrorist legislation. Otherwise, many countries have either passed specific sections of general laws covering terrorism, including the increased use of different types of visas, or criminalized certain political actions. On the domestic front, countries such as the former West Germany, the Netherlands, the United Kingdom, Israel, and the United States, in particular, treat terrorism as a criminal act, refusing to acknowledge its political dimensions (see Wardlaw 1982; Turk 1989). This type of legislation has had controversial effects. For instance, in the United States, terrorism has led to the withering away of the War Powers Resolution (Rubner 1987), and in some contexts has violated citizens' human and civil rights (Hocking 1988, 86).

Governments have also emphasized *international law* as a means to control terrorism. However, disagreements between various countries hinder its utility. In particular, the problems of asylum and extradition vary from country to country. As Sofaer argues, "The law, as presently formulated, cannot reasonably be expected effectively to repress international terrorism" (1986, 922). This kind of political violence is still supported by some states as a legitimate means of struggle against regimes deemed by them to be "colonial," "alien," or "racist." And as long as the international system remains divided along ideological, political, economic, and other axes, overall cooperation will be difficult (Murphy 1982). Therefore, the suppression of terrorism is mainly confined within the jurisdiction of individual states. Furthermore, as long as mutual interests between states continue, bilateral and regional agreements and cooperation will lead to a more realistic approach to combating terrorism.

Since terrorism was internationalized, it seems natural to expect countries to engage in *international collective agreements* to abolish or respond to this phenomenon (see Sayre 1984). A series of documents—concerned with legal protection for diplomats, foreign officials and nationals, international organizations, and civil aviation—focus on the international level of terrorism (Murphy 1985, 1).[19] During the 1960s and 1970s, several international conferences were convened to establish rules and laws through which all countries would abolish or respond to terrorism. Most of these conventions were unsuccessful despite their participants' mutual interests in combating terrorism (Lillich 1982; Gal-Or 1985, 127–35; Murphy 1985).

Even though most international agreements to combat terrorism failed, some *bilateral and regional agreements* are still in effect (Lillich 1982, 157).[20] Whether or not such treaties act as a deterrent is hard to determine. Nevertheless, hijacking between many countries (e.g., United States and Cuba) declined. But most of these agreements generally contain provisions specifically excluding political offenders from the extradition and expulsion process.

2. Tactical approaches

Governments respond to terrorism in a tactical manner as well as the legal manners described above. Police forces, militaries, national security/intelligence agencies, a variety of paramilitary units, and numerous government-managed security outfits have attempted to thwart acts of terrorism. Different strategies have been advocated and implemented. In the main, there are eight responses: preemptive and retaliatory strikes, expulsion of terrorists, interstate terrorism, development of special forces, improved negotiation, increased surveillance, greater cooperation among government agencies, and target hardening.

Preemptive and/or retaliatory strikes at terrorists, their training camps, and sponsors are often considered and occasionally used to fight terrorism. In September 1970, Jordan used this tactic against Palestinian terrorists in its own country. In April 1986, the United States used these types of strikes against Libya. And Israel has applied this strategy often in Lebanon, Syria, and Jordan (see Miller 1990b; United States Senate 1985). During the 1970s, it was alleged that the Mossad (the Israeli intelligence service) tracked down and killed the organizers and perpetrators of the 1972 Munich massacre (Zohar 2002). When viewed negatively, these vigilante-type actions are labeled "quick-fix" solutions and derided as tactics that can lead to the injury and death of innocent noncombatants. Moreover, there is no conclusive evidence that these types of strikes are effective in fighting terrorism (see Alon 1987).

Closely related to negotiation and strikes is the *expulsion of terrorists*, suspected terrorists, or those supporting or suspected to help terrorists. For example, in 1986, West Germany, Spain, and France deported Libyan diplomats believed to be aiding terrorists. In 1992, Israel expelled members of Hamas suspected of participating in terrorist activities.

Another closely related tactic is *interstate terrorism,* which comes as a reaction to another country's implication in state-sponsored terrorism. This has had unfortunate consequences, particularly with "runaway" interstate terrorism. In other words, some terrorist groups trained by intelligence organizations eventually act independently or sever the relationship with their "handlers" and engage in terrorist actions, such as the anti-Castro Cubans or the groups that attempted an assassination on Hamas leader Sheik Fadallah (Dinges and Landau 1980; Adams 1986, 23). As a result of terrorism, some countries have virtually become "national security" (Lasswell 1950) or "rogue" states (Klare 1996).

The *creation of special forces,* specialized antiterrorist units (for example, the Delta Force in the United States or GSG9 in Germany, among others), also called "third forces," to cope with terrorist attacks has been most prevalent over the past three decades (Thompson 1986). These are specially created armed units of a police force, military, or national security organization trained to deal with terrorist incidents. They are typically used when negotiations have broken down or used as a psychological counterbalance (Thompson 1986). Their mere presence may help to intimidate terrorists in these situations. Over the years, numerous special units have carried out successful raids in places such as Entebbe (1976) or Mogadishu (1978).

Improved negotiating techniques apply conflict-resolution skills to hostage-taking situations (Hughes 1990; Miller 1990b). In response to these types of incidents, many police forces and antiterrorist units have specialists who are trained and experienced in conducting negotiations and crisis management. Such methods of diffusing the incidents require flexible techniques. Typically, police forces and security agencies send their "best men" off to training schools or programs to learn these techniques. Additionally, several computer-based negotiation support systems have been developed for use both as training and negotiating tools (see Kersten et al. 1981; Kramer and King 1986; Matwin et al. 1987).

Simultaneously, terrorism has led to *increased surveillance* and intelligence gathered on terrorists and individuals suspected of being sympathizers or supporters (Ofri 1984; Amit 1989). In several advanced industrialized countries, many Libyan, Iranian, and Palestinian individuals and groups are monitored and, in some cases, harassed by national security agents (for example, in 1986, funds of Libyan students studying in the United States were frozen). This tactic includes stepped-up border patrols, immigration inspection, and more stringent visa and passport requirements.

Greater cooperation among government agencies is another tactical dimension at the government level. There is a real attempt by governments and their agencies to foster domestic and international security cooperation (see Hocking 1988; Amit 1989) beyond paper agreements and exchange of information or intelligence. According to Amit (1989), this effort includes "various possibilities from international cooperation to inter-service cooperation" (8). For example, British Prime Minister James Callaghan sent a group of specially trained military officers "to aid the West Germans in their assault on their hijacked airliner at Mogadishu" (Carlton 1979, 225). Sometimes this involves the rationalization of relationships between diverse governmental departments responsible, in whole or in part, for dealing with terrorism. This appears to be the intent of the creation of the Department of Homeland Security under the Bush administration.

Finally, armed guards and various security systems provide obstacles to terrorist organizations—that is, they *harden actual and potential targets.* This hardening has increased domestically and internationally over the past four decades. During the early 1970s, security measures were increased at airports, bus and train stations, corporate headquarters, government buildings, and nuclear facilities. Some of these measures included more and better x-ray baggage screening devices, walk-through scanning mechanisms, police and private security officers, and security procedures around these facilities. During the 1980s, newer, tougher security measures included stronger walls, blast-resistant windows and doors, obstacles on approach and exit roads, electric monitoring equipment, and emergency satellite communications systems.

3. Policy formation and implementation

Since terrorism is viewed as a political issue, it is up to the government and national security agencies of targeted countries to consider, assess, and ultimately decide upon a course of action. Governments are bound by domestic and international laws and rules. Leaders have to determine the what, when, where, how, and why of responding to terrorism.

Policy formation is the initial step in the response pattern; it creates a set of rules and programs upon which the government will act in a given situation. Next, the parties responsible for implementing the rules and programs must be identified. The international nature of terrorism has required the attention of state and foreign ministries, as well as the department of the interior or of domestic affairs of many countries. This necessitates the creation of separate bureaucracies to address terrorism, and naturally, budgets and personnel to staff these organizations have increased.

Ultimately, the government is the final actor in the effects or response model outlined here. Government reactions are a major determinant in the success or failure of a terrorist organization. But the numerous structural and psychological effects of terrorism on victims, citizens, observers, practitioners, and politicians described above are not mutually exclusive; a person or organization may experience a broad continuum of effects at various points in time during and after a terrorist incident.

Conclusion

This chapter has outlined five actor-based models. Each one includes the variety of responses to terrorism. To that end, the stimulus-response model provides a conceptual framework that best represents the interwoven relations between terrorist groups and the effects of their activities upon the targeted actors. Within this schema, the stimulus is an event generated by one actor, which in turn causes a reaction by the others. Thus, the response is also an action (or series of actions) that closes the initial cycle of stimuli-response, but generates an ongoing, interactive process. The underlying assumption in these models is that all actors are engaged in protracted decision making and behavior, thus perpetuating a cycle of stimuli and responses. The dynamics of that relationship can last a long time, during which each actor considers a variety of options and/or engages in a number of different behaviors, hoping to achieve the desired outcome, whether that outcome is a coup d'état or the cessation of terrorism.

Even though we've outlined various responses systematically, many obstacles still remain before we can approach a comprehensive theory. Among the challenges are operationalizing the variables, collecting appropriate data, testing hypotheses, and making adjustments, if necessary, to the hypotheses. Some of the steps along the way include, but are not limited to, building on existing events databases, interviewing the actors outlined in each model, incorporating clinical or psychological tests of terrorists and victims, conducting surveys of the general public, business community, and government employees; and constructing comparative case studies. Eventually, the resulting research can include an intensive analysis of business and government policies and corresponding expenditures. Due to data limitations and available resources, it could be that each model may require a different methodology to test its embedded hypotheses.

We must address one final issue: not the effects, but the *effectiveness* of terrorism. Some observers have tried to answer this question. Wilkinson (2003), for example, has noted, "History shows that terrorism has been most effective as an auxiliary weapon in revolutionary and national liberation struggles" (31). In this case, he cites the use of terrorism by the Stern Gang and Irgun during the British occupation of Palestine, EOKA (the National Organization of Cypriot Fighters in Cyprus), and the FLN (the National Liberation Front) in Algeria. In general, these groups got what they were after; they were effective in kicking out colonial masters in their base of operations and becoming the ruling party.

The following chapter compares the causes of political terrorism in different places, cultures, and time periods to see if the model developed in the causal chapter applies to all or several different contexts.

Questions, Chapter 4

PART ONE: MULTIPLE CHOICE

1. In the Lichbach model, which of the following is true?
   a. action leads to reaction
   b. terrorism is dynamic
   c. terrorism is a cyclical process
   d. a and b
   e. all of the above

2. All of the following are general public effects of terrorism except
   a. anger
   b. fear
   c. demographic shifts
   d. identifying with the terrorists
   e. nationalism

3. Which model did Lichbach develop?
   a. stimulus-response
   b. action-reaction
   c. cost-benefit
   d. all of the above
   e. none of the above

4. Of the seven typical responses in the actor-based model, a terrorist most often responds with
   a. negotiation
   b. training opportunities
   c. tactical violence
   d. intelligence acquisition
   e. group identity-building exercises

5. What is the name of the process whereby victims who are captured express feelings such as sympathy, camaraderie, closeness and friendship towards their captors?
   a. tactical violence
   b. love
   c. sympathy
   d. Stockholm syndrome
   e. Oslo syndrome

6. Lichbach's model is inappropriate to explain terrorism because it
   a. excludes civil disobedience
   b. excludes demonstrations
   c. is underinclusive
   d. is overinclusive
   e. both c and d

7. When terrorists attack nongovernment targets, what is the act considered to be?
   a. indirect communication
   b. domestic violence
   c. random violence against the public
   d. direct communication
   e. all of the above

8. Which model did Ross and Miller use to base their explanation of the effects of terrorism?
   a. action-reaction
   b. cost-benefit
   c. stimulus-response
   d. all of the above
   e. none of the above

9. What are appropriate synonyms for the process of effects?
   a. products
   b. results
   c. actions
   d. conclusions
   e. none of the above

10. What is a third force?
    a. a reggae band that sang a famous song on terrorists
    b. a terrorist group
    c. a special weapons and tactical unit
    d. a weapon of mass destruction
    e. none of the above

PART TWO: SHORT ANSWER

1. List the five actors of the reaction model.

2. What is Stockholm syndrome?

3. List three conventions signed between the United States and other countries in the field of terrorism.

4. What are two possible models which may serve as a basis for understanding the effects of oppositional political terrorism?

5. What are five possible effects that oppositional political terrorism may have on victims and friends?

6. List four actors who are involved in the effects of oppositional political terrorism.

7. In times of crisis, governments pass "emergency legislation." Identify two of these laws that have been used in recent years and comment on their advantages and disadvantages.

PART THREE: ESSAY

1. How does the issue of decline integrate into the effects of terrorism?

2. What are three differences between the action-reaction and stimulus-response models?

3. Which actor in the effects model is the most important and why?

CHAPTER FIVE

Three Case Studies: Al-Fatah, FARC, and PIRA

This chapter applies the structural components of the Psychological-Structural causal model developed to three different campaigns of oppositional political terrorism. Although several terrorist groups were possible candidates for inclusion, the organizations selected are geographically distinct, with slightly different objectives, and are well known to the general public, counterterrorism experts, and scholars alike. Moreover, they are still in operation at various levels of intensity. In most respects, our approach conforms to what is typically called a "most-similar" systems design (Lijphart 1971; 1975). In short, this method restricts comparisons made among entities which share several commonalities in order to make generalizations which are relatively valid.

First, the Palestinian-Israeli conflict (Shipler 1986) has spawned a number of terrorist organizations fighting for the creation of a separate homeland for the Palestinian people, including al-Fatah, the Popular Front for the Liberation of Palestine (PFLP), the Popular Democratic Front for the Liberation of Palestine General Command (PFLP GC), the Abu Nidal group, and Hamas. One of the most well-known and earliest established groups is al-Fatah (or Fatah for short). Formed in 1957, this organization, led by Yasser Arafat, has been responsible for 198 incidents, with 1,322 injuries, and 417 fatalities (MIPT, June 30, 2005). In 1972, although Fatah officially announced that it would no longer engage in terrorism, it still supports other groups, such as the al-Aqsa Martyrs Brigade (referred to in some circles as the armed wing of Fatah), which engages in suicide bombings.

Second, the Revolutionary Armed Forces of Colombia (FARC), established in 1964, is one of the oldest terrorist groups in South America. Its mission is to replace the existing government of Colombia with a regime run on Marxist-Leninist principles. In 1984, after countless deaths and injuries to police, the military, and noncombatants, the Colombian government began to negotiate with FARC, in hopes of transforming this organization into a respectable political party. Although some members of FARC conceded with government requests, others remained steadfast in their approach and tactics to further the mission of the group. One of the consequences, however, was that disgruntled members of Colombia's military started an unofficial war against the legitimate FARC candidates. In 2002, FARC resumed its terrorist campaign against the government.

Third, although the Northern Irish troubles have a long history, formed in opposition to the British government, it was not until 1968 that Catholic militants—motivated by repressive laws, police actions, and Protestant antagonism—resuscitated the once-dormant Irish Republican Army. Later broken off into different factions, the Provisional IRA (PIRA) carried out numerous attacks in Northern Ireland, England, and elsewhere to motivate the British to leave Northern Ireland. The last decade has brought a series of peace treaties and attempts at disarmament.

The case studies that follow examine the history of these three groups and review the relevant structural components that led to their establishment.

Al-Fatah

On November 29, 1947, the United Nations passed Resolution 181, which effectively partitioned Palestine (occupied by the British since the fall of the Ottoman Empire in World War I, circa 1918) into two states: a Jewish one (Israel) and a Palestinian one for the Arab majority living in the area. Although the plan was accepted by the Jewish Agency (responsible for monitoring the negotiations), it was rejected by the Palestinians and the neighboring Arab states acting on the Palestinians' behalf. Violence between Arabs and Jews broke out in Palestine. On May 14, 1948, the British removed their troops. Israelis, through the efforts of their army, the Israeli Defense Force, immediately consolidated their power and repressed the Palestinians living within their borders (Chomsky 1984; Morris 2001).[1] Many left to the neighboring countries of Egypt, Lebanon, Syria, and Jordan.

In 1957, Yasser Arafat and approximately twenty other individuals from different clandestine Palestinian groups formed al-Fatah in Kuwait (Iyad 1981; Hart 1984; Mishal 1986). They were influenced by the success of the Algerian Revolution, in which nationalists used an urban guerrilla campaign to successfully force the French out of Algeria. Over time, Fatah—also known as the National Palestine Liberation Movement—has become the "largest, oldest, and most influential Palestinian resistance organization" (Long, 1990, 36). Fatah has approximately twelve to fifteen thousand fighters and numerous support personnel (Livingstone and Halevy 1990, 72). Fatah focuses on Palestinian nationalism; it does not support any particular political ideology or religious doctrine, despite the fact that many of its leaders are Muslims (Long 1990, 36). It has received resources from "Arab governments, criminal activities, and profits from its extensive portfolio and other business activities" (Livingston and Halevy 1990, 72).

Fatah has offices located throughout world, particularly in the Middle East, Europe, and Asia. This terrorist organization is broken down into subunits, one of which, known as the Western Section, "was headed, until April 1988, by . . . Abu Jihad. It is an operations body set up to promote armed struggle . . . in the occupied territories. Once headquartered in Amman, Jordan," and for a while in Baghdad, "it has about four hundred members. Since the death of Abu Jihad, Yasser Arafat has assumed full control of the Western Section" (Livingstone and Halevy 1990, 73).

In 1964, with the support of other Arab countries, Egypt established the Palestine Liberation Organization (PLO), the governing body of the Palestinian people. In June 1967, the neighboring Arab countries of Egypt, Lebanon, Jordan, and Syria waged a combined military attack against Israel. In what is popularly known as the Six Days' War, the Israelis not only thwarted the aggression on their own territory, but also took control of additional land in the Arab countries, securing the Gaza Strip, the Sinai Peninsula, Golan Heights, East Jerusalem, and the West Bank or Occupied Territories. Fatah gained control of the PLO in 1968 after the setbacks of the Six Days' War and the Battle of Karameh (Jordan) (March 1968), during which they made several military gains against an encroaching Israeli army.

In the 1960s and 1970s, both as a source of revenue and for political reasons, Fatah trained other Middle Eastern, European, African, and Asian terrorist groups, who then committed violent actions in support of each other's causes. Many Middle Eastern countries, including Saudi Arabia, Kuwait, and other Persian Gulf states, provided aid to Fatah during this time.

In September 1970, fearing a loss of political power, Jordan's King Hussein expelled high-ranking Palestinians living in his country. What made this all the more strange was that Palestinians and Jordanians are ethnically very similar. The majority relocated to southern Lebanon, where Fatah established a strong presence that they used to their advantage to attack northern Israeli settlements.

At several points during its existence, al-Fatah committed terrorist actions alone or had one of its subunits do the "dirty work." For example, the breakaway group Black September was born out of the ashes of the Jordanian expulsion. This organization planned and committed several spectacular terrorist events, including "the murder of eleven Israeli athletes at the 1972 Munich Olympics and of two American diplomats, Ambassador Clio Noel and his deputy chief of mission, Curtis Moore, in Khartoum in March 1973" (Long 1990, 38).

Shortly after the 1973 Yom Kippur War (in which Egypt and Syria attempted to retake the land lost in the 1967 conflict), prominent Palestinian terrorist organizations lost confidence in the Egyptians' and Syrians' ability to serve as benefactors. Fatah announced it would cease engaging in international terrorism, particularly hijacking, because they believed that it was not helping their cause and blamed the sporadic attacks which happened after this declaration to be the work of offshoot organizations (Halevy and Livingston 1990). In 1974, in a signal that both he and his organizations were achieving international legitimacy, Yasser Arafat addressed the United Nations. This was coterminous with the dissolution of Black September (Dobson 1974).

In the mid-1970s, the Israelis (bolstered by United Nations forces) set up a security zone inside Lebanon on Israel's northern border. Starting in 1975, however, and lasting until 1990—with factions such as Marionite Christians, (represented by the Phalange), Shiite Muslims, Hezbollah, Druze, and members of the PLO—a bloody civil war took place in Lebanon.

In 1979, the governments of Israel and Egypt (with the assistance of then-U.S. president Jimmy Carter) signed the Camp David peace accords. The PLO (and by extension Fatah) recognized that it would have to deal with Israel directly and engage in some sort of compromise.

In June 1982, however, Israelis became exhausted with cross-border attacks by Hezbollah and Palestinian factions and invaded Lebanon beyond the security zone. Within days Israeli tanks made their way to Beirut. During the occupation, the Phalange, a Lebanese political party and militia, primarily composed of Christian Marionites, (under the control of the Israeli army), made its way into the Sabra and Shatila refugee camps in Beirut, ostensibly to root out Palestinian gunmen. Instead, the

Phalange, who were loosely under the control of the Israelis, massacred 460 to 800 individuals, 35 of whom were women and children.

In 1982, the United States brokered an agreement for the Israelis and Palestinians to leave Lebanon, and for American, French, and Italian peacekeepers to maintain order. Palestinian fighters relocated to Algeria, Iraq, Tunisia, Yemen, and other Middle Eastern countries (Mishal 1986). Meanwhile, "Arafat and the PLO leadership had to be evacuated to Tunis" (Laqueur 2003, 102).[2]

Starting in 1987, many Palestinian activists living in the occupied territories engaged in what was called the Intifada (Schiff and Ya'ari 1989). The Intifada's resistance consisted primarily of youths attacking the Israeli soldiers in the Gaza Strip and in the West Bank with rocks and stones. When the Israeli army overreacted by injuring and killing participants, many of the world's media outlets were present to broadcast the army shooting what appeared to be defenseless youths. In the furor of the times, an Islamic fundamentalist group which goes by its acronymn Hamas was born. Although Hamas was originally a self-help organization (providing welfare and social services to needy Palestinians) in 1992, it started engaging in terrorism five years later (Mishal and Sela 2002). Since that time, Hamas and Islamic Jihad, (the later of which derives its name from the Islamic word and practice "Holy War") have carried out numerous suicide attacks against the Israeli army and Israeli civilians, inside both the occupied territories and Israel proper. These two splinter groups of the PLO want to establish an Islamic country in these areas and do not recognize Israel's right to exist as a sovereign state.[3] Not only are they seen as a threat to Israel, but also to the leadership of the PLO, and many Western countries because they are perceived to be more violent and less susceptible to negotiation.

In April 1993, the PLO and Israeli government signed the Declaration of Principles (also known as the Oslo accords). The Oslo accords set out a number of agreements to foster peace between the two groups and the normalization of relations with the other Arab countries. Among the concessions were that Fatah would give up terrorism, and that the Israelis would permit the Palestinians limited autonomy in the Gaza Strip and West Bank. Both Israeli Prime Minister Yitzhak Rabin and Palestinian leader Yasser Arafat received the Nobel Peace Prize for this accomplishment. According to the plan for limited Palestinian autonomy, the Palestinian National Authority (PNA) formed in 1994 to administer the Gaza Strip and West Bank, with Arafat as its head. Despite the accords, it has been alleged—and there is reasonably reliable information to back the allegation—that Fatah financially and politically supports armed factions or wings such as Force 17, the Hawari Special Operations Group, Tanzim, and the al-Aqsa Martyrs' Brigade. In 1998, things looked promising for peace; a deal brokered by President Bill Clinton, called the Wye River Accords, was signed by Arafat and Israeli Prime Minister Benjamin Netanyahu. Essentially, per the accords, the Palestinians were going to crack down on terrorism, Israel would return land to Palestinians, and Palestinians in Israeli prisons would be transferred to the PNA. This was popularly seen as a land-for-peace deal. Due to increased tension, however, in 2000 a second Intifada began, coupled with suicide bombings in crowded areas in Israeli cities.

According to Newman (2003), "Hamas and Jihad are responsible for attacks on Israeli citizens on the West Bank and Israel proper" in discos, restaurants, bus stations, and shopping malls (155). Israeli retaliation for the attacks killed a great number of people. "Equally for most Israelis," Newman points out, "the failure of Arafat to clamp down on Hamas and Jihad was a clear indication that the renewed violence was taking place with the tacit approval of Arafat. . . . While this may have been true at the beginning of the Al-Aqsa Intifada, by 9/11, Arafat lacked total control over all the Palestinian factions and he would have been unable to prevent every suicide bombing" (2003, 155). In fact, by the summer of 2001, the popularity of Fatah and the PNA had finally been eclipsed by Islamic fundamentalist and other Palestinian nationalist groups (Newman 2003, 156).

In the wake of 9/11, the United States has continued in its efforts to broker a new peace agreement. About a week after 9/11, "Bush forced Sharon and Arafat to agree to a cease-fire and it was announced that if the cease-fire held for 48 hours, Foreign Minister Shimon Peres would reopen peace talks with the Palestinian Leader" (Newman 2003, 157).

Since March 2002, the Israeli Defense Forces have occupied the West Bank; and surrounded the city of Ramalla (West Bank), and at various points in time surrounded Arafat's compound, which has been heavily affected by shelling. Several assassinations and assassination attempts have been carried out against the leadership of al-Aqsa Martyrs' Brigade and Hamas. Meanwhile, suicide bombings take place on a regular basis inside Israel.

On November 11, 2004, two weeks after being transported to a hospital in France because he was suffering from an intestinal disorder, Yasser Arafat slipped into a coma and died. Many international leaders are hoping that Arafat's death will pave the way to increased peace in the Israeli-Palestinian conflict.

Revolutionary Armed Forces of Colombia (FARC)

Three so-called narco-terrorist groups operate in Colombia: the United Self-Defense Forces of Colombia (AUC), the National Liberation Army (ELN), and the Armed Forces of Colombia, or Fuerzas Armadas Revolucionarias de Colombia (FARC). FARC is the largest, best trained, and most deadly of the three. FARC is an extreme, left-wing, communist-inspired group with a reported membership of twelve to eighteen thousand (Simonsen and Spindlove 2004, 341; http://www.farcep.org). Established in 1964, this group is led by Manuel Marulanda (formerly known as Pedro Antonio Marin, a.k.a. Tirofijo ("Sureshot"), who is in his seventies, and six others, including senior military commander Jorge Briceno, a.k.a. Mono Jojoy. Although its origins are murky, the group first came to public attention in 1966 "as the military wing of the Colombian Communist Party" (Simonsen and Spindlove 2004, 341).

Part of the reason for FARC's success is that it has developed a loyal following among Colombia's poor, especially the peasants and indigenous people who live in relatively remote rural areas (Stafford and Palacios 2002). In some respects, FARC is better described as a guerrilla organization that uses terrorism to further its objectives (e.g., Chaliand 1983; Marighela 1971). However, because of its killing of civilians it should be considered a terrorist organization. This group has accumulated significant resources through the drug trade (i.e., coca, opium, and marijuana), either through cultivation or through providing security for traffickers (Ehrenfeld 1992).

Its primary objective is to overthrow the Colombian government. Other demands include increased equality, a reduction in unemployment, an end to privatization, and a redistribution of wealth. FARC is also anti-American; it believes that the United States is an imperialist country, especially because of its intervention in Colombian affairs. Ironically, FARC believes Colombia should legalize drugs. They believe this would reduce the violence and bad effects of these illegal substances. Because of its connection to the drug trafficking, FARC maintains links to criminal gangs in Ecuador, Panama, and Venezuela.

FARC engages in kidnapping, extortion, bank robbery, and drug trafficking in order to finance the organization, but in terms of pure terrorism, it has been responsible for assassinations, bombings, and the hijacking of an airliner. It focuses on a wide range of targets including the police, military, politicians and civilians. FARC's attacks on government targets has led to the development of death squads, paramilitary organizations that engage in extrajudicial killings and disappearances, as well as torture of actual or suspected members of the terrorist organizations or their sympathizers. Most of its violence has been confined to Colombia; rarely has FARC engaged in terrorism outside of the country.

In the later 1980s, FARC established the Patriotic Union (UP), a political party, but the UP fell victim to right-wing death squads sponsored by drug lords and members of the Colombian military. Apparently, some three thousand UP members were killed, including its 1990 presidential candidate, Bernardo Jaramillo Ossa.[4]

In 1998, Colombian President Pastrana granted FARC a 42,000–square kilometer safe haven, which was essentially their base of operations, as a concession to sit down to peace talks. The negotiations proceeded slowly as FARC continued to build up their resources (through gun running, coca production and smuggling, etc.). In the meantime, the group kidnapped and killed a leading and well-liked presidential candidate Ingrid Betancourt and other politicians. In 2001, Pastrana once again began talks with FARC about a peace treaty. However, "as negotiations became bogged down, the Pastrana government threatened to end the deal that had created a demilitarized zone" (Simonsen and Spindlove 2004, 341). In February 2002, the government ended the talks, revoked the political status of FARC, issued warrants for the arrest of its leaders, and instructed Colombia's military to retake the area occupied by FARC.[5] The military offensive called "Operation Black Cat" has used both aircraft and helicopters (Simonsen and Spindlove 2004, 341).

From 2002–04, FARC was "believed to be in a relative/temporary strategic withdrawal due to increasing military and police actions of new hardline president Alvaro Uribe Velez, which led to the capture or desertion of many fighters and medium-level commanders, one of the most important of which has been that of 'Simon Trinidad' . . . in Jan. 2004, a former banker turned rebel, who had participated as a high-profile negotiator in the recent Pastrana peace talks."[6]

During its forty-plus years of existence, FARC has also developed enemies beyond Colombia's national government, including the National Liberation Army (ELN), the smaller of the two main Marxist terrorist organizations in Colombia. FARC seems to have very little international support and thus must rely on its own businesses, as we have noted: drug trafficking, kidnapping, and extortion.[7]

Provisional Irish Republican Army (PIRA)

The IRA struggle is centuries old (Bell 1997; Toolis 1997). In order to understand this conflict, one needs to be familiar with the history and the political and economic role of Ireland. The Irish Catholics' desire for autonomy from British rule has waxed and waned due to a variety of circumstances. At certain points in history, the effort has appeared to have a religious basis; at other times, it has aired grievances that are simply economic and political (i.e., the subjugation of Catholics to Protestant and British rule). This has prompted some analysts to suggest that the conflict has ethnic, rather than religious roots (Bruce 1993; 1995).

A few highlights are in order. After a popular rebellion led by such figures as Michael Collins, the Irish Free State (now known as the Republic of Ireland) was established in 1921. This encompassed twenty-six out of thirty-two counties; the remaining six northern counties came under British protection and are called Northern Ireland (popularly referred to as Ulster). From the time of the split until the mid-1960s, the civil rights of Catholics living in the north decreased (White 2003, 86). A disproportionate number of Catholics have poor jobs as well as inferior housing and education, which affects their ability to get ahead socio-economically. Since 1968, close to 3,600 individuals have died in this conflict. The dead include not only British military, but also police officers and innocent civilians.

During the 1960s, partially inspired by the civil rights movement in the United States, both Protestants and Catholics began to press for improved housing conditions and educational opportunities. But the repression by the Northern Irish government exacerbated matters: "Catholics were not allowed to demonstrate . . . if they attempted to do so, they were attacked by the RUC and its reserve force known as the B-Specials. At the same time no attempts were made to stop Protestant demonstrations. The Catholics believed the RUC and B specials were in league with the other anti-Catholic unionists in the North" (White 2003, 87). Catholics and pro-unionist (Republican) Protestants were essentially at each others' throats (Talbot 2003, 335).

In August 1969, riots erupted in Belfast and Londonderry. Local police were relatively ineffective against this kind of civil disturbance. As a result, the British government increased the numbers of soldiers stationed there. The army—interpreting the situation as a colonial war—quickly allied itself with the Protestants, which only served to polarize the population (Hocking 1988). The British military also uncritically allied itself with the Royal Ulster Constabulary (RUC). The army would surround Catholic neighborhoods, break down doors, and throw tear gas and smoke bombs, all in a combined effort to draw out terrorists and their sympathizers. The Catholics wanted the army out, and many Protestants believed that they could act with impunity against the Catholics (White 2003, 88). As a result of this sectarian violence, the Irish Republican Army (IRA) reconstituted itself and started engaging in terrorist actions. In December 1969, the IRA split into the "Officials" and the "Provisionals." Confusion was rampant, as both organizations had military and political wings (Silke, 1999). Then in January 1972, during a peaceful civil rights parade in Derry (short for Londonderry), 13 unarmed people were shot dead, while 14 others were wounded by British paratroopers. This event, popularly referred to as Bloody Sunday, galvanized many Irish Catholics against the British presence in Northern Ireland.

In the summer of 1972, the "official" IRA declared a ceasefire. It placed its energy into supporting Sinn Fein, the political party established to seek independence for Northern Ireland from Great Britain. Since that time, "the term IRA was used for the organization that had developed from the 'Provisional IRA'" (Simonsen and Spindlove 2004, 78). Membership in the IRA increased to approximately fifteen hundred to two thousand members during the 1970s and dropped to three to five hundred after the 1994 ceasefire was signed (Simonsen and Spindlove 2004, 78).

In 1973 the British government passed the Northern Ireland (Emergency Provisions) Act, which allowed the military greater powers of search and detention of terrorist suspects. The army could enter anyone's house at any time during the day without obtaining a warrant. During the same year, PIRA launched a campaign of bombings on the British mainland in cities including Brighton, Guildford, and London. Since then, violence in Northern Ireland has "intensified in cyclical waves: in 1972, in 1974, in the early 1980s; in the late 1980s, and in the early 1990s" (Talbot 2003, 335). Talbot says, "Loyalists have indulged in significant sectarian violence, attacked the Royal Ulster Constabulary (RUC) and the Army and have also assassinated Republican leaders. After early sectarianism, PIRA concentrated primarily on the British states' representatives, the RUC, the Army, unionist and British Politicians, and the British Royal Family. However, by the early 1990s both PIRA and loyalists had become engaged in a mounting series of 'eye for an eye' type sectarian murders" (Talbot 2003, 335).

PIRA has received financial support, weapons, and intelligence from countries such as Libya, Spain, and the former Soviet Union,

Exhibit Box 17
In the Name of the Father

This 1993 movie, directed by Jim Sheridan, details the exploits of Gerry Conlon, a petty thief suspected of being a member of the IRA. Based on Conlon's autobiography, *Proved Innocent,* the movie depicts Conlon leaving Belfast for London and going to a squatters' house. He and a friend then breaks into a prostitute's apartment, steals her money, and they return to Belfast, after which Conlon and his friends and family are implicated in the IRA's Guildford pub bombing (October 5, 1974) in which five people were killed and seventy-five were injured.

In response to the bombing, the British Parliament hastily passed the Prevention of Terrorism Act, which allows the government to detain an individual for seven days without charging him or her. Through their interrogation techniques (particularly sleep deprivation), the national security agency managed to make Conlon confess to the bombing. His father, Giuseppe Conlon, and other relatives and friends were also arrested and incarcerated for lengthy prison terms.

The film depicts Ms. Gareth Pierce, a prominent human-rights lawyer, coming to visit the prison. Gerry explains his innocence and that of his father (Giuseppe's health deteriorates, and he eventually dies). Pierce is allowed to inspect the Giuseppe Conlon files in a government archive, where she discovers a file that says "not to be shown to defense." The evidence implicates the government detectives in a cover-up to secure Conlon's conviction, and the case against Conlon is dismissed. Conlon was incarcerated for fifteen years before he and the others who were incarcerated in the same case were released.

along with aid from formerly communist Eastern bloc countries. It has received finances through its aid organizations located in the United States (Adams 1986). PIRA has established safe houses in Europe and has been documented training FARC in bomb-building techniques.

Over the last decade and a half, several positive steps have occurred in the long-standing conflict (Dingley 1999). In 1985, the United Kingdom and the Republic of Ireland signed a peace accord regarding the governance of Northern Ireland. Known as the Anglo-Irish Peace Accord, "the agreement seeks to bring to an end to terrorism by establishing a joint system of government for the troubled area" (White 2003, 90). In 1998, the PIRA signed a peace agreement with Great Britain popularly known as the Good Friday (or Belfast) Agreement, and in the following year, a power-sharing agreement (now suspended) started in the Northern Ireland Assembly. The suspension was a result of allegations that the IRA continued to engage in gun smuggling and spying on its political opposition. In 2001, the PIRA began to decommission its weapons and in 2002, Martin McGuiness and Gerry Adams (PIRA leaders and representatives) were offered seats in the British Parliament. They refused, as acceptance would necessitate signing an oath to the Queen of England, which they virulently opposed. Things went from bad to worse when in December 2004 the IRA was accused of $50 million robbery of bank in Dublin, and in January 2005 the IRA was involved in a pub brawl in which a Catholic man was stabbed to death in a Belfast.

In July 2005, shortly after the suicide bombings in London's Tube (subway) allegedly caused by Islamic fundamentalists, and amongst skepticism from leading Northern Irish Protestants, the IRA formally declared that it will give up its three decade long violent struggle to unite with the Republic of Ireland and achieve its goals through peaceful means.[8]

Comparisons

Making comparisons among the three terrorist groups is not easy. They have different ideologies, capabilities, and geographic and political circumstances. For example, whereas the PIRA and Fatah are nationalist-separatist organizations, FARC has a Marxist-Leninist ideology. Nevertheless, some insights can be garnered from comparing the degree to which the causes outlined in chapter 3 are applicable to each group.

Permissive causes

1. Modernization

All three countries in which these organizations predominantly operate have different levels of modernization (Huntington 1968). Determining just how "modern" the host countries are is not so clear cut. Short of utilizing weapons of mass destruction (WMD), all three groups have tried to acquire and use sophisticated technology, including weaponry and communications. The majority of their most significant attacks have occurred in urban locals, and their leadership is usually highly educated and trained professionals.

2. Type of political system

The majority of Palestinians (and by extension, Fatah members) live under Israeli rule (ostensibly a parliamentary democracy). Those Palestinians who live in Gaza and the West Bank are living under conditions of martial law imposed by the Israelis. Otherwise, the vast Palestinian diaspora—those who have emigrated to other countries—live under a wide variety of political systems. The PIRA live disproportionately under British rule, also a parliamentary democracy (with symbolic remnants of a monarchy), which as of early 2005 had draconian antiterrorism legislation (such as the Prevention of Terrorism Act). The Colombian political system is in a state of flux (Stafford and Palacios 2001); Colombia signed a new constitution in 1991 that was supposed to usher in new, expanded political participation. Although currently a presidential system with direct elections, the system is characterized by political patronage and clientelism.

3. Level of urbanization

Our three case-study groups operate in areas with different levels of urbanization. Although it has frequently carried out terrorist attacks in the cities of Colombia, particularly Medellin (Killyane 1990), FARC has conducted its activities primarily in rural and generally remote locations, drawing a disproportionate number of their fighters from those areas. The PIRA and Fatah have flourished in cities (and in the case of Fatah, refugee camps scattered throughout the Middle East and occupied territories where they recruit), though they also draw their supporters and membership from the smaller towns and enclaves throughout their respective country.

Precipitant causes

1. Social, cultural, and historical facilitation

Since these terrorist struggles have endured for a considerable amount of time, they have numerous social and cultural traditions and a rich history on which to draw. The PIRA need not look further than the Republic of Ireland to its south for a constant reminder of what the power of political violence can accomplish. The PIRA also has many members who have achieved international notoriety (e.g., Bobby Sands and the hunger strikers of the 1970s). The FARC is born out of the bloody civil war that engulfed Colombia during the 1950s and the tumultuous history of the Colombian Communist Party. And Fatah can trace its origins to the British mandate (the occupation of Palestine starting at the beginning of the twentieth century). All three of these terrorist groups have developed websites to manage their public image and to disseminate information and propaganda to members and supporters.

2. Organizational split and development

Although Fatah never broke away from a larger group, it certainly has led to many splits not only in its own organization but in the PLO. Similarly, the PIRA has encouraged divisions due to its approaches; "in the fall of 1997 one faction accepting the new Good Friday Agreement, and the other, a newly formed splinter of PIRA, the Real IRA . . . continuing armed resistance to the British occupation of Northern Ireland" (Simonsen and Spindlove 2004, 74–75). Other groups include the Continuity IRA and Real IRA; their connection with the political wing of Sinn Fein is undoubtedly confusing; understanding the platforms and objectives of the respective subdivision is difficult at best. FARC itself was the result of organizational development, having grown out of an alliance between liberals and communists after the civil war that engulfed Colombia between 1948–58; later, FARC stimulated the growth of several new leftist guerrilla or terrorist organizations, including the ELN and the EPL.

3. Presence of other forms of unrest

Colombia, like Northern Ireland, has been wracked with all sorts of labor difficulties and criminal violence. According to the Henning Center for Labor Relations, since the mid-1980s, 3,800 union leaders and activists in Colombia have been assassinated by far-right paramilitary organizations.[9] Labor unrest is also a bone of contention for Palestinians. They are typically underpaid and a source of cheap labor for some Israeli business who care to hire them.

4. Support

Fatah has been supported by wealthy Palestinians, Arab states, and the former Soviet Union. FARC has made a considerable amount of money through kidnappings, assassinations, and working for the drug cartel, especially as the cartel's strong arm. The PIRA has allegedly received training and weapons from Libya and Fatah has been involved in several kinds of criminal activities, including drug trafficking, extortion, and protection services.

5. Counterterrorist organization failure

At various times, the Colombian, British, and Israeli national security and intelligence agencies that monitor terrorist groups have failed to detect terrorist cells and actions. With each security lapse, these government entities try to improve policies and procedures. In most cases, new approaches are put into place, just as terrorist organizations are constantly looking for holes in the existing security systems.

6. Availability of weapons, explosives, and materials

In recent years Fatah has been accused of making its own bombs, and there is even some credible evidence of cooperation between the PIRA and FARC, in terms of sharing bomb-making expertise. Meanwhile, Hamas has been building Katusha rockets and firing them on Israel; whether they pass this technology on to Fatah or their splinter groups is unknown.

7. Grievances

Although things are complicated by geography (i.e., the state of Israel lies between the West Bank and the Gaza Strip), Fatah seeks to establish a homeland for the Palestinian people, a group taht has been under Israeli control since the partition. FARC wants a complete communist revolution in the state of Colombia, and the PIRA wants the British army to leave Northern Ireland, which would then allow the Irish Catholics to establish a separate country.

Conclusion

By reviewing the history and motivations behind these terrorist groups, formed and continuing to commit acts of political violence, we can determine similarities and differences in causal patterning. In sum, what this analysis points to—the trait they share most in common—is the powerful effect of grievances. While the other factors are important, none can sustain a terrorist group without the perception of some sort of hurt or damage to an organization, culture, race, or ethnicity: a wrong that is widely felt, long-standing, and unresolved. These grievances have been a source of contention despite changes in leaders and generations. Unless some sort of meaningful accommodation is made by the countries where they started, these conflicts will persist and possibly worsen. New generations will carry on the struggle, and both sides (victims and perpetrators) will suffer injury, senseless property destruction, and death.

Questions, Chapter 5

PART ONE: MULTIPLE CHOICE

1. What is the name of the al-Fatah subunit that engages in suicide bombings?
   a. al-Aqsa Martyrs' Brigade
   b. al Qaeda
   c. Hamas
   d. Islamic Jihad
   e. PFLP-GC

2. What is the dominant religious affiliation does al-Fatah support?
   a. Christian
   b. Jewish
   c. Muslim
   d. Secular
   e. none of the above

3. Which of the following countries was NOT involved in the Six Days' War?
   a. Jordan
   b. Lebanon
   c. Iraq
   d. Syria
   e. Israel

4. Where is the Gaza Strip?
   a. borders with Lebanon
   b. borders with Syria
   c. borders with Jordan
   d. borders with Egypt
   e. none of the above

5. Which of the following Palestinian terrorist organizations have the largest number of members?
   a. al Qaeda
   b. Fatah
   c. PFLP
   d. Hammas
   e. PLO

6. Who is the current head of PIRA?
   a. Gerry Adams
   b. Bill Idol
   c. Jerry Garcia
   d. Billy Holliday
   e. none of the above

7. What was Bloody Sunday?
   a. the popular name given to the 1974 incident in which a bomb exploded in an English pub
   b. the day on which the NILA formed
   c. IRA attack on members of Parliament in Brighton
   d. the incident where the British military fired openly on protesters
   e. the stock market crash of 1929

8. Which terrorist group were the Guildford Four accused of being members of?
   a. Baader-Meinhoff gang
   b. *Brigatte Rose*
   c. FLQ
   d. IRA
   e. Italian neo-fascists

9. What is the name of the agreement that was brokered between the PIRA and the British government?
   a. Olso agreement
   b. Good Friday accords
   c. Bloody Sunday
   d. *In the Name of the Father*
   e. none of the above

10. What act was used to hold and interrogate the Guildford Four?
    a. PATRIOT Act
    b. Prevention of Terrorism Act
    c. War Measures Act
    d. War Powers Act
    e. Defense of the Realm Act

11 How many people died in the Guildford bombing?
   a. 4
   b. 5
   c. 14
   d. 15
   e. 20

12. What day did the Guildford bombing take place?
    a. October 25, 1964
    b. October 15, 1968
    c. October 5, 1975
    d. October 15, 1976
    e. none of the above

13. In which country does FARC operate?
    a. Argentina
    b. Colombia
    c. Cuba
    d. Ecuador
    e. Venezuela

14. What is the dominant ideology of FARC?
    a. nationalist/separatist
    b. left-wing/communist
    c. right-wing
    d. all of the above
    e. none of the above

15. Of the three principle groups discussed in this chapter, which one has had the longest existence?
    a. al-Fatah
    b. al Qaeda
    c. FARC
    d. PFLP-GC
    e. PIRA

16. In terms of structural causes, which one is the most dominant?
    a. grievances
    b. the type of political system
    c. the presence of other forms of unrest
    d. geographical location
    e. none of the above

PART TWO: SHORT ANSWER

1. What is the name of the al-Fatah organization that formed when Jordan's King Hussein ran the Palestinians out of Jordan?

2. In what country/ies would you find the Hezbollah?

3. When did the Algerian Revolution take place?

4. In what year was al-Fatah formed?

5. Who was the original leader of al-Fatah?

6. What are the names of the groups that al-Fatah allegedly supports?

7. What are the Good Friday accords?

8. What are three causes for the rise of the PIRA?

9. From which religious group does the IRA draw?

10. List four terrorist groups that have operated in Northern Ireland.

11. Who is the leader of FARC?

12. How has the FARC supported itself?

13. In recent years, what sort of accommodation did the government of Colombia offer FARC?

14. How old is FARC?

PART THREE: ESSAY

1. If grievances remain the most important *cause* of terrorism, what is the most important *effect* of these groups?

2. To what extent can understanding the different causes of terrorism help us control it?

3. How useful is it to have both a political branch (such as a political party) and a military branch (such as a terrorist subunit) of an organization?

4. Why do you think it has been difficult for the Palestinian people to succeed in establishing their own homeland?

5. What do you suspect are three problems with the Prevention of Terrorism Act of 1974?

CHAPTER SIX

Terrorism in the United States

Moving closer to home, this chapter examines the history of terrorism in the United States. This includes the rise of the Ku Klux Klan and the events of the turbulent 1960s, which brought to public attention terrorist groups such as the Weathermen/Weather Underground, the Symbionese Liberation Army, and the Black Liberation Army. It continues with a discussion of white supremacist organizations like the Aryan Nations and the bombing of the Murrah Federal Building by Timothy McVeigh and his accomplices. We'll conclude with a brief discussion of émigré/nationalist-separatist and single-issue groups and individuals who resorted to terrorism (Smith 1998).

During the 1960s and the early 1970s, several race riots and violent antiwar student demonstrations (opposing the Vietnam War) took place in the United States. These actions, in part, set the conditions for the growth of a number of terrorist groups with ideological leanings (toward the left *and* the right). Some of the other terrorist groups from this period were affiliated with émigré or nationalist-separatist movements (such as the anti-Castro Cubans, Croatian Separatists, and Puerto Rican and Armenian nationalists). Finally, some organizations are appropriately labeled "single-issue" groups. They borrowed ideological or philosophical nuances from legal groups (for example, political parties), social movements (such as environmental movement) or popular causes (pro-life, pro-choice, animal rights). We'll review these groups in chronological fashion.

Left-Wing Terrorism

In the 1960s and 1970s, several left-wing terrorist organizations formed in the United States. Among the most prominent were the Weather

Underground, the Symbionese Liberation Army, the United Freedom Front, and certain black militant groups. They were opposed to American participation in the war in Vietnam, capitalism, police violence, and the lack of progress that was being made in the granting of civil rights to minorities particularly African Americans.

Weathermen/Weather Underground

In June 1969, the Students for a Democratic Society (SDS)—at the time the largest alternative new left organization opposed to the American presence in Vietnam—held its annual convention in Chicago. Many activists present considered this an extremely frustrating experience, as the processes for decision-making and expressing opposing viewpoints were extremely disorganized. Three months later, during the Democratic Convention in October, a series of violent protests known as the "Days of Rage" occurred. Young men and women, including college students, some of whom were identified with the countercultural hippie and yippie movements participated. Shortly after these two events, a number of individuals (including Bill Ayers, Bernadine Dohrn, Brian Flanagan, David Gilbert, Naomi Jaffe, Mark Rudd, and Laura Whitehorn) who were disappointed with the SDS and the possibility for nonviolent political change in the United States formed the Weathermen (later renamed the Weather Underground). They supposedly got their name from one of Bob Dylan's lyrics: "You don't need a weatherman to know which way the wind blows." Part of the Weather Underground's ethos included giving up their bourgeois lifestyle, engaging in group sex, and a rejection of monogamous relationships.

After trying to organize working-class youths, and planning a series of demonstrations, the Weathermen, and beginning in December 1969, the Weather Underground bombed government (including police and military) and corporate buildings, offices, and vehicles, starting in California and then moving to New York and other states. In its first year, the group was credited with five hundred bombings. Their actions were denounced by the SDS and the radical Black Panther Party.

On March 6, 1970, the New York cell contained two Weather leaders, Kathy Boudin and Cathlyn Wilkerson, as well as Diana Oughton and two other active Weathermembers, Terry Robbins and Ted Gold. This unit was involved in a now-famous bomb explosion, when Oughton and Gold were killed when a bomb they were assembling went off prematurely, killing them and damaging the group's Greenwich Village house in New York City.

The Weather Underground tried to develop relations with many radical groups that were active during their existence. It had an interesting relationship with the Black Panther Party (BPP). The Weather Underground believed they shared similar ideological goals but were publicly rebuffed by then-leader of the BPP, Fred Hampton, later shot to death in December 1969, in a predawn raid by Chicago Police Department officers (Churchill and Vanderwall 1988, chapter 3) . The Weather Underground were perceived by many activists as outlaws, similar to the characters portrayed in the popular 1960s films *Butch Cassidy and the Sundance Kid* and *Bonnie and Clyde*. In 1970, about forty of their members went underground; some believe that going into hiding fueled the name change from the Weathermen to the Weather Underground. Others have suggested that the name Weathermen could be perceived as sexist, as there were numerous women in the organization's ranks (see exhibit box 18).

In September 1970, after allegedly being paid twenty thousand dollars, the group helped Timothy Leary (a 1960s psychologist and icon who advocated and popularized the use of LSD) to escape from a prison in San Luis Obispo, California, and run to Algeria (Vetter and Perlstein 1991, 52–53). Then, in 1971, the Weather Underground placed a bomb in the United States Capitol Building, but it was discovered and safely defused. Also in 1971, to protest the shooting of prominent African American writer George Jackson, who was allegedly escaping San Quentin Prison, the group placed a bomb at the California Department of Corrections building in San Francisco; this time it exploded.

Although the group "officially" disbanded in the mid-1970s, many of its members were still in hiding or committing periodic crimes. The reasons behind the group's demise included the existence (and relative success) of more mainstream groups like Vietnam Veterans Against the War, the debilitating effects of living on the run, and the final pullout of United States troops from Vietnam. The need for an antiwar movement had dissipated. The organization felt marginalized; no one cared about its ideology anymore (Ross and Gurr 1989).

In the late 1970s, some of the remaining membership who had been in hiding reconstituted themselves into a group called the May 19th Communist Organization (M19CO). They allied themselves with members of the Black Liberation Army and individuals of a group called the Republic of New Africa. They were responsible for "liberating" a handful of so-called political prisoners from American jails and prisons (Smith 1994, 99–107). On October 20, 1981, members of M19CO were involved in a $1.6 million Brinks truck robbery in Nyack, New York. This operation culminated in the shooting death of a Brinks employee and two police officers, as well as the wounding of a security guard, and eventually led to the arrest of four individuals, including former Weather Underground members Katherine Boudin and David Gilbert. Both Boudin and Gilbert have been in prison for the past twenty-three years and have been denied parole in connection with the robbery and shooting.

By 2001, most of the members had been arrested, were in prison, or had been released back into the community. Bernadine Dohrn is currently a professor of law at Northwestern University. Her husband, Bill Ayers, is a professor of education at the University of Illinois. David Gilbert continued with the Black Liberation Army and is serving a lengthy prison sentence in Attica Penitentiary. Boudin did time at the Bedford Hills Correctional Facility in New York. Finally, Mark Rudd is a math professor at TVI Community College in Albuquerque, New Mexico.

The Symbionese Liberation Army

The Symbionese Liberation Army (SLA) was responsible for numerous murders and bombings and achieved notoriety by kidnapping Patricia Hearst, the daughter of the wealthy newspaper and communications corporation tycoon Randolph Hearst. Hearst's kidnapping took place in Berkeley, California, on February 4, 1974. As Sloan has noted, "In the ensuing months this small and previously unknown group skillfully used the media. The SLA's sense of the dramatic would be a harbinger of the terrorist 'spectaculars' that would seize the world's headlines throughout the decade" (Sloan 1993). Shortly after Hearst was abducted, something strange occurred; at a number of bank robberies, security cameras recorded what appeared to be Patti Hearst toting a submachine gun. She was eventually arrested and served time in a California prison. As discussed in an earlier chapter, in a bizarre twist of fate—or, as her defense argued, in a case of the Stockholm syndrome—she had apparently sympathized with her captors.

The United Freedom Front

Between 1976 and 1984, one of the most active new left terrorist groups was the United Freedom Front (UFF). This organization consisted of only eight people (four white males, three white females, and one African-American male, who eventually broke with the organization. They had a generic new left ideology. "In addition to a series of bombing incidents, UFF members were involved in the 1981 murder of a

Exhibit Box 18
Weather Underground

Released in 1976, Emile de Antonio's film *Weather Underground* provides an opportunity to listen to the viewpoints of some of the original and key members of this terrorist organization. It includes their rationales, motivations, and ideological views, and uses their life histories to provide context for their actions, capturing both the positive and negative sides of the group. *Weather Underground* also provides an attenuated history of the civil rights movement, labor strikes, and U.S. foreign policy, including the dates and background necessary to understand them. These events are crucial conditions under which terrorism thrived in the United States. The film also examined the group's solidarity with the black struggle. In terms of drawbacks, there was not much critical analysis of Weather Underground members' viewpoints. The movie was also a little too long and, in many cases, the points were redundant and repetitive. Additionally, in order to minimize their potential capture by authorities, none of the faces of people interviewed were completely displayed.

In 2004, independent filmmakers Sam Green, Bill Siegel, Carrie Lozano, and Marc Smolowitz made a follow-up documentary *The Weather Underground,* which integrates news reports, film footage, and interviews. The interviews include most of the surviving key players. They talked and reminisced about their days as part of the terrorist organization. In order to contextualize things the filmmakers interviewed Todd Gitlin, the former head of the SDS and now a respected academic, former Black Panther Kathleen Cleaver, and FBI agent Don Strickland who was assigned to investigating the Weather Underground.

New Jersey State Police officer and the attempted murders of two Massachusetts State Police officers in 1982. The group also reportedly committed armed bank robberies" along the eastern seaboard (Vetter and Perlstein 1991, 54). Between November 1984 and April 1985, the remaining seven members of the group were arrested (Vetter and Perlstein 1991, 54). One of the most charismatic is Tom Manning who is currently incarcerated at Leavenworth prison (http://www.geocities.com/capitolhill/parliament/3400/).

Black Militants

During the 1960s, despite numerous clashes between African Americans and the police—including controversial attempts by police to kill

Black Panthers in shootouts (see Churchill and Vanderwall 1988)—few African-American groups engaged in domestic terrorism. For example, the Black Panther Party (BPP), the most radical of the groups, did not engage in political violence. One group that *did* pursue this strategy was the Black Liberation Army.

Formed as splinter group from the BPP, between 1969 and 1973, the Black Liberation Army murdered (or attempted to kill) policemen, and robbed banks in New York City, Atlanta, Chicago, and San Francisco. Among their many exploits were attempts to free their incarcerated members from jail or prison. Many of their members were killed in shootouts with police (http://thetalkingdrum.com/freedomfighters. html). And in 1977, about a dozen members of the Hanafi Muslim group, a militant Black Muslim organization, took over the district building (city hall), the B'nai B'rith, and the Islamic center building in Washington, D.C. (Tanenbaum and Rosenberg 1979/1994). A total of 134 individuals were held at gunpoint for 39 hours. Then Washington Mayor Marion Barry was shot in the chest, and a local radio reporter was killed. The standoff ended when ambassadors from three Arab countries negotiated with the hostage takers. Apparently the Hanafis were seeking revenge for the 1973 murder of five of their group at the hands of the Nation of Islam. Those involved were handed down prison terms, including Khalifa Hamaas Abdul Khaalis, who was sentenced to 21 to 120 years.

Right-Wing Terrorism

There is a long tradition of right-wing violence in America. Some of the more dominant right-wing terrorist groups include the Ku Klux Klan and the Aryan Nations (Smith 1994, chapters 4–5). This section discusses these groups, as well as some of their offshoots, and concludes with a discussion of Timothy McVeigh and the Oklahoma City bombing.

The Ku Klux Klan

The Ku Klux Klan (KKK) was formed in the aftermath of the Civil War (1861–65). Its organizational base consisted of white Southerners who were upset with the results of emancipation, particularly their loss of status and power. The white supremist organization promoted Protestantism and took their anger out on defenseless blacks through a ruthless campaign of terror that included assault, cross burning, and lynching. During its one hundred and fifty years of existence, the KKK has gone through several different permutations due to internal competition and corruption.

In the 1960s and early 1970s, the Klan was involved in countless "murders, beatings, cross burnings, and other acts intended to intimidate and harass civil rights workers in their attempts to enroll black workers. . . . FBI investigations led to the successful prosecutions in the federal courts, and by the late 1960s and early 1970s, many white Southerners . . . were alienated by the Klan's terrorist activities. The KKK has endured, however, and so does the susceptibility of some Americans to racial and religious extremism" (Vetter and Perlstein 1991, 57).

In the 1980s, the Klan was primarily a loose collection of state-based organizations under the watchful eye of local law enforcement, the FBI, and several national watchdog organizations, like the Southern Poverty Law Center and the Anti-Defamation League of the B'nai B'rith organization. Lawsuits depleted their resources, and as a consequence the frequency of their violent actions diminished. The Aryan Nations would soon take over the Klan's goals.

The Aryan Nations and its splinter groups

During the 1980s, acts of violent, right-wing terrorism were carried out by various groups loosely affiliated with the Aryan Nations, including the Order, the Covenant, the Sword, and the Arm of the Lord (CSA). Aryan Nations, which at its height had approximately a thousand members, was based in the Pacific Northwest, particularly in Hayden Lakes (near Coeur d'Alene), Idaho, and like many similar groups, practiced or adhered to "Identity Christian" beliefs (Aho 1990; Smith 1994, chapter 4). "This is a label applied to a wide variety of loosely-affiliated groups and churches with a racialized theology. Most of them promote a militant white supremacist and neo- Nazi version of Christianity. Their key commonality is British Israelism theology, which teaches that white Europeans are the literal descendants of the Israelites, and that the Israelites are still God's "Chosen People" (http://en.wikipedia.org/wiki/Christian_Identity).

In the late 1970s, the Aryan Nations established what appeared to be a survivalist training camp in Hayden Lake Idaho, which became the home or stopping-over point for all sorts of individuals on the radical right (such as right-wing skinheads, bikers, Klansmen). In short, this group picked up where the Klan left off.

The Order (also known as the Bruder Schweigen or "Silent Brother-hood") was formed in 1983 by Robert Matthews and drew its inspiration from a book entitled *The Turner Diaries* (1978), written by William Pierce, a disaffected former college professor of physics who was the founder of the now-defunct National Alliance, a right-wing political party. This manuscript was a blueprint designed to enable a band of right-wing sympathizers to overthrow the U. S. government.[1]

The Order's members were responsible for "bombings, assaults on federal officers, and the murders of a suspected informant, a Missouri state police officer, and a Denver talk-show host named Alan Berg"[2] (Vetter and Perlstein 1991, 59). To keep the organization running, the Order committed a number of armed robberies and engaged in counterfeiting. "Between Oct. 1984 and March 1986, thirty-eight members of the Order were arrested. On Dec. 7, 1984, Matthews was killed in a shoot-out with federal authorities on Whidbey Island, Washington," located in Puget Sound (just outside of Seattle) (Vetter and Perlstein 1991, 59).

In the 1970s, the Covenant, the Sword, the Arm of the Lord (CSA) formed by James Ellison, a former minister. Initially "a fundamentalist church with beliefs common to many Americans, had turned into an armed enclave resentful of those with different beliefs or physical traits, deeply suspicious of the federal government, and despairing federal authority" (Smith 1994, 1–2). Soon they offered paramilitary training, made their own weapons (silencers and automatic weapons), committed bombings and arsons against buildings (including a synagogue and churches), armed robberies, and murdered a black Arkansas state police officer. In April 1985, the FBI raided the CSA compound in the Ozark Mountains of Arkansas. After a three-four day standoff with roughly 100 members, arrests were made, and eight of the leaders were convicted and imprisoned (Vetter and Perlstein 1991, 60; Smith 1994, 1; www.mipt.org).

In the mid-1980s a number of groups loosely tied to the militia movement began to emerge. Leonard Zeskind, "(the director of the Atlanta-based Center for Democratic renewal), an organization which monitors militia activity, uses the metaphor of a 'conveyer belt' . . . to depict a process whereby individuals are initially recruited into groups like the militias on the basis of their opposition to legislation outlawing firearms but gradually come to embrace increasingly extreme violent positions that, in turn, are legitimized by appeals to scripture and theological imperatives" (Hoffman 1998, 106). Some of this process is detailed in the movie *American History X*. At the Aryan Nations compound, for example, recruits would receive training in firearms and indoctrination in the group's philosophy and strategy. New members were recruited through word of mouth or through gun shows. Later, militia-associated groups included the Arizona Patriots and the White Patriot Party. In general, though, they lacked the organizational resources to carry out any significant span of terrorist activities (Smith 1994, chapter 4).

Timothy McVeigh and the Oklahoma City bombing

On April 19, 1995, Timothy McVeigh bombed the Alfred P. Murrah Federal Building in Oklahoma City. With the assistance of Terry Nichols (and, to a lesser extent, Michael Fortier), McVeigh—a decorated Gulf War veteran—parked a Ryder rental truck containing a powerful homemade bomb in front of the building. When the device exploded, it virtually leveled the entire structure and caused considerable damage, injuries, and the deaths of 168 people. Although McVeigh had visited Aryan Nations compounds, most accounts suggest that he was acting without their assistance (Hamm 1997).

McVeigh and Nichols were apparently upset with the joint FBI–Alcohol, Tobacco, and Firearms assault on Randy Weaver's house in Ruby Ridge, Idaho (August 2, 1992), as well as the federal government's raid on the Branch Davidian compound in Waco, Texas (April 19, 1993).

Weaver was an anti-Semite who lived with his wife and four children, periodically attended Aryan Nations meetings, and had an outstanding warrant for his arrest because he had allegedly sold a sawed-off shotgun to an ATF informer. In August, 1992, because Weaver failed to appear for a court date, federal marshals decided to forcibly arrest Weaver. Despite what appeared to be comprehensive preparations, the marshals were quickly pinned down from the Weavers' gunfire, and one of them was killed. The FBI were called in to manage the situation. They engaged in an eleven-day standoff at Weaver's home, and in the end, Weaver's forty-two–year-old wife, twelve-year-old son, and dog were shot dead by the FBI.

The Branch Davidians, on the other hand, were a breakaway group from the Seventh Day Adventists that has a history dating to the 1929. They studied the bible as literal truth. In 1954, the Davidians gathered in Mount Carmel, Texas. There was a split in their ranks. In 1991, under the leadership of David Koresh, they built a new church. It was a multiracial community that practiced sexual polygamy and possessed firearms. This riled the local community. Since 1991, Koresh started buying and selling weapons. Contrary to federal government assertions, he was not stock-piling guns. On February 28, 1993, the Bureau of Alcohol, Tobacco, and Firearms (BATF) started a no-knock raid at the main Davidian building. There was a standoff and the Davidians responded by shooting back. 130 Branch Davidian members were inside the compound. When the BATF could not end the siege, the mission was turned over to the FBI. After 51 days there was a tank and tear gas attack. 75 died in the aftermath. In 1995, as a response to the tragedy there was congressional investigation which appeared like a post hoc justification.

In June 1997, McVeigh was convicted of conspiracy to blow up the Murrah building. He was given the death penalty, while Nichols was sentenced to life in prison and Fortier to twelve years in a federal peni-tentiary. McVeigh was executed on June 11, 2001. Although some ana-lysts and keen observers (Hamm 1997; Jones and Israel 1998) point to a wider conspiracy among McVeigh, Nichols, and Fortier, federal author-ities appear to have closed the book on this investigation. Nevertheless, shortly after the Oklahoma City bombing, federal authorities began to crack down on the militia movement (Dyer 1997).

Émigré and Nationalist–Separatist Terrorism

The history of terrorism in this country predates the 1960s; some would even say that it is coterminous with the founding of the United States. Many immigrants and foreigners have played out their homeland ten-sions here. Since the mid-1970s, we have experienced bouts of terrorist activity from groups sympathetic to the people and countries of Croa-tia, Armenia, Cuba, and Puerto Rico.

Croatian terrorism

In September 1976, "five Americans of Croatian descent skyjacked" a plane, had the pilot fly to Europe, and "demanded that leaflets on behalf of Croatian Independence be dropped over Chicago, London, Montreal, New York, and Paris" (Vetter and Perlstein 1991, 61–62). This small group, known as the Croatian Freedom Fighters, wanted a totally free Croatia (from Yugoslavia). The hijackers were captured in France and rapidly extradited to the United States, "where they were con-victed and sentenced to lengthy prison terms" (Vetter and Perlstein 1991, 61–62). A total of seven incidents are attributed to this group.

Exhibit Box 19
Timothy James McVeigh (April 23, 1968–June 11, 2001).
Born on April 23, 1968, in Pendleton, New York, Timothy James McVeigh, along with co-conspirators Terry Nichol and Michael Fortier, and possibly others, holds the distinction of being responsible for the worst case of domestic terrorism in the United States. His bombing of the Edmund Murrah building in Oklahoma City (April 19, 1995) led to the death of 168 people and injuries of numerous others. After finishing high school McVeigh enlisted in the army just in time to participate as a gunner on a Bradley Fighting Vehicle with the Army's 1st Infantry division, during the American involvement in the Gulf War (1990–1991). As a result of his exemplary performance, he received the Bronze Star Medal. After Operation Desert Storm (the military name for the War), McVeigh attempted to join the Army's elite Special Forces, but failed the physical part of the test. Apparently he was devastated by this news. He left the military, worked briefly as a security guard, but then "his lifestyle grew increasingly transient." It was during this time period he met Nichol and Fortier, and members of an Aryan-oriented group that was later picked up for a series of bank robberies.
McVeigh was arrested shortly after the Oklahoma City bombing by a state trooper, because his car did not have a "license plate and [he was] carrying a loaded firearm. Three days later, while still in jail, McVeigh was identified as the subject of the nationwide manhunt." On June 2, 1997, McVeigh was convicted of the murder of eight federal employees" who were in the Murrah building. It was up to the state of Oklahoma to try him for the remaining deaths if the federal case fell through. McVeigh was sentenced to the death penalty.
During his prison time he insisted that he acted alone, filed an appeal, but instructed his lawyers not to plead insanity. The appeal was denied, and on June 11, 2001, he died by lethal injection. He appeared to want to be perceived as a martyr for his cause. It was the first time that the Federal government had executed someone in 38 years. (http://en.wikipedia.org/wiki/Timothy_McVeigh)

Armenian terrorism

In January 1982, the Justice Commandos for the Armenian Genocide (JCAG)—a splinter group from the ASALA—assassinated the Turkish consul general in Los Angeles. In May 1982, the honorary Turkish consul general was assassinated in Boston. Later that year, this group's activities terminated with the arrest, prosecution, and conviction of its members, including Hampig (Harry) Sassounian, who was sentenced to life in prison for the Los Angeles murder (Gunter 1986).

Anti-Castro Cuban terrorism

Cubans who were either loyal to the former Batista regime (a corrupt authoritarian government with strong links to the United States) or opposed to the Castro (communist) government (1959–present) have carried out acts of violence against pro-communist entities in the United States and abroad (e.g., Canada). Four principle terrorist groups have been responsible for the violence: Alpha 66, El Poder Cubano, the Cuban National Liberation Front, and Omega 7. Many of these organizations have been supported by the United States government, materially, financially, or through training. It appears that when these groups became more independent or hurt American citizens, the CIA stopped dealing with them.

"The oldest anti-Castro group," according to Vetter and Perlstein, "is Alpha 66, which is still led by members of the Cuban militia who participated in the ill-starred landing at the Bay of Pigs" (1991, 62). Vetter and Perlstein go on to describe other anti-Castro groups: "Between 1968 and 1975 such groups as El Poder Cubano (Cuban Power) and the Cuban National Liberation Front were responsible for a series of bombings, assaults, and an assassination. Between 1975 and 1983, a group called Omega 7 was the main source of Cuban émigré terrorism and a serious threat to the U.S. and Latin American states that support Fidel Castro. Seven key members were arrested in 1982 and 1983, including Eduardo Arocena, the group's leader. Arocena was convicted and sentenced to life imprisonment" (Vetter and Perlstein 1991, 62). Shortly after his arrest, Omega 7 terrorism appeared to stop (Vetter and Perlstein 1991, 62).

Puerto Rican terrorism

Puerto Rican terrorism can be traced back to 1868, when Puerto Rican nationalists engaged in violent actions in an attempt to gain independence from Spain. Puerto Rico is a protectorate of the United States that has commonwealth status, meaning it has local autonomy but is voluntarily united with the United States; the justice system is run by the United States, and all Puerto Ricans have title to American citizenship. In general, Puerto Rican nationalist groups oppose what they perceive to be American imperialism; they want complete independence, and they share Marxist-Leninist political ideology. Some observers and analysts believe that, since the 1960s, Puerto Rican terrorists have been supported by the Cuban government.

Several terrorist incidents carried out by Puerto Rican groups have occurred both in Puerto Rico and on the U. S. mainland. Some of the more daring events included the 1950 assassination attempt on former president Harry Truman and the 1954 shootings of five congressmen in the House of Representatives. Since the late 1980s, the greatest concentration of Puerto Rican terrorism has been on the island. In the United States, the groups have engaged in activities in cities in which a great number of Puerto Ricans live, including Chicago, Miami, New York City, and Washington, D.C.

Various terrorist groups have emerged over the years to carry on the campaign for Puerto Rican independence, and there is good evidence that individuals may be members of several different organizations. In the late 1960s, members of the Comandos Armados de Liberacion (CAL) and Movimiento Independencia Revolucionario Armando (MIRA) claimed credit for numerous bombings in Puerto Rico and New York. Some attacks were aimed at American companies that owned property on the island; others sought to discourage American tourism on Puerto Rico. Although the bombings stopped after a series of arrests, the surviving members reorganized themselves as Fuerza Unida Revolutionaria Pro Independencia Armando (FURIA), which later reconstituted itself once more as the Fuerza Armandas de Liberacion Nacional (FALN).

In the 1960s and 1970s two principle Puerto Rican terrorist groups formed: *Moviemiento Independencia Revolucionario Armando (MIRA)* and *Comandos Armandos de Libercion (CAL).* They focused their energies on Puerto Rico, "where they attacked American-owned commercial enterprises in hopes of convincing American capitalists to invest elsewhere. The local police managed to crush most of the opposition and the survivors regrouped under the name FURIA (Fuerza Unida Revolutionaria pro Independicia)" (Sater 1984, 5).

FURIA later became *Fuerza Armandas de Liberacion Nacional (FALN).* FALN was one of the strongest and most active Puerto Rican terrorist organizations operating in the United States and, to a lesser extent, in Puerto Rico. FALN was unknown to law enforcement until October 1975, when it claimed responsibility for five bombings in New York City. Over the next decade, this organization was credited with "72 actual bombings, 40 incendiary attacks, 8 attempted bombings, 10 bomb threats, resulting in 5 deaths, 83 injuries, and over $3 million in property damage."[3] Some observers believe that the FALN's bombings of large American corporations has led to a decrease in both tourism and foreign investment in the island.

FALN's activities were not limited to New York City; they engaged in terrorist acts in Washington, D.C., Chicago, Miami, and Newark. Three of their more famous attacks include the bombing of Fraunces Tavern in New York City in January 1975, which took four lives and injured fifty-three people; the December 1979 ambush of a United States Navy bus in Puerto Rico, in which two sailors were killed and ten other servicemen injured; and the March 1980 seizure of the Carter-Mondale campaign headquarters in Chicago and Republican Vice President–Elect George H. Bush's office in New York City. In April 1980, eleven FALN members were arrested, including Carlos Torres, their leader at the time. Since then it appears that they have ceased to exist.

On the island of Puerto Rico, the *Ejercito Popular Boricua (EPB)* (more popularly known as the *Macheteros*—the "machete wielders") is the most effective, and most violent of all the Puerto Rican terrorist groups. Formed in early 1970s, this group has been responsible for numerous murders and bank robberies. In January 1981, they bombed nine planes belonging to the Puerto Rican National Guard and set off a bomb that injured one and killed three American naval officers on leave on the island. The Macheteros targeted mainly the American military (either officers or buildings). In September 1983, Victor Gerena Ortiz, an employee working for Wells Fargo in West Hartford, Connecticut (who turned out to be a Macheteros mole), absconded with $7.1 million (Fernandez 1987). In August 1985, U. S. federal agents made a major crackdown on the organization and came up with nineteen indictments against real or alleged members of the group, among them the founder of the Macheteros, Filiberto Ojeda Rios; he was spirited away or escaped from the island and remains on the FBI watch list. The trial resulting from the 1985 arrests of their members concluded with a number of those indicted put behind bars. In August 1999, then-president Bill Clinton, in a controversial decision, granted clemency to sixteen Puerto Rican terrorists from FALN and the Macheteros.

Single-Issue Terrorism

Occasionally, appropriately motivated individuals are willing to resort to terrorism in the United States and elsewhere. Since the 1980s, members of the Animal Liberation Front or Army, the pro-life movement, the Jewish Defense League, and eco-terrorist movements have committed acts of terrorism.

Animal Liberation Front/Army

Attacks by animal rights activists under the banner of the Animal Liberation Front (ALF) and Animal Liberation Army (ALA) have occurred in many large American cities. Although the group formed in 1976 in England, terrorist incidents in the United States started in 1980. These attacks have included property destruction and what activists call the "liberation" or "rescue" (others call it theft) of animals being used for research. Animal rights activists and members of the ALF and ALA have also damaged the property of furriers and companies that sell clothing made out of fur, and butcher shops. One of their more costly attacks was in 1987 when they destroyed a research facility in California. This caused millions of dollars in damage.

Pro-life terrorists

Between 1984 and 1994, individuals opposed to abortion and a group calling themselves the Army of God bombed or committed arson against one hundred abortion and birth control clinics or providers of abortion. As Vetter and Perlstein report, "Nationwide, abortion clinics have been invaded, vandalized, burned, and bombed. Patients are harassed as they enter clinics . . . one Illinois physician and his wife were kidnapped and held for eight days" (1991, 64).

On July 26, 1996, a bomb exploded at the Olympic Centennial Park during the summer Olympics in Atlanta, Georgia. The bomb killed one person and injured 111 others in attendance. Although there was considerable confusion with respect to the suspect, the FBI finally determined that it was most likely Eric Robert Rudolph. Rudolph had been under suspicion for the bombings of an abortion clinic and a lesbian nightclub, and was also responsible for a slew of other attacks between 1996 and 1998. After eight years on the run, Rudolph was finally captured in May 2004. In April 2005, he was sentenced to life in prison.

Rudolph, who explained his motivations for the bombings in an eleven-page screed during his plea-bargained sentencing, is a product of his times. He revolted against the Bill and Hillary Clinton neo-liberalism of the 1990s, when the federal government was taking abortion rights and gay rights seriously, and appointed an unprecedented number of women and minorities to some of the highest positions of power.

Many of Rudolph's extreme views, in a strange and disturbing way, dovetail with those of the Christian right—a source of strong popular support for the Bush administration, and arguably the deciding factor in 2005 in gaining Bush a second term. Rudolph's diatribe was anti-gay and anti-abortion; he described himself as carrying out his "fundamental duty" as a citizen to use force to stop what he believed were crimes against society, perpetrated by a corrupt government. To many, Rudolph was a folk hero, like Paul Bunyan or Jesse James, rebelling against an allegedly out-of-touch and demonized Washington.

While he was on the run, Rudolph seemed to capitalize on his folk-hero status by having others help him to hide, on the romantic image of the lone guy striking back at the "big bad feds," and a society running amok, wrongs that could only be set right through violent action. Shirts emblazoned with the slogan "Run Rudy Run" were printed and worn with pride by some of his supporters. It could also be argued that the FBI's rush to judgment with respect to security guard Richard Jewel, the initial suspect in the Olympics bombing, only fueled empathy for Rudolph's cause. The longer he eluded capture, the more he appeared to be above the law. Rudolph's beliefs echoed those of a loose group of individuals, including "Identity" Christians, who were quick to draw parallels between him and Randy Weaver, who, as we've discussed, also attained a kind of celebrity status from some in the conservative right.

Although these pro-life terrorists might be classified more generally as ultra-rightists, their focus has generally been much narrowly focused on abortion-related targets.

The Jewish Defense League (JDL)

In 1968, the now-deceased Meir Kahane, an outspoken Brooklyn New York rabbi, established the JDL. Originally intended as a self-defense organization for Jews against street gangs and incidents of anti-Semitism, the JDL soon developed groups in other cities in the United States. Eventually the JDL formed a connection with the Kach movement and party in Israel. Kach advocated that all Arabs leave Israel and that the state of Israel become a Jewish theocracy. During the 1970s and 1980s, the JDL harassed numerous individuals and organizations, conducted several break-ins, engaged in vandalism, and placed or exploded bombs at Soviet-related targets in the United States. Between 1977 and 2005, the

JDL have been implicated in 72 terrorist incidents (www.tkb.org). In 1987 many JDL members were convicted and sent to jail or prison on terrorism-related charges. This was a major setback for the organization. In 1990, Kahane was assassinated by an Arab extremist. By about 2000, the JDL had close to two hundred members. In 2001, then-leader Irv Rubin and member Earl Krugel were charged with conspiracy to bomb Arab-American Congressmen Darell Issa's office and the King Fahd Mosque in Los Angeles. In the fall of 2002, while Rubin was in jail awaiting trial, he apparently fell from a tier and died. The death was ruled as a suicide.[4] In 2003, Krugel pled guilty to charges, and sentenced to federal prison. In November 2005 he was killed by another inmate. Over the last few years it appears that the group has ceased to exist.

Eco-terrorists

We also need to take into account the eco-terrorists (Nilson and Burke 2002). Beginning in the 1990s, a number of individuals became willing to engage in violence against individuals and corporations they accused of damaging the environment (through logging, mining, real estate development, and so on). Their retaliation included tree spiking, arson, and other kinds of property damage. Although Greenpeace and Friends of the Earth, because of their aggressive tactics, have been typically implicated in these acts, these two groups are, for the most part, nonviolent. On the other hand, some of these individuals have been associated with an organization called Earth First or the Earth Liberation Front; in fact, in 1990, a car in which two Earth First members were traveling exploded when a bomb they were carrying prematurely went off. In early 2000, someone set fire to a resort in Vail, Colorado, and to SUV dealerships in California.

Although Theodore (Ted) Kaczynski, the "Unabomber," did not have an affiliation, his letter and parcel bombs make clear that he had sympathies for the ecology movement and was against the wholesale adoption of technology. Between 1978 and 1998 he was responsible for sixteen mail bombings, which killed three people and injured twenty-three. Initially, he sent bombs to airline executives and professors of science and engineering; the FBI called him the "Unabomber" because of this combination of universities and airlines as targets.

In 1995 Kaczynski sent the *New York Times* and the *Washington Post* a thirty-five-thousand–word manifesto explaining his rationale for the bombings and outlining his stance against technology and modern science. The papers consulted the FBI about the appropriateness of publishing the piece, and the authorities thought it might lead to someone who knew him. This is, in fact, what happened. His brother identified Kaczynski, and on April 3, 1996, he was arrested. Theodore Kaczyniski had been living in Montana, in a one-room cabin without electricity or plumbing.

Broad Overviews of Terrorism in the United States

Although several reviews of domestic terrorism during the tumultuous 1960s and 1970s have been written (Bell and Gurr 1979; Gurr 1988a), and commentaries on research on these efforts (Ross 1993b), perhaps one of the best was *Terrorism in America: Pipe Bombs and Pipe Dreams*, written by Brent Smith (1994). He provides a history of terrorism in the United States between 1980–1993 and profiles the different individuals and types of groups involved, primarily those identified by the FBI as terrorists, as well as the government reaction to and prosecution of them. Smith examines the problems with the FBI definition of terrorism, but also points out its utility in conducting the kind of in-depth research he performed. Smith identifies eighteen domestic terrorist groups and ten foreign terrorist organizations from which one or more members were indicted by the FBI. He also reviews the histories of 168 people who were indicted. In order to conduct his research, he analyzed the criminal case histories of the events. Among his numerous findings are that during the 1980s, leftist terrorism declined, while incidents committed by right-wing organizations and the environmental movement increased.

Another equally important book is Hewitt's *Understanding Terrorism in America: From the Klan to al Qaeda* (2003). Hewitt has prepared a comprehensive database analyzing close to three thousand terrorism-related attacks. He notes that terrorists are usually between the ages of eighteen and thirty, and are disproportionately middle class in origin. Additionally, he examines the links between terrorist groups, how they are financed, and the government response to them.

Conclusion

Regardless of the underlying causes, domestic terrorism in the United States will probably always be present. Of recent note has been the idea, particularly in radical right terrorist groups, of the leaderless resistance. In this kind of approach, terrorist acts are committed and terrorist organizations exist without the benefit of a clearly identifiable key player (Beam 1992; Michel and Herbeck 2001).[5] This minimizes the possibility of capture and destruction of an entire terrorist network.

Perhaps the greatest threat in the early twenty-first century, however, is not domestic, but rather foreign terrorist activity. The next chapter turns to a discussion of 9/11 and al Qaeda.

Questions, Chapter 6

PART ONE: MULTIPLE CHOICE

1. Which of the following groups is the oldest, most active, and strongest of the Puerto Rican terrorist organizations?
   a. CAL
   b. FALN
   c. MIRA
   d. FURIA
   e. none of the above

2. Which of the following groups would be considered left-wing terrorists?
   a. the Weather Underground
   b. the United Freedom Front
   c. selected Black Militant groups
   d. the Symbionese Liberation Army
   e. all of the above

3. In 1950, on which U. S. president did terrorists make an assassination attempt?
   a. Truman
   b. Johnson
   c. Kennedy
   d. Bush
   e. Jackson

4. Which of the following is not a single issue from which terrorist groups have formed?
   a. pro-life/anti-abortion
   b. protection of the environment
   c. animal rights
   d. Judaism
   e. Weather Underground

5. Who trained the anti-Castro Cuban terrorists?
   a. Castro
   b. Nicaragua
   c. the Central Intelligence Agency
   d. the Soviet Union
   e. none of the above

6. Which of the following were émigré/nationalist-separatist terrorist groups operating in the United States?
   a. anti-Castro
   b. Armenian
   c. Croatian
   d. Puerto Rican
   e. all of the above

PART TWO: SHORT ANSWER

1. What are *The Turner Diaries?*

2. List three examples of single-issue terrorism in the United States.

3. What two reasons have been cited for McVeigh and Nichols's act of terrorism?

4. What did Leonard Zeskind mean when he used the metaphor of a "conveyor belt" to describe the action of recruits to American militias?

PART THREE: ESSAY

1. Explain the Black Panther Party's relationship with the Weather Underground.

2. What issues united the left-wing terrorists of the 1970s, and why did they feel it was necessary to resort to terrorism?

3. How did the Ku Klux Klan differ from the Aryan Nations?

4. How much does ideology play in the commission of terrorist acts in the United States?

CHAPTER SEVEN

9/11, al Qaeda, and Osama bin Laden

Few incidents of terrorism can compare to the level of horror and to the number of injured and dead resulting from the September 11, 2001, attacks carried out by members of Osama bin Laden's terrorist organization, al Qaeda. The 9/11 incidents highlighted the vulnerability of the United States to international terrorism: although Americans had been the victims of terrorist attacks abroad, rarely had they been targeted by international terrorists at home.

No sooner did the attacks take place than hypotheses about their causes began to circulate. Explanations ranged from the simplistic to the irrational. Some relied on history, others invoked the supernatural. Several questions were posed. Were foreign governments involved? It was suggested that Iraqi president Saddam Hussein assisted bin Laden in his efforts. Could unsuspecting Americans or foreigners have unwittingly helped the hijackers? If so, was there something they could have done to prevent the attack? It has since come to the public's attention that some of the terrorists received instruction in flight centers throughout the United States, and others even considered using crop dusters to spray an area with chemical or biological weapons. Americans, made wiser by the incident, wonder how these supposedly isolated slips in national security occurred.

This chapter reviews the circumstances leading up to 9/11 and discusses the perpetrators as well as alternative explanations of the causes. It also introduces some of the more dominant effects of the attacks and outlines possible scenarios that may occur in order to provide additional security.

Prelude: The 1993 World Trade Center Bombing

New York City's World Trade Center building was a symbol of American capitalism and progress, which are anathema to fundamentalist Muslims, bin Laden, and his organization al Qaeda (Gunaratna 2002; Burke 2003; Glantz and Lipton 2003). On February 26, 1993, Ramzi Yousef and his accomplice Mohammad Salameh, members of the al Qaeda terrorist organization, drove a rented Ford Econoline van laden with explosives into the basement parking lot of the World Trade Center in New York City. It was a primitive bomb with a long fuse, but it managed to ignite and explode at midday, and the explosion was powerful enough to destroy five floors of the building directly above it and short out all electricity in the structure (Reeve 1999, 11–12).

Initially, many people thought it was simply a fire or an electrical transformer explosion. But when workers exited the building, some were "crushed underfoot as panic began to spread" (Reeve 1999, 13). The New York City Fire Department "sent a total of 750 vehicles to the explosion, and did not leave the scene for the next month. It took hundreds of firefighters two hours to extinguish the blazes and more than five hours to evacuate both towers" (Reeve 1999, 14). Six people were killed and 1,042 injured. According to Reeve, the incident led to "more hospital casualties than any other event in domestic history apart from the Civil War. Many of those who escaped without apparent physical injury will be scarred mentally for life, and yet it is almost miraculous that in such a huge bomb attack even more were not killed or injured" (1999, 15).

Yousef wanted to cause one of the buildings to fall into the other. If he had been successful, he would have ended up killing almost a quarter of a million people working in the buildings that day. According to Yousef, "Only carnage on such a level would be sufficient punishment for supporting Israel, America's friend and ally, and the fundamentalists' sworn enemy because of its treatment of the Palestinians" (quoted in Reeve 1999, 24). After the attack, Yousef almost immediately left the country for Karachi, Pakistan. Investigators combing the scene found the van's vehicle identification number relatively quickly and were able to determine that it was rented by Salameh.

Salameh, unlike Yousef, foolishly went back to the rental company to recoup his deposit. There, waiting for him, was an FBI officer posing as a rental agent. After a series of questions, Salameh was arrested.

Then, based on this initial investigation, the FBI took into custody a number of co-conspirators. In order to capture Yousef, the authorities disseminated the information worldwide, and he was later captured on February 7, 1995, in Pakistan (while plotting to launch a major offensive against the American presence in the Philippines) and returned to the United States.

While the trial in connection with the bombing progressed, the FBI determined that much of the conspiracy was drawn around a local blind man, Egyptian-born Sheikh Omar Abdel-Rahman, who at the time was living in New Jersey. Abdel-Rahman, a spiritual leader at a Jersey City mosque, preached inflammatory messages about the United States, Israel, and Jews. The Sheikh was eventually arrested and in 1996 convicted of conspiring to bomb a number of New York City landmarks.

Later, on August 7, 1998, bin Laden and al Qaeda were implicated in the bombing attacks on American embassies in Nairobi, Kenya, and Dar es Salaam, Tanzania, which killed 237 and injured 5,000 people—not only Americans, but also citizens of these countries. And on October 12, 2000, al Qaeda allegedly bombed an American naval ship docked just off the port of Aden, Yemen; the attack on the *USS Cole* caused seventeen deaths and thirty injuries. Despite international arrest warrants for bin Laden and several members of al Qaeda, the United States and other participating countries were unable to capture them.

September 11, 2001

On the morning of September 11, 2001, shortly after take off, seven members of the al Qaeda organization managed to commandeer four large jet airplanes. At approximately, the same time two crashed separately into the twin towers of the World Trade Center in New York City, one into the Pentagon, and the last crashed in a field in rural Pennsylvania. Close to 3,000 people died. Responsibility for this attack was placed squarely on the al Qaeda terrorist organization.

Participants: Bin Laden, al Qaeda, and their Supporters

Osama bin Laden and his organization, al Qaeda, facilitated the rise of the Taliban (the Islamic and Pashtun nationalist movement, and former leadership of Afghanistan). Born in 1957 into a wealthy Saudi family, and trained as civil engineer, Osama became increasingly disaffected with the family business and members of his family. He turned to his Islamic faith. During the 1980s he used his inherited fortune to assist the mujahidin fighters (i.e., a military force of Muslims engaged in a jihad; a holy/religious war against nonbelievers or so-called enemies) in Afghanistan. In 1984 his organization Maktab al-Khadamat (MAK) funneled arms, money and recruits to the insurgency. In 1988 bin Laden began a new organization popularly known as al Qaeda. It included the more militant members of MAK.

Although countless histories of al Qaeda, the Taliban, and the Soviet invasion and occupation of Afghanistan exist (e.g., Griffin 2003), the facts can be summarized as follows. In 1979, the Soviet Union invaded Afghanistan. As a response, young Muslim fundamentalists from around the world joined forces with mujahadin rebels to fight a guerrilla-type insurgency. This campaign received covert support from the United States, Great Britain, and the Gulf States (Qatar, Bahrain, etc.) (Reeve 1999, 2). In February 1989, the Soviets pulled out of Afghanistan no longer willing to suffer the cost both economically and in term of deaths that it had sustained over the previous decade. When the Soviets were defeated, the Taliban emerged as the dominant leaders of Afghanistan and established a theocracy (a government run by a religious rule) (see Exhibit Box 20).

Meanwhile, many Afghan Arabs, as they were called, were emboldened by their success in fighting back the Soviets and sought additional international targets. Reeve notes that "estimates of the total number of Afghan Arabs vary. One source . . . claims the number is close to 17,000, while the highly respected British publication *Jane's Intelligence Review* suggests a figure of more than 14,000 (including some 5,000 Saudis, 3,000 Yemenis, 2,000 Egyptians, 2,800 Algerians, 400 Tunisians, 370 Iraqis, 200 Libyans, and scores of Jordanians)" (1991, 3). Two of the Afghan Arabs were Ramzi Yousef and Osama bin Laden.

According to Reeve, "Some of these men are now responsible for much of the global terrorism threatening the West, while others returned from the Afghan war to start or lead guerrilla movements in their own countries against governments they perceive as being un-Islamic, corrupt, or despotic. These veterans of the Afghan jihad have taken the war home to more than 25 countries, including Algeria,

Exhibit Box 20
What happens when the state is a theocracy?

Many analysts and observers have prognosticated about how long it should take the United States to fight the Taliban, capture Osama bin Laden, and bring some degree of normalcy to Afghanistan. President George W. Bush has suggested that the "war on terrorism" will be long because of the sophistication of the enemy. What many Westerners, both citizens and policymakers, don't realize is that we are not dealing with a "normal" state. Unlike a presidential or parliamentary system, or even a military junta, in which there is a well-defined chain of command, in the current crisis, those in power do not assume the traditional positions of leadership with which we are accustomed to negotiating. The Taliban, for example, created a theocracy, one that makes decisions based on consensus and religious edicts, and those decisions are slow to be made. Since 2001, the Taliban is under siege, and it is surprising that we get any information from the group at all.

It must also be understood that there are different types of theocracies and each has varying degrees to which religion and religious rulers have power over everyday affairs. Although the term first appeared in the first century and was originated by Josephus Flavius, a Jewish historian, it has taken on progressively poor connotations. "After that 'theocracy' has been mostly used to label certain politically unpopular societies as somehow less 'rational' or 'developed'" (http://en.wikipedia.org/wiki/Theocracy).

Azerbaijan, Bangladesh, Bosnia, Britain, Burma, Chechnya, China, Egypt, France, India, Morocco, Pakistan, the Philippines, Saudi Arabia, Sudan, Tajikistan, Tunisia, the USA, Uzbekistan, and Yemen" (1991, 3).

Bin Laden was considered a hero of the insurgency. He eventually took up residence in Sudan, and along with training new recruits, invested in several business ventures. Bin Laden's group is estimated to have five thousand members, "all of whom seem willing to kill and die for the Islamic cause. His soldiers are men . . . young, full of zeal, technically skilled to a high level, and determined to bring terror to the West" (Reeve 1991, 4). In the meantime, al Qaeda sponsored and committed a number of anti-American attacks (Bodansky 2001; Rashid 2001).[1]

Causes of 9/11

Many individuals and organizations have tried to identify the causes of 9/11. It is difficult distinguishing between the group's stated causes— i.e., what bin Laden himself says on publicly released videotapes—and the group's causes as understood by keen observers and terrorism experts. The following is a brief analysis of the general and single-issue causes which can be ascertained.

Global causes

Some explanations, like those produced by the conservative U. S. Council on Foreign Relations[2] and *The 9/11 Commission Report* (United States 2004), have been global in nature. These examine the role of Muslim militant extremism, the presence of American troops in Saudi Arabia, American assistance to repressive regimes, UN sanctions on Iraq, American support of Israel, Arab politics, the clash of civilizations, and world poverty. These explanations provide a template from which to analyze why a group like al Qaeda might resort to international terrorism, but they need to be contextualized and analyzed for their merits.

Single-issue causes

Other explanations, like the one below, have been at the group or individual levels. We'll examine nine reasons that can explain why bin Laden and al Qaeda committed the terrorist acts of 9/11.

1. American abandonment of Muslim fundamentalists

The United States, through the CIA (which covertly aided the mujahadin), abandoned the Muslim fundamentalists after the Soviets finally pulled out of Afghanistan (Cooley 2002; Baer 2003; Coll 2004). Having accomplished their short-term goals, bin Laden and al Qaeda may have felt used and wanted to teach the United States a lesson.

The problem with this proposition is that the Muslim fundamentalists were most likely happy that the American and other Western advisors left them to go about their business without the watchful eyes of outside powers. It also appears that al Qaeda was very successful in forging a strong relationship with the ruling Taliban, who were also fundamentalists. They were the most ideologically similar to al Qaeda and could allow them to operate with minimal supervision.

2. Bin Laden's banishment from Saudi Arabia

According to this explanation, bin Laden wanted to get back at the United States, because he suspected them of having a hand in 1995 of convincing the Saudi Arabian government of revoking his citizenship. But it is more likely that the ruling Saud family was afraid of bin Laden, and that American insistence probably had nothing to do with it. Alternatively, the Saudis might have had an easier job monitoring bin Laden's activities if he had been under their control (perhaps in prison or under house arrest) rather than outside the country. Additionally, there is also the possibility that bin Laden does not recognize citizenship to any state as his loyalty seems to be to Islam which does not acknowledge state borders.

3. Presence of American forces in Saudi Arabia

After the Gulf War ended in 1991, the United States failed to remove its troops from Saudi Arabia, where Mecca and Medina, the holy cities of Islam, are located. According to Muslim lore, the House of Saud (the Saudi ruling family) is considered to be the protector of these sacred places. Some argue the fact that America, the "Great Satan" as some call it, is still close to the holy sites almost a decade later, upsets Muslim fundamentalists.[3]

But if this is the case, then why, for example, did al Qaeda not engage in a similar spectacular terrorist event, like 9/11 against the American troops stationed in Saudi Arabia, or toward the House of Saud, which has repeatedly been accused of corruption and of being too cozy with the Americans (Unger 2004)? True, security in Saudi Arabia is tight, as recent history has demonstrated, but there are always lapses.

4. American support of "corrupt"or un-Islamic regimes

Another theory is that 9/11 was a response to American support of Middle Eastern countries like Egypt, Kuwait, Saudi Arabia, and the Gulf States that maintain corrupt regimes (monarchies) that stand in the way of the implementation of Islamic law. But the United States is not the only Western country that has helped those states. Many have considerable economic investment and military support from European and other Group of Eight (G-8) countries (i.e., the leading industrialized and democratic countries: Britain, Canada, France, Germany, Italy, Japan, Russia, and the United States). If foreign help provided to Arab monarchies was the terrorists' main grievance, any of the trading partners could have been singled out for attack.

5. American support of Israel

Many Islamic fundamentalists are opposed to the creation of the state of Israel and wish that in the subsequent military conflicts it would have been "driven into the sea" (an expression used by Arab leaders during the 1967 war). The fact that the United States helps Israel financially and militarily has clearly been a grievance of Palestinians in their struggle with Israel. This could possibly be important, but if the real enemy was Israel, why have there been no reported attacks against Israel by al Qaeda over its two decades of existence?

6. American targeting of bin Laden

After the first World Trade Center bombing (1993) and the Kenyan and Tanzanian embassy bombings (1998), the American government instituted a reward for bin Laden's capture; thus he had a "price on his head." So, this theory suggests, rather than be captured or killed, bin Laden decided to strike first against the United States. He must, however, have had some sense of how the United States, and particularly the American people, would react if the World Trade Center was bombed. He knew that attacking "the enemy" before they attacked would only anger Americans and their allies, thus bolstering anti–bin Laden sentiments.

7. Timing

This argument suggests that it was only a matter of time: it had been a while since al Qaeda attacked a large target, and for a terrorist group to be credible, it must periodically engage in political violence. Al Qaeda is respected in many Muslim quarters, so in order to maintain its status, its members may have believed that they had to pull off an incredible terrorist event that would showcase their strength and skills.

This is a strong possibility. It had been eleven months since the attack on the USS Cole, and unfortunately, the United States had not yet formulated a military response.

8. American economy and capitalism

Some argue that bin Laden believed that by hitting, if not destroying, the World Trade Center, his organization could seriously injure the American economy and capitalism. Perhaps, but within days the stock exchange was up and running through satellite offices throughout New York City and across the Hudson River in New Jersey. Additionally would he and his organization not be hurting themselves as it was learned, shortly after the attacks, that al Qaeda, through its legitimate affiliates was trading stocks to finance their operations. Although the economy has been affected by 9/11, these effects have primarily limited to particular sectors like the airline and tourism industry, and areas such as New York City.

9. American culture

American power—in the form of its culture (e.g., so-called equality between men and women, promiscuity, etc.), capitalism, military power, and foreign policies—is considered to be a threat to Islam and the Muslim way of life.

This is perhaps the most convincing of the arguments and is what probably drove bin Laden and his organization to the events of 9/11. Bin Laden believes he is fighting for all of Islam, and that the whole conflict is nearly identical to the Crusades (Reeve 1999; Bodansky 2001). Outside of the United States, Americans are often hated by foreigners (hence the concept of "the ugly American"—a disposition to be insensitive to local customs), something not lost on Muslim fundamentalists. Anti-Americanism is high in many countries throughout the world. Why, for example, has al Qaeda not attacked other advanced industrialized democracies, like Canada, America's neighbor to the north? Some have suggested that 9/11 was motivated not by Islamic fundamentalism, but by anti-Americanism. American foreign policy is

Exhibit Box 21
Significant dates in the history of al Qaeda and Osama bin Laden

1957: Osama bin Laden is born into a wealthy Saudi family, and trained as civil engineer,

December 1979: The Soviet Union invades Afghanistan. Young Muslim fundamentalists from around the world join forces with mujahadin rebels to fight a guerrilla-type insurgency against the Soviets. Their campaign receives covert support from the United States.

1984: Bin laden establishes an organization known as Maktab al-Khadamat (MAK) which funneled arms, money, and recruits to the insurgency.

1988: Bin Laden began a new organization popularly known as al Qaeda. It included the more militant members of MAK.

February 1989: Soviets, defeated, pull out of Afghanistan. Taliban achieves power.

August 1, 1990–April 1991: Gulf War (when Iraq invaded Kuwait). Afterward, the United States leaves significant number of troops in Saudi Arabia.

February 26, 1993: Al Qaeda members Ramzi Yousef and Mohammad Salameh drive a rented van, laden with explosives, to the basement parking lot of the World Trade Center in New York City. It explodes, injuring 1,042 people and killing 6.

August 7, 1998: Al Qaeda bombs American embassies in Nairobi, Kenya, and Dar es Salaam, Tanzania, killing 237 and injuring 5,000 people—not only Americans, but also citizens of these countries.

October 12, 2000: Al Qaeda allegedly bombs the USS Cole, an American naval ship that was docked just off the port of Aden, Yemen, causing 17 deaths and 30 injuries.

September 11, 2001: Nineteen al-Qaeda hijackers commandeer four airplanes, crashing two into the World Trade Center, one into the Pentagon, and another into a rural field in Pennsylvania.

perceived to be overly aggressive, and American corporations are thought to exploit foreign workers (see Exhibit Box 21).

Effects of 9/11

When we consider what the effects of 9/11 were and should be—how did we respond in the short term, and what we will do in the long term to prevent a second attack. The first question to answer is, Did the prevailing antiterrorist prevention system fail? And, if so, to what degree?

Hindsight

As the pieces of the puzzle began to fit together, it became clear that those plotting the 9/11 attacks had been in the United States for a considerable period of time before the event, undetected by law enforcement authorities and national security agencies. Maybe American security intelligence was blindsided by the activities of the nineteen or more hijackers because they were focused on other issues or crises.[4] In the six months preceding the attacks, in the aftermath of the contested presidential election of George W. Bush, there was a change in the administration of American national security organizations; Louis Freeh, director of the FBI, announced that he would be stepping down. When the country talked about terrorism, it was usually in connection with the circumstances around the execution of Timothy McVeigh. Additionally, it came to the attention of the CIA, FBI, and the public that they had traitors among their ranks (e.g., Robert Hansen, who for close to a decade had been covertly providing the Soviets, then Russians, classified intelligence). The investigations and the judicial actions that followed dominated agency agendas. More than likely, there were numerous security glitches; counterterrorist measures that should have been implemented have since been identified (Clarke 2004). Many of these issues were eventually discussed during the 9/11 Commission which dominated much of the spring 2004 domestic news coverage (United States 2004).

It might be possible that there is very little governments and citizens can do when individuals like those implicated in the 9/11 attacks are so committed to their cause. Maybe no antiterrorist agency can ultimately deter a determined individual or group of individuals. America has suffered domestic terrorist attacks in the past (e.g., anarchists, the Weather Underground) as well as attempted and successful assassinations of political leaders, and each time government agencies have put into place a series of countermeasures. Perhaps these responses are obsolete in an age that carries with it more sophisticated technology for weaponry and communication.

As we have learned, when organizations and governments increase security, they traditionally resort to target hardening—more blast-resistant materials, architectural designs that can withstand the impact of a highly charged bomb, and reconfiguring traffic patterns. Since the 1960s, the United States and many other democracies have taken measures to prevent attacks from occurring and have instituted safeguards to minimize damage. During the 1960s, as a response to hijackings, sky marshals (a program that has recently expanded) were used to protect civilian aviation from this kind of activity. There was also an increase in the number of metal detectors, and luggage and bag inspections in order to prevent hijackings (Ross and Miller 1997).

Short-term effects

No sooner than the events of 9/11 took place, the United States went into a lockdown situation. Planes were grounded and trains were stopped. More police were visible guarding transportation hubs and the national guard was called up to patrol critical infrastructure targets.

Long-term effects

For ideas about solutions and examples of strategies, we might look at how other countries have handled their terrorism problems. It is not uncommon, for example, to see armed police or the military in European airports, train and bus stations, nor is it unusual for passengers to have their bags thoroughly searched and to be subject to what might appear to be inane questions when flying many foreign airlines.

Unintended consequences

Maybe, despite media reports to the contrary, the events of 9/11 are behind us; bin Laden and his organization have made their point and, despite their saber rattling and the American military response, realistically, we have nothing more to fear from al Qaeda. Historical evidence has proven otherwise with dramatic bomb attacks against civilians in Jakarta (August 2003), Madrid (March 2004), and London (July 2005). The incidents, however, may have served to embolden other individuals or organizations to engage in so-called copycat acts of terrorism. In fact, this is what is being currently suggested: many people, experts and citizens alike, are quick to blame al Qaeda (and bin

Laden) for every terrorist attack since 9/11. This process of *contagion* is well known to terrorism experts (see Midlarsky, Crenshaw, and Yoshida 1980). For example, we have not heard much lately from right-wing organizations like the Aryan Nations, and this may be an opportune time for them to step back into the public spotlight. Leaders or members of these groups may ride the coattails of increased anti-Arab sentiment in America and achieve a measure of respect with some right-wing constituencies.

One of the biggest fears amongst the public, politicians, and security personnel is that after 9/11, the heightened security will be relaxed, and life will return to *business as usual*. The concrete barriers will slowly and inconspicuously be removed from popular tourist attractions, prominent government buildings, and transportation hubs. The increased precautions that we have now instituted at entrances (known collectively as "access control") will be lifted. And then, it will be the perfect time for another terrorist attack.

Future consequences

As noted earlier, perhaps there is not much we can do when individuals and groups are so firmly committed to the idea and practice of overthrowing the values, institutions, and government of the United States. At times it may seem that all we can do is bury our heads in the sand or engage in mindless hedonism, if we believe "the end is near." This is not an uncommon reaction. During the 1970s, the survivalist movement, for example, was a response to the fear many Americans had of widespread civil and racial unrest in our cities (Dyer 1997; Hamm 1997). On the other hand, some commentators have suggested that the 9/11 attack narrowed the racial divide, that traditional antipathy between blacks and whites may have temporarily subsided because of a common enemy.

Regardless of which measure(s) we take, there will be costs (financial, psychological, and political in terms of lost civil liberties) attached to each official response. Some debate that we run the risk of developing a garrison state (e.g., Lasswell 1962), as in Britain and some totalitarian countries, where surveillance of citizens (particularly through the use of closed-circuit television) appears pervasive. Americans, used to broad protections of privacy, will have considerable difficulty with this new state of affairs. Compared to their European allies, Americans have a disproportionate amount of freedom or liberty with respect to mobility and political association. Having this curtailed or giving this up will take a major accommodation.

Conclusion

The events of 9/11 have demonstrated that America, the world's largest superpower, is not invincible. Many people thought the United States would never be attacked on its home soil by foreign-based terrorists. If nineteen individuals can create so much damage and wreak so much havoc armed only with their fists—and, in some cases, boxcutters—we need to rethink our country's approach to counterterrorism. In short, Americans can no longer assume they are immune from terrorist attacks at home. In order to deal with this insecurity, they will have to spend valuable resources and challenge values they hold so dear, including their cherished and protected civil liberties, which they will have to partially forfeit in order to maintain some degree of security.

A multiplicity of factors caused 9/11, but three factors clearly stand out. The first issue consists of problems connected to American foreign policy, which has routinely been accused of being unnecessarily aggressive (Chomsky 2001; Johnson 2004). The second factor is the so-called clash of civilizations (Barber 1996; Huntington 1998). Here Americans are characterized as having difficulty dealing with non-Europeans, coming off as the "ugly American," abrasive and insensitive to foreigners. The third item is the failure of national security organizations to properly analyze the signs and signals and institute proper countermeasures in a timely fashion.

The recent attacks may foreshadow some of the possible terrorism that many countries will be subjected to in the coming years. Not only does it appear that a variety of possible targets are susceptible to terrorist attacks, but well-founded fears exist surrounding the methods by which innocent civilians will be hurt and/or lose their lives. The possibility of biological, chemical, and nuclear incidents (especially because of revelations that the 9/11 terrorists were checking out crop dusters as "delivery vehicles," and the anthrax-filled letters sent during the fall of 2001), increase already high levels of fear and paranoia (Tucker 1996; 1999; Miller, Engelberg, and Broad 2001; Allison 2004). In short, America is a changed nation, and its citizens and national security establishment may never be the same.

Questions, Chapter 7

PART ONE: MULTIPLE CHOICE

1. When was the first terrorist attack on the World Trade Center?
    a. June 12, 1990
    b. July 20, 1998
    c. February 26, 1993
    d. March 10, 1980
    e. September 11, 2001

2. In 1998, bin Laden and al Qaeda were implicated in the bombing attacks of which two American embassies?
    a. Ghana and Algeria
    b. Kenya and Tanzania
    c. China and Japan
    d. Nairobi and Ethiopia
    e. Zimbabwe and Nigeria

3. What is the name of the very first individual who unsuccessfully tried to blow up the World Trade Center?
    a. al Qaeda
    b. Andreas Baader
    c. Ulricke Meinhoff
    d. Ramzi Yousef
    e. Mohammed Atta

4. What is the popular name for the group of the young Muslims who went to Afghanistan to fight against the Soviets?
    a. al Qaeda
    b. Afghan Arabs
    c. Taliban
    d. mujahadin
    e. none of the above

5. How many people died in the first attack on the World Trade
    Center?
    a. 3
    b. 6
    c. 12
    d. 25
    e. 100

6. What is a theocracy?
    a. government led by a king
    b. government led by a royal family
    c. government run by religious leaders
    d. government elected through participatory elections
    e. none of the above

7. After the first World Trade Center bombing, who returned to
    the rental company to retrieve the deposit?
    a. Ramzi Yousef
    b. Mohammad Salameh
    c. Osama bin Laden
    d. Timothy McVeigh
    e. Terry Nichols

PART TWO: SHORT ANSWER

1. What are three reasons why Osama bin Laden and al Qaeda
    may have attacked the World Trade Center?

2. What is the name of the Islamic nationalist movement that
    Osama bin Laden supported?

3. What are three single-issue causes of 9/11?

4. What are three future consequences of terrorism in the United
    States?

PART THREE: ESSAY

1. Would there have been more or less terrorism against American targets under a Bush or Kerry presidency?

2. How can we prevent people like bin Laden from coming to power again?

3. How can the United States minimize its perception of being overly aggressive or insensitive in its foreign policy?

4. In the aftermath of 9/11, the United States has spent considerable resources (especially money) on public safety (through law enforcement and national security). This has had a number of effects, including the war in Afghanistan and Iraq. Some analysts have suggested that the United States will be in a deficit position for generations to come. How can we ever maintain a balanced budget in the future?

CHAPTER EIGHT

The Role of the Mass Media

The mass media is an extremely powerful actor in the dynamics of terror-ism. Since the late 1970s numerous studies have looked at the role of the media in connection with terrorism (e.g., Johnpoll, 1977; Schmid and de Graff 1980; 1982; Friedlander 1981; Jenkins 1981; Wilkinson 1981; Miller 1982; Midgley and Rice 1984; Martin 1985). This chapter goes beyond how the news media (typically newspapers and television) portray terrorism, and into how Hollywood, foreign movies, and popular fiction report on this phenomenon. The balance of the chapter will examine if and how public opinion is affected by media reports on terrorism.

One of the most controversial relationships under debate is the con-nection between terrorism and the media, particularly the power of newspapers, radio, and television during ongoing campaigns and dur-ing the context of incidents (Jenkins 2003, chapter 8). Any understand-ing of the connections between this type of political crime and violence and the media must be embedded in broader discussions of the power of media; the relationship between journalists, authorities, and terror-ists; empirical analyses of the media; and the connection between ter-rorism and public opinion.

The Power of the Media

The power of the media has been clearly and unmistakably identified by several researchers and observers of the press (e.g., Shaw and McCombs 1972). Arno, for example, says, "Systematic, purposive involvement in conflict situations is the most immediately salient feature of the anatomy and behavior of the news media in relation to other contemporary social entities. They insert themselves or are drawn into virtually every kind of conflict because, in a basic sense, conflict is news" (1984, 1). Part of the interest in media analysis revolves around the possibility that communication about certain kinds of issues creates, intensifies, or diminishes conflict (Alexander 1973; 1977; Clutterbuck 1983; Arno 1984).

Measuring the power of the media

Although we can easily acknowledge the power of the media, it is more difficult to identify which type is the most effective for communicating a particular message, and how influential each medium is (Dowling 1986). Advertisers, for example, know that in order to get their message across they need to use the media effectively, either through the strategic use of paid advertising or by creating media events that may lead to news stories. Moreover, there isn't just one important media outlet that is important—there are several that can have an effect on the public. "The various media," as Arno points out, "are interrelated in the process of conflict management because they can reach different sectors with different messages, on a particular issue" (1984, 4). But we must realize that the media are not everything. Interpersonal communication is extremely important in the diffusion of ideas about products and issues, as is the nature of the audience (Rosen 2000).

Origins of the power of the media

According to Hoffman, "The modern news media, as the principal conduit of information about such acts, thus play a vital part in the terrorists' calculus. Indeed, without the media's coverage, the act's impact is arguably wasted, remaining narrowly confined to the immediate victim(s) of the attack rather than reaching the wider 'target audience' at whom the terrorists violence is actually aimed" (Hoffman 1998, 132). Because of increased competition for our attention, the terrorist events that we notice appear to be, and most likely are, carefully planned in order to capture considerable public attention. Jenkins (1974), for example, suggested, "Terrorism is theatre"; later, in another context, he added that "terrorists want a lot of people watching, not a lot of people dead" (Jenkins 1979, 169).

In some respects, the growth of terrorism has paralleled the invention, manufacture, and purchase of new communication technologies. The media-terrorism connection has much to do with the invention in 1812 of the steam powered printing press and broadcast technologies (radio and television), as well as with the launching of communication satellites (Hoffman 1998, chapter 5). New technology (faxes, cell phones, the Internet, etc.) allows the news media to report not only more quickly, but also more accurately and more in depth. Over time, the price of technology decreases, making it within the means of the average consumer—including cash-strapped terrorists and their respective groups. Also, the increasing miniaturization of communication technologies means that it's more portable, enabling reporters and terrorists alike to do more and giving their audiences increased access to information. Indeed, the creation of the Internet has increased the media's ability to widely and quickly disseminate news and terrorist groups' ability to communicate with the public (Weimann 2004).

In the late 1870s, in large part due to changes in technology, the newspaper business rapidly expanded. This allowed terrorist organizations to promote their causes to a larger audience. The Russian group Narodnaya Volya and the anarchist terrorists were the immediate beneficiaries of this change (Hoffman 1998, 136), but the effects continue to the present day.

Almost a century later, in 1968, the United States launched the first television satellite, which would expedite the transmission of terrorist images throughout the world. Also important were the inventions and introductions of the "mini-cam[,] . . . [the] portable battery-powered video recorder, and the time-base corrector" (Hoffman 1998, 137). These inventions were important in the coverage of the hostage takeover in the 1972 Munich Olympics and later, after the 9/11 attacks, in the creation of videotaped communiqués provided by bin Laden and his top-ranking subordinates.

Analyzing the power of the media

The power of the media to communicate insurgent messages, affect audience perceptions, and influence others to engage in particular terrorist or supportive behaviors is intimately connected to terrorism (Schmid and de Graff 1982).[1] Yet the question still remains: Does the media influence people to commit terrorist actions, or does the publicity that terrorists receive help further their cause, motivating them to engage in additional actions? Obviously opinion on this matter is divided. According to White, for example, "The media may magnify the threat of terrorism to the government, and conversely reports of violence may encourage more terrorism" (2003, 262). Undoubtedly, there is a continuum of interpretations, based primarily on anecdotal (and occasionally on empirical) evidence to suggest that the media causes terrorism, or is one of the biggest reasons why terrorism exists.

Often called the *contagion effect,* (Midlarsky, Crenshaw, and Yoshida 1980) many analysts, such as Mazur (1983), believe that reporting on terrorism leads to more threats. Mazur looked at the relationship between the number of threats on nuclear facilities versus press coverage. He examined "bomb threats against nuclear facilities from 1969 to 1980, comparing them with the amount of coverage devoted to nuclear power on television and in newspapers. He found the number of threats proportionately matched the number of news stories. When coverage increased, bomb threats increased, and the converse was also true. When coverage decreased, bomb threats decreased" (White 2003, 260). This research, however, primarily refers to *threats,* which may or may not result (or be intended to result) in terrorist *actions.* Alternatively, Schmid and de Graff (1982) believe that the media are a major cause of terrorist acts.

This perspective is not easily tested. One way of approaching this question is to analyze the types of media that influence people who have committed terrorist acts or are predisposed to commit terrorist acts (which would be a Herculean, if not impossible, task). It might be worthwhile to do a content analysis of the media that *could* be influential. Which source, for example, has the most amount of influence upon its readers? Answers to this question depend on a number of collateral factors: the motivation level of people reading this material; the degree to which it can reinforce existing opinions; circulation, literacy, readership, listenership, and/or viewership; and the extent to which terrorists are more influenced by one type of medium than another (e.g., Weaver and Mauro 1978). On this last point, it may be that broadcast media has had the largest effect on its audience due to its historical importance, particularly with the illiterate members of the society (Berger 1979; Guttman 1979; Elliot, Murdock, and Schlesinger 1983; Wurth-Hough 1983).

Terrorist understanding of media dynamics

Many terrorist groups know how to achieve media attention. They are very sensitive to the timing of news stories and audience dynamics, and structure their actions accordingly. Several reviews of how terror-ist groups take the dynamics of the media into account include the 1974 kidnapping of Patricia Hearst by member of the Symbionese Lib-eration Army; the 1977 Baader-Meinhof gang suicide in Stammheim prison; the kidnapping in 1977 of the Italian prime minister, Aldo Moro, by the Red Brigades; the 1983 ASA attack against the Turkish ambassador in Lisbon, Portugal; and the 1984 bombing of the Grand Hotel in Brighton by the Provisional Irish Republican Army (Poland 1988, 51–60).

But perhaps one of the most salient terrorist events covered by the media was the kidnapping of Israeli athletes during the 1972 Olympics held in Munich; members of Black September realized that the world's major media organizations would be at the Games and decided to use the event to stage their incident. Similarly, the November 1979 takeover of the American embassy in Teheran by Iranian activists helped focus the world's attention on the power of Islamic revolution, especially by stretching the event over 444 days (Sick 1985).

Terrorist organizations taking over or "owning" the media

Some terrorist groups have taken over broadcast stations. This is per-haps why, in the wake of 9/11, we saw large television stations in big American cities protected by around-the-clock law enforcement and private security personnel. Authorities were possibly afraid that some terrorist cell might try to commandeer a large television broadcast out-let. Indeed, some media become channels through which terrorist groups talk to the public.

Alternatively, if resources permit, terrorist groups will run their own communication vehicles. According to Weinberg and Davis (1989), "The PLO has its own radio station, the Voice of Palestine. Dur-ing Italy's recent terrorist episode, Radio Sherwood . . . and other pro-fessionally revolutionary stations made announcements on behalf of the leftist terrorist groups. There were also newspapers and other widely circulated publications with links to the New Left movements that performed a similar task in acting as sources of 'counterinforma-tion'" (126–27).

A mid-range position is the fact that some media outlets are sympa-thetic or appear overly accommodating to certain terrorist organiza-tions. For example, in the aftermath of 9/11, al Jazeera (located in Bahrain) broadcast a handful of Osama bin Laden's videotapes.

Problems with Media Coverage

There are six basic difficulties with the coverage of terrorism by the media. They are, from least to most important, selective reporting/self-censorship, editorial discretion, the increasing dominance of consolidated media companies, misinformation fed to reporters by national security/intelligence agencies, news media getting in the way of security forces, and sensationalization.

Selective reporting and self-censorship

In an effort to gain access to terrorists, journalists are sometimes subject to blackmail and intimidation (Weinberg and Davis 1989, 128). Once contact has been established, terrorists and their groups typically establish certain conditions under which they will speak. This may lead to selective reporting and/or self-censorship if reporters want continued access or fear that danger will befall them or their families. This reaction is well founded, as journalists have been kidnapped and killed in their efforts to talk with terrorists. The most recent example was Daniel Pearl of the *Wall Street Journal* who, during the spring of 2002, while working in Lahore, Pakistan, received a tip that a high-ranking member of al Qaeda was willing to talk with him. Unfortunately, this was simply a ruse with the express purpose of killing him.

Editorial discretion

Just because a story is written or shot it does not mean that it will be published or broadcast (Fishman 1980). In addition to the relationship between reporters and sources, a complex understanding exists between journalists and their various editors or producers. This interaction affects the assigning, researching, writing, editing, and printing or broadcast of articles or stories on terrorism. In deciding if, how, and when a story will be run, most editors or producers make decisions about the reliability and "abnormality" of the piece, its sources, other competing articles that they deem newsworthy, and other stories that are on schedule, or were written or shot for that day's news (Ross 2000, 18).

Increasing dominance of consolidated media corporations

Although some cable and satellite stations have managed to carve out economically viable niches, increasingly, media outlets are owned by a limited number of large multinational corporations (e.g., Time Warner, General Electric, Walt Disney Company, Viacom, etc.). Through this process of consolidation, competition is minimized or eliminated. This is why much of what is reported on one news station seems the same as what's reported on the next news outlet. As a result, journalists are less willing and able to take on controversial subjects or dig deep below the surface and report on subjects like the causes of terrorism rather than simply reporting terrorist events.

Misinformation fed to reporters by national security agencies

Many stories that are printed in the press or broadcast electronically originated with official government sources. According to Jenkins, "Most materials that appear in the media can be traced to a small number of official agencies, and indeed, subunits of those agencies, which enjoy a very high degree of credibility. . . . Media reliance on law enforcement sources is not difficult to understand because, for all their flaws, agencies like the FBI should in fact be the best-informed group in the country, with access to abundant evidence from moles, infiltrators, and surveillance materials" (Jenkins 2003, 140). But reporters are often used by these agencies to further their own purposes, particularly through so-called strategic leaks: "over the last two years, the news media have often reported what 'official sources' say about Iraqi involvement in terrorism, with stories variously claiming or rejecting such activity. Virtually all such leaks can be traced to the ongoing war within the Bush administration" (Jenkins 2003, 140). This is especially true after 9/11, when federal agencies scrambled to do "damage control," hoping to prove to the American public that they were not sleeping on the job.

News media obstructing counterterrorist efforts

The media has a difficult task in covering terrorism. Occasionally, they have even inadvertently hindered antiterrorist efforts to negotiate or resolve a hostage-type incident successfully or quickly. Press corps members, for example, "have entered lines of fire and secured zones, and hostage and rescue forces have been pictured on live television as they moved in for an assault" (White 2003, 263). Holed-up terrorists need only to turn on a television or listen to the radio to gain the upper hand. There are countless examples of this taking place, including during the 1993 battle of Mogadishu (the Somalian capital), when warlords and their supporters only needed to turn on CNN to get an idea of U.S.

Exhibit Box 22
Hanafi Muslim takeover of B'nai B'rith headquarters

On March 9, 1977, 12 members of the Hanafi Muslim sect, a black power organization that had split from the Nation of Islam, took over the B'nai B'rith headquarters in Washington, D.C. The B'nai B'rith is an international Jewish organization that promotes tolerance and peace, and monitors anti-Semitism. In addition to the organization, the Hanafis took over the District building (city hall) and the Islamic Center. A total of 134 hostages were taken; 107 at the B'nai B'rith building. In the process, the group pistol whipped a handful of hostages, shot and paralyzed a city employee, shot former Washington, D.C., Mayor Marion Barry in the chest, who at the time was a city councilman, killed a reporter, and wounded two others

The Hanafis wanted the government to release five Black Muslims who were convicted of killing a Hanafi family in 1973. They also wanted theatres to stop showing the movie *Mohammed, Messenger of God*, because they believed it was disrespectful. The siege lasted 39 hours. During the negotiations, a reporter from a local radio show managed to get in touch with one of the terrorists. The police argued that this involvement unnecessarily interfered with the protracted negotiations. Apparently, the reporter asked the leader when he planned to execute the first hostage, but the terrorist had not even considered this as an option until the reporter suggested it. Three diplomats from Muslim countries intervened and brought the siege to a relatively peaceful ending. The Hanafis were sentenced to prison.

positions and the 1977 Hanafi Muslim takeover of the B'nai B'rith building mentioned in the last chapter (see Exhibit Box 22).

The fear of terrorism's influence on the media has resulted in a number of controls established by law enforcement, national security, and media organizations on media reporting of terrorism. There are essentially two positions: first, that the government needs to intervene, and second, that the media should regulate itself. The public and the media are appropriately quick to cry censorship whenever the government proposes some kind of intervention. Schlesinger (1981), for example, basing his opinion on media coverage of the Northern Ireland terrorist problem, says that the media naturally support a hands-off approach. In the United States and in many other advanced industrialized democracies, we value free speech, which is protected by the First Amendment to the Constitution.[2]

Kehler, Harvey, and Hall (1982) argue that members of the media should regulate themselves. Jones and Miller (1979), using a historical analysis of case law, say that government attempts to restrict coverage during an emergency do not necessarily prevent the media's right to unfettered access to the perpetrators (in this case, terrorists). Finally, many newspapers, professional organizations to which journalists and broadcasters belong, together with some scholars (e.g., Scanlon 1981; 1982) have developed a series of guidelines to which reporters and news organizations should adhere when covering terrorist events. Scanlon also emphasizes that the counterterrrorist practitioners need to treat the journalists professionally (and honestly) in order to garner their cooperation.

Sensationalization

There is considerable competition amongst news organizations to be the first to report any news (Tuckman 1978), which, in turn, has an effect on the way news is obtained and portrayed (O'Neil 1986; Chermack, Bailey, and Brown 2003). "This could be accomplished basically in one of two ways, by being the first on the scene or by being the first to report some hitherto undisclosed information," Hoffman points out (1998, 138). He elaborates: "Hence, having broken the story and captured viewers' attention the priority becomes to hold that attention with equally gripping follow-up reports. Accordingly, for the duration of an important story's life, the media's focus invariably shifts from reporting of the limited and often dwindling quantity of 'hard' news to move human-interest type feature stories, mostly involving exclusive interviews . . . or the breathless revelation of some previously unknown or undocumented item of related news—no matter how trivial or irrelevant" (Hoffman 1998, 138).

Hoffman goes on to trace a pattern of effects: "The quest to keep a story alive leads inevitably to a disproportionate fixation on the 'human interest angle' most often, the grief and anguish of family and friends of terrorist victims and/or hostages" (Hoffman 1998, 138). The result, he finds, is that "there is accordingly a discernible proclivity among network executives to look more to the 'bottom line' than to journalistic priorities for guidance and hence to emphasize entertainment value over good reporting" (Hoffman 1998, 140). It appears that what matters most is the economics, particularly controlling costs drives the media's decision about which stories to cover and how it should be done.

Some would also argue that terrorism has helped the careers of well-known journalists. For example, the popularity of ABC's *Nightline* increased after Ted Koppel took over as the lead anchorman, when he focused on the Iranian hostage crisis (October 1979) in the wake of Iranian Revolution. Every night since the capture of the hostages he would do in-depth coverage. Some would also say the career of former CNN producer Peter Bergen was improved because he is credited with having the first television interviews of Osama bin Laden, whose organization al Qaeda is implicated in the 9/11 attacks.

Empirical Analyses of Media Coverage

A growing number of empirical analyses explore the connection between the media and terrorism. The most important type of research uses content analysis; this usually entails counting and statistically analyzing how terrorism is mentioned in the context of a particular form of communication (Holsti 1969; Krippendorf 1981). In the field of terrorism studies, content analyses have primarily used four types of sources: newspapers, personal statements and communications, public appeals, and popular culture. Typically, however, content analyses entail counting the number of articles on terrorism that appear in newspapers per issue, month, and year, and then determining the relationship between the numbers of stories on terrorism and acts of this form of political violence. Kelly and Mitchell (1981) suggest that "through content analysis, the sort of subconscious judgments which one naturally makes . . . [through] evaluating books, newspapers, and other forms of communications, are made more carefully recorded and analyzed to reveal underlying trends and orientations" (275).

Occasionally, the sources of those articles are evaluated as part of the analysis. For example, Herman and O'Sullivan (1989) looked at who the media interviewed to obtain background details for articles on terrorism. They found that 42.3 percent were U. S. government officials, 24.4 percent were private-sector experts, and 18 percent were others— "mainly the 'victims' of terrorist acts" (Herman and O'Sullivan 1989, 194). Although the authors claim that "objective" sources were generally overlooked, their study suffers from methodological problems in terms of sample size (Ross 1991b).

The majority of papers analyzed for coverage of terrorist events originate in Western countries and are considered the elite press. For instance, Kelly and Mitchell (1981) reviewed the *New York Times* and the *Times* of London. Fuller (1988) examined the *Christian Science Monitor*, and Picard and Adams (1991) studied the terrorist coverage in the *Los Angeles Times*, the *New York Times*, and the *Washington Post*. Generally neglected are ethnic, racial, and/or religious-based newspapers directed toward members of a particular community and connected, in some sense, with places where a significant number of terrorist actions have occurred. There are numerous monthly, bimonthly, quarterly, or semiannual newsletters printed in major urban centers by religious groups, nonsectarian associations, and even individual citizens. Additionally, few content analyses of radio and television broadcasts (e.g., delli Carpini and Williams 1987) have been conducted that focus on terrorism.

Because of the sporadic nature of these articles, it is doubtful that they are capable of instigating terrorist activities. None of the information reported is exceptional or exclusive of these sources; it can also be found in other venues. At the most, the press may reinforce perceptions already held by their readers. The deciding factor in the ability of the press to motivate terrorism may thus lie in the preexisting mind-set or receptivity of the audience.

Finally, more sophisticated methodologies could be used to address this issue of the media's influence. These might include improved processes for electronically downloading entire periodicals onto a computer to allow for better textual analysis of the issue in question, surveys of journalists covering terrorism, or other empirical analysis of incarcerated terrorists to track their media consumption patterns prior to and during their terrorist activity.

Public Opinion

We should also keep in mind that just because terrorists are successful in getting the media to communicate their messages does not necessarily mean that the public is afraid of these groups are convinced of their merits (Snyder 1978; Weimann 1983; Hewitt 1990). Countless events and processes can intervene. According to Hoffman, "There is a belief that the media has an effect on public opinion and whether that leads to particular actions on the part of the citizenry. . . . The real issue, however, is not so much the relationship itself, which is widely acknowledged to exist, as whether it actually affects public opinion and government decision-making, as the media's critics claim, in a manner that favours or assists terrorists" (1998, 142).

Few studies measure public opinion before and after terrorist events. Nevertheless, authors like Weinberg and Davis (1989, 133–35) warn us about this kind of research. Despite the numerous polls about how people feel about terrorism, we are not sure exactly how or if the media affects them. Additionally, the issue of salience or prominence is often not taken into consideration; although people may think that terrorism is a problem, often it is not the most pressing, compared with other social issues. Moreover, many public opinion polls have a hard time comparing the fear of terrorism between and within different countries. After reviewing a handful of studies, Weinberg and Davis concluded, "The problem with these responses, though, is that they were based on snap shots taken at single points in time. The questions were usually asked during or just after a particularly dramatic terrorist event or events, that is, at a time when the public was most likely to be aroused by the violence and where media coverage was likely to have been of the crisis variety" (1989, 135). Capturing public opinion about terrorism over time through longitudinal studies is rarely done. This would help us to better understand if fear of terrorism has increased or the public has become desensitized.

The Commodification of Terrorism

Undoubtedly, one result of the rise in public consciousness of terrorism is the use of its images in and on products in order to sell them, and vice versa (Selzer 1979). According to Jenkins, "Whether we are looking at films or television movies, reading novels or true crime accounts of terrorism, popular culture plays a critical political role in shaping American attitudes toward terrorism" (Jenkins 2003, 150). It shapes attitudes elsewhere, too—in parts of the Middle East, you can buy Osama bin Laden towels and paraphernalia.

But nowhere is the commodification of terrorism more evident than in contemporary American (and foreign films) that use or deal in part with political terrorism. We have seen numerous Hollywood films (Williams 2002), television series, documentaries, and novels that use terrorism either as a central feature or a backdrop to tell a story. Commercial movies like *In the Name of the Father* and *Year of the Gun* and documentaries like *Germany in Autumn* are often filled with historical inaccuracies and thin plots (see Exhibit Box 23). The terrorists' grievances are rarely analyzed, as this would detract from the

Exhibit Box 23
Commercial movies with a terrorist theme

A. Terrorism in Canada and the United States

American History X
Black Sunday
Les Ordres
Mississippi Burning
The Siege

B. Terrorism in Europe

Defense of the Realm
The Lost Honor of Katherine Blum
Hidden Agenda
In the Name of the Father
The Crying Game
The Legend of Rita
Michael Collins
Some Mother's Son
Year of the Gun/
Germany in Autumn/ Deutschland im Herbst
Marianne and Julianne
Shake Hands with the Devil
The Informer
The Devil's Own

C. Terrorism in Latin America

Collateral Damage
Four Days in September
Missing
State of Siege
Toy Soldiers
The Official Story

D. Terrorism in the Middle East

The Battle of Algiers
Delta Force
Raid on Entebbe
Victory at Entebbe

"good versus evil" framework into which these films so easily fall. The portrayal of the terrorists is routinely an exaggeration of reality. To a certain extent, terrorists have become the enemy du jour, replacing Soviet and Chinese communists as our cinematic foes (Ross 2002b). Unfortunately, all too often, these products and services may glorify or sensationalize terrorism, or delegitimitize terrorists' underlying grievances.

"In American cinema," Jenkins suggests, "terrorists have provided thriller villains rivaled only by 'drug lords.' In many ways . . . the realities of the terrorism issue have been systematically distorted by commercial and political pressures on writers and filmmakers" (Jenkins 2003, 150). He further argues that the "message from popular culture is that the problem is chiefly the work of a handful of very evil individuals, and understanding this menace is perhaps less difficult than comprehending the diverse factors (political, social, economic, spiritual) which drive the faceless terrorists of real life" (P. Jenkins 2003, 151). "The choice of movements and conflicts covered has been very patchy," and, he says, "No correlation exists between the actual seriousness or potential harm of a terrorist movement and the attention it receives in popular media, mainly because there is little interest in covering groups not seen as relevant to U. S. conditions" (P. Jenkins 2003, 152).

Jenkins reviews domestic (and foreign films) that depict terrorists or have a terrorist theme, focusing both on groups often depicted and those ignored in Hollywood films. The author also points out how powerful interest groups can affect the content of these movies, noting how certain themes are almost always ignored in films, including American terrorist organizations, particularly the radical Weather Underground and the anti-abortion movement. Jenkins finds:

> Two separate reasons help explain the neglect of America's domestic terrorist movements. First, extremism is a difficult product to market commercially. The domestic movements were often very controversial at the time, and the violent protest of the late 1960s was so divisive that fictional treatments would not have been commercially viable. Also it is difficult to imagine how the characters could have been treated. If the radicals were portrayed as anything short of mad bombers, the films would probably have alienated mainstream audiences. On the other hand, if they were presented as crazy or evil, such a simplistic portrayal

would have deterred many potential young adult viewers. (P. Jenkins 2003, 155–56)

Second, Jenkins says, "portrayals of terrorist movements tend to alienate ethnic or political groups who might not sympathize with the actual violence, but who see themselves as part of the same ideological spectrum as the militants" (P. Jenkins 2003, 156).

Jenkins also documents how the image of Arabs as terrorists has changed over the past three decades, noting that the "image of the Arab terrorists was at its height in the late 1970s and 1980s, when numerous films portrayed American agents or soldiers avenging terrorist atrocities by massacring Arab commandos" (P. Jenkins 2003, 158). As a response, Arab Americans, both individuals and their organizations, attempted to dispel this image through lobbying and public relations campaigns (Shaneen 1984; P. Jenkins 2003, 159). The considerable lobbying surrounding the Arnold Schwarzenegger film *True Lies* was a wake-up call to Hollywood producers that they needed to treat the image of Arabs more sensitively. In another ironic twist, a series of movies produced over the last decade have used the threat of terrorism as a backdrop, but the affiliation of the individuals or the groups is barely detectable. These movies include *The Sum of All Fears* and the *Die Hard* series.

Conclusion

This chapter has reviewed the power and nuances of the media's interaction with terrorists, their organizations, and official sources. In the final analysis, the media does not cause terrorism; however, it may facilitate it. Terrorists use the media as a tool to gain increased coverage and communicate their message, but throughout history, many terrorist organizations without access to the media have been nonetheless successful in communicating their message. The Sicarri, the Assassins, and the Boxers, for example, were responsible for considerable death and destruction and were able to instill fear among the population close to their attacks, without any media comparable to that which has existed for the past century and a half. In this context, an appreciation of the social construction of terrorism is important (Jenkins 2003).

Questions, Chapter 8

PART ONE: MULTIPLE CHOICE

1. In what year was the first American television satellite launched?
   a. 1966
   b. 1968
   c. 1978
   d. 1986
   e. 1988

2. Which steam-powered machine was in 1812 heralded as the start of the modern mass media?
   a. computer
   b. telephone
   c. telegraph
   d. printing press
   e. car

3. What TV show was born out of the 1979–80 hostage crisis in Tehran?
   a. *America Today*
   b. *America's Most Wanted*
   c. *Biography*
   d. *Investigative Reports*
   e. *Nightline*

4. Which terrorist group established Radio Sherwood?
   a. Abu Nidal Group
   b. FARC
   c. PIRA
   d. FLQ
   e. none of the above

5. What is the principal way that scholars study the power of the media?
   a. content analysis
   b. survey experts
   c. cross-national research
   d. case studies
   e. none of the above

PART TWO: SHORT ANSWER

1. When was the first known use of the media by terrorists?

2. List four of the five problems with the media's coverage of terrorism.

3. How does the media typically cover terrorism?

4. By the 1970s, what three critical pieces of television equipment made it possible for reporting news events in "real time"?

5. Does the mass media cause terrorism?

PART THREE: ESSAY

1. Is the media a structural or psychological cause, and what type is it?

2. How can the media both capture a wide audience and minimize the sensationalistic aspects of terrorism?

3. In terms of causes of terrorism, how important is the media? Could terrorist groups function without it?

CHAPTER NINE

Combating Terrorism

A variety of strategies are mobilized in combination to prevent, deter, respond to, and combat terrorism. In this chapter, we will examine the more important of these responses and their relative effectiveness. First, however, we must review important conceptual and contextual issues.

Conceptual Issues

Some analysts have suggested that there is a difference between antiterrorist and counterterrorist measures. The former responses are proactive (or defensive) actions designed to prevent or deter terrorist incidents from happening and include, among other things, special legislation (Alon 1987). The latter are reactive (or retaliatory) measures a government takes after terrorism has occurred, and usually use force, as in air strikes or selective assassination.[1] Other observers and practitioners have blurred the distinction and use these terms interchangeably (Townshend 2002, 114–15).

Another, related difference is between passive versus active measures (see Tovar 1986). Passive measures, Townshend notes, "are shaped by the nature of terrorist acts—airport security is a response to hijacking and sabotage of aircraft, defensive steps labeled 'target hardening' a response to bomb attacks, the 'safety net' of individual security measures a response to kidnapping. . . . They are an effort to shrink the windows of opportunity available to terrorists" (2002, 120–21). Active approaches, on the other hand, engage "terrorists with the aim of capturing or destroying them," but as Townshend notes, "The only chance of success in this direction lies in an effective intelligence system, using techniques such as infiltration and surveillance to acquire accurate information" (2002, 121).

We must also recognize that in any security environment, trade-offs must be made between the risk of attack, including its possible effects, and the cost of preventing the incident (Sloan 1993). Most security decisions are made in a political and economic context where reason often is subjugated to expediency (Schneier 2003). If, for example, you examine the history of emergency legislation passed in Canada, the United Kingdom, and the United States one of the threads that connects these events is that they were passed immediately in the wake of major terrorist incidents without the benefit of calm and rational discussion.

Contextual Issues

The reactions to terrorism in general, and to counterterrorism in particular, come from a host of political actors (policymakers, practitioners—law enforcement and national security personnel—and citizens) with competing resources, agendas, and interests. Interpreting and balancing what these constituencies want and need is no easy task. One central question is whether government agencies should or must adhere to the rule of law, or—given the unusual nature of terrorism—whether they may circumvent state-based constitutions and internationally mandated human-rights documents and practices by responding with extraordinary force (Ross 2002a). The dilemma is not easily resolved in a manner that makes all parties happy.

Another question asks whether we should approach terrorism as a policy problem to be addressed primarily by government organizations that deal with issues of justice, or as a security issue to be answered by bureaucracies that oversee national security. The answer will determine, to a large extent, which state agency should take the lead role. In the United States, the natural choices have been between the FBI and the CIA. The first is responsible for monitoring major crimes, particularly those which affect more than one state, including domestic terrorism. The second is responsible for gathering intelligence that would aid foreign policy, including monitoring external threats like terrorists from abroad. Traditionally, if terrorism occurred in the United States, it was an FBI matter, and if it was external to the country, it was a CIA concern. Now, with the creation of the Department of Homeland Security (DHS), this kind of distinction becomes a bit blurry. Additionally, since local law enforcement is often a "first responder" (the first point of contact in a crisis), its appropriate role in terrorism is also under debate.

The primary opportunity to control terrorism is in the country of origin, at the hands of their own governments. This is done through local, state, and federal police forces or a public security agency like the Canadian Security Intelligence Service in Canada, or the newly established DHS in the United States. Things become more complex at the global level. One of the international bodies that have stepped up to the plate in the fight against terrorism is Interpol, the international police agency. As some analysts have pointed out, however, "Interpol's effectiveness is limited by several factors. First although it maintains a data bank on criminal activity around the world, it is under-funded and understaffed. Second, it is generally not supposed to get involved in political problems—and most international terrorist activities are highly political. The European Union has developed a European police force (Europol) with similar aims. However, it will be years before Europol has the political, technical, and financial support needed to tackle not only organized crime but terrorism as well" (Duncan et al. 2002, 283).

Since the 1960s the methods through which countries combat terrorism have changed. With each rash of incidents, new countermeasures are implemented, and in time, terrorist organizations find new weaknesses to exploit.

Problems in Combating Terrorism

Some of the difficulties (mentioned in earlier parts of this book) that stand in the way of countering the terrorist threat include a lack of a definition commonly accepted by government agencies, and a lack of cooperation—not only among state agencies with an interest in monitoring and responding to terrorism, but also among countries that may have helpful intelligence. Most of these entities are reluctant to share information, especially national security agencies, unless they believe that it is in their own short-term political interests.

Countries and their national security agencies must also carefully balance citizens' individual freedoms in their pursuit of terrorists. Too much repression leads citizens to question the legitimacy of the existing regime. In reprisals for terrorist actions, there is always the possibility of collateral damage, especially when innocent civilians are detained, injured, or killed, or when property is damaged or destroyed (Ross 2000a; 2000b). This outcome is an all-too-familiar consequence of America's involvement in Afghanistan and Iraq, and was plainly evident in Great Britain's shoot-to-kill policy.

Finally, measuring the effectiveness of combating terrorism is a thorny issue. According to Townshend, "If we look for precise evaluation of the effectiveness of antiterrorist policies we find it is surprisingly thin on the ground. Very few indeed of the many writers on terrorism have produced a statistical analysis of key countermeasures" (2002, 133). Policymakers and practitioners would be well advised to keep these factors in mind when they comment on or propose and implement measures designed to combat terrorism.

Typical Measures

There are eleven major ways through which governments have countered terrorism. They are, from least to most important or frequently used, appeasement; development of databases and collection of relevant intelligence; cutting off financing; hardening of actual and potential targets; creation and use of "third forces," special military units or SWAT teams to handle terrorist situations; changing police policies and practices regarding the use of force; development and use of antiterrorist technology; approval and implementation of new international treaties; approval and enforcement of new laws against terrorism, both nationally and internationally; increased use of intelligence and surveillance of suspected terrorists and their supporters; and military responses.

1. Appeasement

If at all possible to do without losing face, governments could decide to appease the terrorists by making appropriate concessions. This approach is also known as addressing grievances or the root causes or problems. According to Wilkinson (2003), "Conflict resolution methods [e.g., negotiation, mediation, etc.] alone will not eradicate the terrorist violence of incorrigible groups fueled on hatred and revenge. But by significantly reducing the underlying causes of deep-seated conflicts, giving politics and diplomacy a chance to succeed, they can save thousands of lives" (35). The problem with this strategy is that in some cases, the demands of terrorists and the concessions promised by governments are next to impossible to achieve. Alternatively, they are difficult to interpret because they are so vague and open to interpretation.

2. Development of databases and collection of reliable intelligence

As reviewed in previous chapters, governments (and the agencies charged with responding to terrorism) have developed, purchased, or have access to databases that track either terrorist incidents or suspected terrorists and groups, through which they can (theoretically) track terrorists' whereabouts, contacts, habits, and trends (Ross 2004). Databases, however, require constant updates in order to ensure that the information is accurate and relevant. The reliability of the database is enhanced if multilingual professionals are assigned to its design, maintenance, and interpretation.

Some commentators have suggested that since World War Two, Western intelligence agencies have disproportionately relied on signals and other technological types of intelligence (such as satellites) and neglected to invest in human intelligence (e.g., infiltration, cultivation of sources) Thus, it was precisely this shortsightedness that allowed individuals like bin Laden to communicate, plan, and carry out 9/11 (Reeve 1999, 264). Developing key infiltrators and informants is crucial for national security organizations.

3. Cutting off financing

Most terrorist groups need a constant supply of resources. One of the most important is regular infusions of money. True, groups can stage bank robberies, but this puts them at risk of being caught or dying in a potential shoot-out with local authorities. It also increases the risk that they will be caught on surveillance video (Adams 1986). During the past decade the United States through the Department of Treasury and not DHS has increased regulations on international money transfers and investigated so-called charitable organizations which have served as a channel to fund various terrorist groups.

4. Hardening of actual and potential targets

Since the 1960s, security measures at various locations—government buildings, corporate locations, and nuclear facilities—have been increased. Added security measures include more technology (x-ray baggage-screening devices and walk-through metal detectors), more personnel (police and security officers), and additional and improved security procedures throughout these facilities (Enders and Sandler 1993). Some analysts are quick to warn us, however, that "if you fortify aircraft, terrorists will attack airports; if you fortify airports, they can bring down aircraft with missiles fired from remote locations; if you defend aircraft, they attack ships; and so on. Overwhelmingly, such security precautions are designed to raise public consciousness, a feel-good strategy without any real effects or benefits" (Jenkins 2003, 111).

A good example of this dilemma was the July 2005 bombings in London. What makes this recent attack all the more incomprehensible is that there is considerable security in London, more so than in most advanced industrialized democracies. Closed-circuit television CCTV is pervasive in London, as is access control in and out of the city. Almost all vehicles entering London have their license plates photographed and compared to central databases. The Brits have considerable experience with IRA terrorism during which these protocols have been developed. But the attacks, like those in London, demonstrate that hardening targets cannot provide security all the time in open democratic societies.

5. Creation and use of third forces

Governments have developed armed forces (staffed by either local law enforcement or army) with specialized training to deal with hostage negotiation, barricade and rescue situations, and other terrorist-related crises (Thompson 1986). For example, in the United States, Delta Force is part of the army. In Canada, the Special Emergency Response Team (SERT) was originally an outgrowth of the Royal Canadian Mounted Police but was disbanded in 1993 in favor of a more clandestine organization called the Joint Task Force Two (JTF2). These teams can minimize the number of injuries and deaths in an armed standoff, but unfortunately, they can also increase a sense of machismo, as portrayed in Hollywood movies like *Rambo.*

6. Changing police policies and practices on use of force

Most police departments make their own unique plans with respect to how it will go about maintaining order and enforcing the law in their respective communities and this is true for combating terrorism. The more enlightened police chiefs make these decisions in consultation with the mayor, local political leaders, and members of the community in which they work.

It is important to understand that policies and practices about police use of force have evolved considerably over the past two decades. Starting with the Supreme Court's decision in *Garner v. Tennessee* (1985), which forced police departments to instruct their officers that they could use deadly force against a fleeing suspect only if they had probable cause to believe that the individual might seriously injure or kill persons nearby.

Then, largely because of the criminal and civil trials, not to mention the riots surrounding the March 1991 beating of Rodney King at the hands of members of the Los Angeles Police Department, most police officers were trained and sensitized to the continuum of force idea. Here, police are taught to react to real and potentially violent suspects only with the amount of force that is necessary to subdue the individual. So if the person is being verbally belligerent, then the officer should limit his or her response to verbal commands. On the other hand, if the suspect pulls out a weapon and it appears that the lives of the officer and/or citizens are in peril, then they can respond with deadly force.

Since the Columbine High School shootings (April, 1999), however, many police departments have changed their approach to hostage takers. Because of lawsuits launched by fifteen families of the incident, and a close review of how the situation unfolded, police have come to the conclusion that it no longer makes sense to wait for the bomb squad or SWAT team to appear. During the Columbine incident, the police who responded within minutes waited for almost 45 minutes before the SWAT team was sent in. A review of the incident determined that the majority of the children who were killed or shot during the first 20 minutes, while the police were waiting outside. A new method generally referred to as rapid response, but also going under the names of emergency response or first responder, has been implemented, whereby those officers who are first on the scene will almost immediately pursue the suspect and "shoot to kill." This practice of emergency response can be extended to the shoot-to-kill approach in connection with a potential suicide bomber. This is not necessarily because they have had experience with Israeli security practices.

True shoot-to-kill tragedies like the one in London (July 2005) happen on a periodic basis. We need not look back farther than the case of Amadou Diallo who in February 1999 was shot to death by four NYPD officers from their "Street Crime Unit." Although the officers were cleared of criminal wrongdoing, the NYPD was charged civilly and they settled the case with the plaintiffs for $3 million. In April of 2002, partially as a result of the Diallo shooting, the NYPD disbanded the unit.

Then again, many big-city police departments have jump-out squads, which make arrests after a criminal activity has taken place, typically a drug sale. There is a considerable amount of adrenalin pumping through the veins of the police officers and they must make split-second decisions.

A number of police departments now have, in addition to SWAT teams, antiterrorism squads. There is little information on how much training they get, how well they are trained, or their policies. Chances are they exist in the bigger and more well-funded cities like New York City and Washington, D.C.

One of the worries, however, about the mistaken shooting of citizens is that this might simply be an outgrowth of racial profiling. Almost every day we hear reports in the media about Muslim-looking individuals being detained. In the spring of 2005 in New York City, for example five British Sikh tourists were handcuffed based on a bus workers' report that they seemed suspicious. Whether this is racial or behavioral profiling it is difficult to determine.

What is known, however, is that not enough money is being spent on police departments for proactive responses to terrorism. It seems as if the federal government through the Department of Homeland Security is more willing to free up money for reactive sorts of things like new bomb-sniffing technology, or walk-through x-ray machines.

Municipal police have always been the poor cousins in the "war against terrorism." Mayors and chiefs of police argue that since local law enforcement are typically first responders to incidents of terrorism, then they should get assistance (financial or otherwise) from the federal government and not simply through local taxpayer dollars or state appropriations.

That is why mayors and governors have been lobbying the Department of Homeland Security for more funds. While most chiefs of police want this for proactive kinds of things like patrols and intelligence collection, the DHS is more willing to place it in things like bomb sniffing or deactivating robots and x-ray machines.

On the other hand, when the money is given, it is not completely clear where this money is going. Is it used to pay for anti-terrorist technology, multijurisdictional task forces, police overtime, or for normal expenditures but cast in the light of homeland security? This means that chiefs and those in charge of securing addition funding are skillfully engaged in creative proposal writing or accounting.

7. Development and use of antiterrorist technology

Members of the private sector, with respectable financial incentives from the government, have increased their research and development of new pieces of technology for detecting bombs, including use of metal detectors, and monitoring the whereabouts of suspect individuals. Consequently, a number of civil liberties organizations have complained about the potential development of a surveillance society (Marx 1990).

8. International treaties

Given that it takes a considerable amount of energy to craft antiterrorist agreements between states, it's more common for several countries to be signatories on international treaties providing for the extradition or trial of captured terrorists, and the suspension of air services to countries providing a safe haven for hijackers (Gal-Or 1985). For example, since the mid-1970s, the United States and Cuba have had a treaty regarding the hijacking of planes. As a result, hijackings between these two states have been greatly reduced.

The most effective cooperation to date has been accomplished in the context of the economic summits through such documents as the Bonn Declaration on aircraft hijacking and the Vienna Declaration on the protection of diplomats. The public, however, must be reminded that "since the 1930s, international cooperation has advanced by quite small stages, always limited by the absence of consensus on the justifications for political violence. In Oct. 1970 the UN General Assembly resolved that it was the duty of states 'to refrain from organizing, instigating, assisting or participating in acts of civil strife or terrorist acts,' but subsequent committees established to define terrorism and recommend methods of preventing it failed to do either" (Townshend 2002, 128). The problem is that many countries value self-determination over the threat posed by terrorism. As Townshend points out, "The most successful international measures have focused on particular offenses, like attacks on 'internationally protected persons' primarily diplomats—and hostage taking; and on the protection of nuclear material and the prevention of transfer of terrorist finances" (Townshend 2002, 129).

9. New laws (national and international) against terrorism

Many of the international laws have had minimal success in deterring terrorism. One of the perpetual problems involves the inability of countries to agree upon an acceptable definition of terrorism. In short, "nations do not want to give up their right to grant asylum to those who commit politically motivated offenses" (Wardlaw 1982). Thus, few states have ratified international agreements. Additionally, international bodies such as the United Nations have little enforcement power. Similarly regional bodies (e.g., League of Arab States, Organization of American States, etc.) have passed "conventions" combating or suppressing terrorism. They suffer from many of the same difficulties as international bodies, mainly because of they are lacking in enforcement powers.

On the other hand, since the 1970s, many countries (e.g., Canada, Israel, Pakistan, United Kingdom, etc.) have passed antiterrorism laws, special enactment legislation, or emergency legislation in whole or as part of specific sections of general laws. These laws give national security forces special privileges to conduct surveillance and to interrogate and detain suspects.

10. Increased use of intelligence and surveillance

National security agencies and local law enforcement have increased the use of a variety of different intelligence-gathering techniques

(Amit 1989). One of the most dominant is closed-circuit television (CCTV), a tool pervasive in many jurisdictions, especially in London. Police observe street corners through CCTV, which photographs license plates and, in a matter of seconds, compares the numbers with a database to determine if the vehicle is stolen or if the driver/owner is wanted by the police.

Since the mid-1960s, individuals from Middle Eastern countries such as Libya, Iran, Iraq, and Palestine have been subject to intense scrutiny and, in some cases, harassment, by American national security agents. In 1987, for example, funds of Libyan students studying in the United States were frozen when the United States bombed Libya. Sometimes this scrutiny or harassment involves infiltration of groups, with dubious ethical repercussions: "In order to investigate terrorism, law enforcement agencies must use various clandestine methods, including infiltration and double-agent tactics. While these means are essential, they often lead to difficulties in assigning the blame for acts, and raise questions about the reliability of official statements and statistics. . . . Agencies wishing to suppress terrorism must, of necessity, operate in a complex and dirty clandestine world" (Jenkins 2003, 111). Additionally, "the more difficult a group is to infiltrate, therefore, the more effective will be its operations, and the longer it will last. This explains why groups like al-Qaeda often use family networks, in which individuals have known each other for many years, and have powerful motives for remaining loyal" (Jenkins 2003, 111). The assumption here is that you can trust your relatives more than you can believe your associates.

11. Military response

Historically, the military reaction to terrorism has been the traditional response to terrorist actions and appears to have intensified since 9/11. In the wake of the 1998 simultaneous bombings of the American embassies in Tanzania and Kenya, then-president Clinton commenced Operation Infinite Reach, which involved the navy launching cruise strikes against what the United States perceived were al Qaeda terrorist training camps in Afghanistan and against an alleged chemical weapons plant in the Khartoum, Sudan. Since 9/11, most of these military activities have been conducted under the guise of the war on terrorism and may in fact be redesigning the shape of the armed services.

Conclusion

The previously reviewed methods to combat terrorism should be interpreted as a menu from which counterterrorist practitioners can choose. The power to experiment with as many strategies as possible—while at the same time keep track of the costs and benefits—will inevitably minimize the future occurrence of terrorism. What remains, however, are regular systematic analyses and testing of counterterrorist strategies (e.g., Hewitt 1984) as terrorism evolves and counterterrorist methods improve.

The post-9/11 bombings mean that we must continue to harden our societies against terrorist attacks, and expand our efforts domestically and internationally to take down and destroy terrorist networks. We need to protect vulnerable targets, improve cooperation with our allies, and minimize or address grievances held by groups that have difficulties with the United States, Great Britain, and their allies. This includes increasing transatlantic cooperation in a number of key areas such as penetrating terrorist organizations, arresting or eliminating terrorist operatives, destroying the links between transnational crime and terrorism, and halting recruitment into terrorist organizations or providing realistic alternatives to young men susceptible to these groups' appeals.

Terrorist attacks require rational responses without abridging rights. This approach seemed to be abandoned as a reaction to 9/11, and we have paid a huge penalty for it. Hopefully the leaders of the G-8 countries will respond in a thoughtful fashion and not advocate policies and practices that unnecessarily violate human and civil rights any more than they currently are. We must also be careful about making analogies between terrorism and war or framing our response as a war on terrorism.

Contrary to some analysts, the Arab world is not seething with anger toward the West—just parts of it are. Focus our attention on those areas before they force us to compromise Western values like protection for human rights and equal protection under the law, to the point where we're no better than they are. Diligence is what we need now, the kind of rectitude and principled decision making that Roosevelt and Churchill exhibited during World War II. What's occurring here is nothing like that in terms of scale or consequence. But applying our collective wisdom now, as we appear to be entering a new phase in the conflict, could prevent this terror campaign from growing wider and deeper. The trick is to be proactive and not simply reactive in combating terrorism.

Questions, Chapter 9

PART ONE: MULTIPLE CHOICE

1. According to this chapter, where is the primary place that terrorism is controlled?
   a. in cities
   b. in rural areas
   c. by governments in foreign countries
   d. by governments in their own country
   e. none of the above

2. What was the Bonn Declaration?
   a. investigation into an al Qaeda cell in Germany
   b. an exile of the Baader-Meinhoff gang
   c. a statement on aircraft hijacking
   d. West German terrorist propaganda
   e. none of the above

3. What is the name of the specialized antiterrorist unit in the United States?
   a. GSG9
   b. SAS
   c. Delta Force
   d. SERT
   e. local SWAT teams

4. Approximately how many ways can a government combat terrorism?
   a. 1–5
   b. 6–10
   c. 11–15
   d. 16–20
   e. 21–25

5. What is CCTV?
   a. a Muslim fundamentalist terrorist group
   b. a type of SWAT team
   c. an antiterrorist organization
   d. a surveillance camera
   e. none of the above

PART TWO: SHORT ANSWER

1. Given what you have learned in this chapter (or elsewhere), what is the best way to counter terrorism and why?

2. What is the difference between antiterrorism and counterterrorism procedures?

3. How do police develop antiterrorist policies and practices?

4. In the context of combating terrorism, what is appeasement?

PART THREE: ESSAY

1. Is the war in Iraq going to increase the terrorist threat against the United States, and how?

2. Are the American efforts in Afghanistan qualitatively different than what the United States is doing in Iraq?

3. To what extent will hardening targets prevent terrorists from committing acts of terrorism?

CHAPTER TEN

Post 9/11: Are We Any Safer Now?

The American government, media, and general public still find it diffi-cult to put the tragedies of September 11, 2001, completely behind them—and for good reason. While the United States declared war on terrorism and sent troops overseas, ostensibly to hunt down those responsible for the attacks, has life in America really changed? Since 9/11, the public was faced with bomb threats, breaches of airline secu-rity, videotapes of bin Laden and high-ranking members of al Qaeda celebrating the attacks, and other intimidating threats.[1] These events certainly caused many to question the state of national security.

For all the debate, activity, and posturing, the question remains: Are we really safer now? How effective are the new security measures enacted across America and around the world? Is the public right to criticize the inconvenience of heightened security measures at airports, especially in light of ongoing news reports about "lapses" in such prac-tices? Is it safe once again to go to the tops of tall structures, such as the Empire State Building and the Sears Tower? How much of a presence do terrorists still have in our country, and are we a target for future attacks? What, if anything, should "we" still fear? Will it ever be safe to go back to how we used to be?

The short answer to the provocative question "Are we any safer?" is, maybe. But you probably already knew that, and perhaps you think there's no need to read further—not so fast! Although some people may feel safer, and others may still live in constant fear, our current state of preparedness in the United States should be contextualized. Accord-ingly, this chapter provides a theoretical background, interprets the reactions to 9/11 using the five-actor model developed earlier, and then reviews what we'll call the "threat of the week" syndrome. We'll also review what federal, state, and local governments have done, as well as some of the key accomplishments in the "war on terror."

Theoretical Background

Although much has been written on the effects of terrorism (Wardlaw 1982; Hewitt 1984; Weinberg and Davis 1989, chapters 5–7; Sederberg 1989, chapter 6), particularly on counterterrorist efforts (Livingstone and Arnold 1986), few comprehensive models of the responses have yet to be developed.

There are some exceptions. As previously mentioned, Ross and Miller (1997) created a series of relatively comprehensive actor-based models that outline the responses to (that is, the effects of) terrorism. The stimulus-response conflict model (Holsti, Brody, and North 1964) served as a framework to sketch these reactions and to specify some of the more important hypotheses. This work provides a tool for exploring and testing the responses, causes, and ultimately, cycles of terrorist-target interaction.[2] Specifically, as we've discussed, five basic actors are involved in the reaction: terrorists, victims (and their families and friends), the general public, businesses, and government. These will serve again as the framework for our discussion in this chapter.

Additionally, the phenomenon of "crime-reporting waves" partially informs our perception of terrorism. During the 1980s, Fishman (1980) introduced and documented the phenomenon that became known as "crime-reporting waves." He demonstrated that the crime rate, which has been acknowledged to be an inaccurate indicator of actual crime, bears little relationship to the frequency of media reporting on crime. More importantly, most people derive their fear and safety not from the actual incidence of crime, or from being personally victimized by crime, but rather from the frequency and attention paid to crime in media reports. Simply put, if the media pay considerable attention to crime (or terrorism for that matter), then viewers will feel scared—regardless of whether they've experienced crime recently or whether crime is, in reality, increasing.

Building on Fishman's work, others—such as Best (1989; 1999) and Jenkins (1998)—have sensitized us to the fact that, although there may be a very real problem with social predators like child molesters or serial killers, the media attention and the public fear that this phenomenon generates is largely out of proportion to the actual number of these types of criminals that exists in society.

In short, the public's fear and safety is directly connected to what is in the media. So, although it sounds simplistic, if you don't want to feel scared, don't pay attention to the media. This leads to another interesting point: in some places in America, there is no or minimal fear at all.

Has Life Really Changed?

As a result of 9/11, life has changed drastically in some quarters, while it appears to be "business as usual" in others. These divergent effects are dependent on a number of factors, including the proximity to the attacks, the pervasiveness of fear in the population, media interpretation of the events, and the susceptibility of the actor. We will address the first two aspects briefly before concentrating the balance of the discussion on the five specific actors.

Proximity to attacks

The results of a 2001 University of Houston poll indicated that those closest to the 9/11 attacks experienced the highest levels of anxiety. Thus, residents of New York City—even if they did not personally know someone who perished in the tragedy—experienced disruption in some shape or form because of job loss, transportation delays, the massive cleanup, or the much-publicized debate over what to do with the site where the twin towers once stood.[3]

General level of fear in the population

It's possible that some people outside of New York City and Washington, D.C., and other similar contexts (e.g., big cities with tall buildings) not experiencing a high level of anxiety were still in a state of denial, blocking out the shocking reality of what transpired; maybe as an attempt to deal with the horror, Americans have become numbed or have subconsciously numbed themselves. Yet, in contrast to this, some rural communities (particularly those out west) have encountered virtually no reported increase in anxiety levels: the local sheriff or small-town police officer still does his rounds without a glimmer of trepidation that he might stumble upon a terrorist cell plotting to blow up the local grain elevator.

Another rarely examined factor in the general population's level of fear is age. Those who are young and have no memory or experience of similar tragedies may have a difficult time placing the events of 9/11 into context. As a result, their susceptibility to fear or fear-inducing messages may be high.

Media Interpretation

The 9/11 attacks were a major news item. Networks both in the United States and elsewhere devoted considerable coverage to the incident. At the time there were also no competing stories that would bump the attacks off the front page. In the months following the attacks it appeared as if all incidents of unexplained violence occurring in the U.S. were somehow connected to 9/11.

Susceptibility of the actor

The events of 9/11 have had both structural and psychological effects. These broad categories of explanations will be analyzed using the five categories created earlier in our discussion of the effects of terrorism: terrorists, victims (and their friends and families), the public, businesses, and government.

1. Terrorists

As of April 20, 2005, there were approximately 520 "enemy combatants," most of whom are members of al Qaeda and the Taliban detained at Guantánamo Bay in Cuba.[4] Additionally, there are numerous individuals in foreign jails and prisons, some of whom are being held at the request of the United States government. When those detainees are captured, regardless of the country, they are interrogated by FBI officers or other representatives of American national security agencies (Cole 2003). There is some speculation that a significant blow has been made against al Qaeda as a result of these arrests. Some claim that in the war on terror, we need to capture or kill enough terrorists to reach what's called the "tipping point," the point at which declining membership acquires inevitable downward momentum toward collapse (in this case, the half-way point) (Gladwell 2002). In an attempt to achieve this objective, at the end of March 2002, Abu Zubaida, a senior al Qaeda member, and several of his subordinates were captured in Pakistan. During the raid, all sorts of relevant intelligence documents and materials were found that might enhance efforts to reach the tipping point by revealing the locations of other members or plans for future attacks (Pincus 2002).

In sum, particularly since the American invasion of Afghanistan, numerous al Qaeda members have been arrested, detained, or killed. But because this organization is widely dispersed, the likelihood of its survival is increased.[5] Failure to completely stop this group, along with periodic highly destructive bombing attacks (e.g., Madrid, March 2004, and London, July 2005) contributes to heightened anxiety among the public, politicians, and counterterrorist experts.

2. Victims (including family and friends)

The number of people who died as a result of 9/11 is close to 3000. Approximately 6,300 others were injured, many of whom will have permanent physical effects from the tragedy. Some may have experienced psychological reactions such as anger, anxiety, insomnia, post-traumatic stress disorder (especially because so many innocent lives were lost), and confusion (because bystanders and "first responders" did not know the best way to respond). The pain and suffering did not stop with the immediate victims. Many people lost a close relative: a wife, husband, father, son, daughter, or sibling. Those affected could amount to over 100,000 people.

Prior to 9/11, most people did not believe that a foreign-based terrorist group had the capability to carry off an operation of that magnitude. Many Americans thought that the country was invincible. Now individuals are more alert about their surroundings, security, and safety. Others may shy away from populated places or events (such as transportation hubs, sporting events, fireworks displays, and so on). Some victims responded positively by expressing their grief and turmoil through creating makeshift and permanent memorials that were set up throughout locations in New York City and Washington, D.C.

3. The public

Among the general community, there were several noticeable effects. Responses perceived as positive include financial support to victims, increased patriotism, and a deeper bond between Americans. Effects perceived as negative include antipathy towards Arab or "Muslim-looking" individuals in the United States and elsewhere, increased expenditures for gas, the loss or temporary absence of family members called up for active duty, an increase in the fear of flying, and criticism of the government for its failure to protect citizens.

In the immediate aftermath of the attacks, members of the public supported their communities by making donations to victims' funds and giving blood. Large public assistance organizations such as the Red Cross and Salvation Army increased their aid programs. Many individuals who had been against the death penalty or sympathetic to national liberation struggles and the grievances of fringe groups became less supportive or questioned their beliefs because of the overwhelming nature of the attack.

Many suggest that the events of 9/11 have led to an increased sense of nationalism and patriotism, made visible in expressions like "These colors don't run." The perception of a nationalistic surge is buttressed by the numerous displays of flags on lapel pins, cars, and houses. Additionally, slogans like "United We Stand" were displayed on postage stamps, posters displayed in shopkeepers' windows, and bumper stickers (Dudziak 2003). Many students redoubled their efforts to get a job with a federal law enforcement agency in order to join the "war against terrorism."

Others claimed that 9/11 brought Americans closer together, creating a brotherly atmosphere that fostered acts of generosity, kindness, and tolerance. Commentators and pundits have gloated over this reaction, going further to imply that if we fail to maintain everyday activities, "surely the terrorists have won."

But, by the same token, there were also negative consequences. 9/11 has probably also led to an increase in prejudice toward foreign-born Americans, immigrants, and visitors, particularly those of Islamic, Arabic, or Middle Eastern ethnicity. Many people have started looking at foreigners with suspicion, including those going about normal business at gas stations, variety stores, and so on.

The public has also felt the pinch by having to spend more money on gas for their cars and other vehicles. It has been suggested that 9/11 has somehow disrupted the West's access to oil from Middle Eastern countries and this has been reflected at the gas pump. Many individuals who were in their state National Guard or in the Army reserves have been activated (i.e., called up for duty) to serve in Afghanistan or Iraq. They have deprived their family, not only a significant breadwinner but emotional and other kinds of support.

Despite increased security many Americans are still afraid to fly both inside the country and outside. While fares have been reduced on some routes, they remain the same if not higher with others.

In some quarters, faith in government has been questioned. 9/11 pointed out the shortcomings of our then-current crime prevention and security apparatus. This was reinforced through the work of the National Commission on Terrorist Attacks upon the United States and their report (United States 2004).

Some individuals, up until 9/11 were otherwise politically apathetic. Now they pay more attention to the news media—and not just sports or entertainment—with greater acuity, noticing what is going on politically in the country and in the world.

In the immediate aftermath of the attack, some investigative reporters (such as Emerson 2002) went on a search for "the smoking gun." Many people are trying to understand why our national intelligence agencies missed the signs and signals of 9/11. After the fact, it became apparent that some FBI agents either had prior knowledge of the possible attacks or were restricted in their efforts to detect them. Many reporters, experts, and pundits concluded that there must have been a "failure in communication." Other individuals developed a new sense of respect for our nation's first responders: the police, fire fighters, and paramedics.

4. Business community

The events of 9/11 prompted a number of reactions by business interests. The stock exchange was closed for four days, and the day it was opened, companies listed on the exchange suffered their largest single-day drop in history. The airline and hospitality sectors were adversely affected economically, while specific sectors—such as private security firms and defense-related contractors—experienced a boom. Some companies (particularly those that were housed in the twin towers) were relocated to begin anew. Terrorism insurance was sold at alarming rates (Fawn 2003).

Initially, the airline and hospitality industry experienced a financial setback when many people cancelled business and recreational trips. Later, the federal government bailed out the airline industry to keep it alive, as so many other businesses depend on it. The stock market was temporarily shocked: prices plummeted, especially those of businesses connected to the travel industry. Many businesses went bankrupt, causing thousands of people to loose jobs. Thus, unemployment increased, along with other economically related social implications such as homelessness.

Although some segments of the economy suffered and people were laid off, many defense contractors were reinvigorated. Lockheed Martin, for example, had laid off much of its workforce, but with new contracts for GPS-controlled robots (to plot out land mines, for example), Lockheed Martin had a new lease on life.

We might assume that because of increased security—primarily through the stepped-up efforts of the Immigration and Naturalization Service (now called U.S. Citizenship and Immigration Services)—those working illegally in the United States will be identified and deported more efficiently. However, an unintended consequence might be a negative effect on the already-beleaguered enforcement service, and upon the agricultural, construction, landscaping, and service industries that rely on illegal laborers.

5. Government

In order to combat terrorism, local, state, and federal law enforcement agencies have implemented a number of measures. By far, the most dramatic and sweeping responses have come from the federal government (Buckley and Fawn 2003). These initiatives are listed from least to most important: readjusting expenditures, hardening of targets, and new policies, practices, and laws, especially the passage of the USA. PATRIOT Act.

Both the federal and state governments have cut back on spending in several sectors like health care, education, and prisons to fund the massive expenses that were incurred in the public safety parts of their state budgets.

As in previous eras, there was considerable target hardening at vulnerable targets. Many people in charge of security have changed security-related policies and practices. This was especially prominent at transportation hubs and around government facilities. For example, more concrete barriers have been placed at airports and critical infrastructures, and different traffic patterns have been established. On the other hand, some targets that analysts might expect would be hardened have not been. The Saudi Arabian embassy in downtown Washington, D.C., for example, does not appear to be any more protected than other targets of opportunity. This may be explained by the fact that Saudi Arabia, well knowing that it might be subject to terrorist attack, by either Islamic fundamentalists, or even Americans who blame the Saudis for complicity in the 9/11 attacks has either recalled most of its diplomatic staff, or relocated them to different offices.

Legislative empowerment allowed the Treasury Department to close or tighten the reigns on the *hawalas*, the Islamic money exchanges believed to be critical in the transfer of money to terrorists and their supporters in the United States. And the Immigration and Naturalization Service (INS) separated into two divisions, one concerned with administration and another with enforcement. The INS was then moved out of the Department of Justice and into the Office (now called the Department) of Homeland Security. The INS has also cracked down on visitors who have overstayed their visas, resulting in the detention of many people suspected of belonging to or aiding terrorist groups. Surveillance has also increased at the Canadian border, leading to questions about the proper role of the National Guard along the 49th parallel. It appears that the U.S. border patrol, which has disproportionately focused their efforts along the Mexican border does not have the appropriate number of staff to police the northern part of the United States.

Perhaps the biggest changes have been in the field of transportation including the use of military or National Guard soldiers at major airports. And almost everyone who has used public transportation has their own horror story; those who have taken an airplane, a train, or a Greyhound bus know that some sectors of transportation have implemented extra security precautions, while others retain a laissez-faire attitude. For example, few, if any, changes have been made to affect bus travel or bus stations. In the immediate aftermath of 9/11, a mentally disturbed individual attacked a bus driver while the vehicle was en route in Tennessee, and as a result of this event, Greyhound started talking about installing geopositioning satellite (GPS) technology tracking devices on their buses. GPS probably would not have prevented the particular incident that inspired its use, but it may have aided in locating the bus if it had been hijacked for more sinister reasons.

However, things have changed slightly in train transportation. More Amtrak police patrol the platforms instead of simply walking around the station. Although passengers need to show identification now to purchase a ticket from a window, they can still buy one anonymously through an automatic ticket machine, conveniently located in most stations. This loophole would be eliminated if passengers were also required to show identification once on board, but this is rarely the case. In Washington, D.C., for example, before passengers are released from the waiting area, they must show their ticket and identification, but the Amtrak gate attendant rarely compares the two. In Baltimore, which is along the same train line, even that flawed safeguard does not exist.

In most of the big airports, by contrast, security procedures have become more rigorous. Depending on the airport, picking up and dropping off passengers is now more of a hassle, and sometimes a more time-consuming and expensive ordeal without curb side pickup and drop-off. Although passengers are still asked a number of questions at the ticket counter, such as, "Has anyone helped you pack your bag?" and "Has your bag been in your possession at all times?" they can easily lie. Airlines are now often restricting carry-on luggage to one item either to increase their revenue by charging for extra baggage that passengers would normally take as carry on, or minimize the items that could possibly be carried on and used as weapons.

In another new safety measure, baggage handlers and screeners have been "federalized" and integrated into a new government agency, the Transportation Safety Administration (TSA) that is part of the Department of Transportation. In general, passenger and baggage screeners (there are now some thirty thousand of them) are doing a more thorough job including testing their personal effects for gunpowder residue, increased metal sensitivity, and regular and random searches.

Checking baggage is also more onerous. New legislation demands that those responsible for baggage handling and inspection will be better trained and more experienced. Many people believe that the procedures are now ridiculous, such as having eighty-year-old women turn over nail clippers or treating quadriplegics as would-be terrorists simply to demonstrate impartiality in screening; not being able to take nail clippers, but allowing disposable razors; not being able to take cigarette lighters but permitted to take box of matches.

Another new program (the utility of which is not yet proven or publicly known) is Computer-Assisted Passenger Pre-screening System (CAPPS II), which examines a passenger's travel history to determine if there are any "unusual" patterns. CAPPS "uses airline reservation computers to identify passengers who may pose a higher risk of being terrorists and subjects them to additional scrutiny" (Levin and Morrison 2001, 2A). CAPPS "examines 26 aspects of a passenger's travel history," but we don't know exactly what those items are because "details are classified" (Levin and Morrison 2001, 2A).

In addition, after the 9/11 attacks, because of its close proximity to the Pentagon, flights out of Ronald Reagan National Airport in

Washington, D.C., were initially suspended, then scaled back, and sky marshals were placed on all flights in and out of the airport. Moreover, passengers are not allowed to leave their seats for the half hour after departure from or during approach to Reagan Airport and Dulles in northern Virginia.

A number of changes have occurred with respect to boarding and onboard procedures as well. Nationwide, when coming on to a plane, certain passengers can be taken aside to have their persons and their carry-on items completely searched. Pilots are now allowed to carry guns, and cockpit doors have been reinforced. The airlines no longer serve food on so-called short-haul trips; one would assume this last precaution is because utensils can be potential weapons, and because not providing food defrays the immediate loss of income incurred after 9/11. Even so, many people are scared to travel long distances, especially if the trip involves flying.

In November 2001, two air-travel security bills were debated in Congress. At the same time, a number of security breaches (incidents of passengers bringing weapons onboard planes) were highly publicized, such as in Chicago, where a man was discovered with *several* weapons in his bags. Secretary of Transportation Norman Mineta has proposed mandating a "National Travel Card" to "verify proof of citizenship and provide photo identification, generating a national database" (Levin and Morrison 2001, 2A). Since 9/11, others have made similar suggestions for national identity cards. It has been argued that since the United States is the only country that does *not* have these sorts of documentation, it would serve to slow down terrorists. If we had these pieces of identification, advocates argue, it would be easier for law enforcement authorities to share information and detect known terrorists and criminals. In the long run, however, such ID cards are probably just like drivers licenses; you can get a fake one and hold on to it long enough to commit a number of crimes. Ultimately, it does not seem necessary to burden society with more rules and regulations to demonstrate a response to a recent threat; instead, we should properly implement the ones we have and not be complacent about enforcement.

Increased cooperation and sharing of data among law enforcement organizations and national security agencies, and between the United States and our allies is always to be encouraged. Better cooperation among customs, U.S. Citizenship and Immigration Service, the FBI, and the CIA would also seem prudent. This was the principal intent surrounding the creation of the Department of Homeland Security.

On November 6, 2001, the Inspector General of the Department of the Justice released a report that said, "Hundreds of foreign nationals who came under suspicion during immigration inspections were allowed into the country under a special program and then disappeared, ignoring requirements to return with missing information"; the report concluded that the INS needed to create "a better system to track deferred foreign nationals."[6]

In the fall of 2002, as mentioned earlier, Congress authorized the establishment of the Office, now Department, of Homeland Security. In essence, Homeland Security is supposed to coordinate national policy and security on terrorism, bringing these functions out of the hands of the FBI. Needless to say, there are a number of potential difficulties, including the increasingly complex communications needs that result from developing one more layer of bureaucracy. In the meantime, a number of new appointments place capable-sounding individuals at the helm of counterterrorism agencies.

In the middle of October 2001, Congress passed sweeping legislation against terrorism in what is now referred to as the PATRIOT Act. Some of the more important highlights include so-called roving wiretaps (tied to certain people rather than to particular telephone lines); nationwide search warrants, instead of those limited to specific jurisdictions; eavesdropping on electronic mail; and the power to detain foreigners for extended periods of time. The bill gives "authorities the ability to hold immigrants suspected of terrorist acts for 7 days without filing charges."[7] Part of the PATRIOT Act also includes longer and more severe sentences and the extension of the "statute of limitations on terrorism cases."[8]

This rather draconian antiterrorism legislation, which few literate Americans have seen or read (and that includes a handful of congressmen and congresswomen who passed the bill), is something to be watchful of—we need to be afraid of an emerging "Big Brother" attitude. Meanwhile, in the wake of 9/11, some people have even suggested that it is unpatriotic to criticize the government.

As of early 2005, Congress was considering very comprehensive antiterror legislation, dubbed PATRIOT II Act. Both the House and the Senate were developing separate terrorism bills that would "enhance domestic surveillance powers, stiffen penalties for terrorism and make it easier for law enforcement and intelligence agencies to share information" (Lancaster 2001). Increased monitoring and regulation of financial institutions is also being considered, as it is recognized that in order to mount a successful campaign, a terrorist organization needs financing

(Adams 1986). Without new legislation, banks are only required to report to the federal government transfers and withdrawals that are over $100,000. Banking legislation may need to be changed, but these would undoubtedly slow down the pace of international capitalism.

Since the attacks, state, local, and federal governments have provided more security around parades and government sponsored celebrations for significant holidays, such as Memorial Day, Independence Day, and New Year's Eve. The federal government has also increased the number of jet fighter patrols over Washington, D.C. Many of the new policies and practices are still in development.

Two of the most important governmental or political responses have been in the area of foreign policy, and those are, of course, the wars in Afghanistan and Iraq. Shortly after the 9/11 attacks, American national security agencies recognized that bin Laden and al Qaeda were responsible, and that when requested, the Taliban, the regime in power in Afghanistan, was not willing to turn him over (Fawn 2003). The United States then assembled a coalition of states, including the United Kingdom and Pakistan, and Afghani political/militia groups (such as the Northern Alliance), to help it unseat the Taliban if negotiations failed. In the fall of 2001, the Taliban failed to concede, and the United States commenced bombing operations. Shortly thereafter, American Special Forces, with the assistance of the Northern Alliance, started a ground war in Afghanistan. In the meantime, videotapes of bin Laden exhorting his followers to wage war against the United States were aired on al Jazeera. Soon, American fighters were joined by British, Canadian, German, and Italian military. Meanwhile, the Pakistani army was busy securing their border against fleeing members of the Taliban and al Qaeda. Despite several setbacks, the United States, with the assistance of the United Nations, was relatively successful in installing a new government in Afghanistan with the semblance of democracy.

The invasion of Iraq, however, is another story. Shortly after the invasion of Afghanistan, the United States accused Saddam Hussein of Iraq of covertly supporting al Qaeda. President George W. Bush and his administration also said that he was hiding weapons of mass destruction (WMD). The United Nations made several inspections of Iraq, but Hussein was unwilling to have them look in certain areas. The United States became frustrated and was unwilling to garner a coalition to help it militarily threaten Iraq. It then issued an ultimatum to Hussein to allow unrestricted inspections. Hussein failed to comply, and so the

United States (along with Great Britain), and without the support of the UN invaded Iraq. As the months went by and American ground forces increased, it became clear that Hussein had no WMD and had not supported al Qaeda. A wide segment of the American and international public not only did not agree with the invasion, but never believed the al Qaeda link or the presence of WMD, and felt the "terrorist threat" was being used to justify pre-existing plans and motivations.

"Threat of the Week" Syndrome

In the days and months following the 9/11 attacks, the American public was subjected to the "threat of the week" syndrome. Many rumors surfaced, facilitated by media attention and increased public access to the Internet, about possible terrorist attacks on the United States. Many of these stories turned out to be false.[9] Some of the rumors clearly originated in the minds of the public, motivated by fear and suggestibility; others were manufactured by mean-spirited citizens. A few can be traced to intelligence collected by the government. Such rumors included the following:

- that missing or unaccounted-for rental trucks (U-Haul, Ryder, etc.) could be carrying explosive materials, ready to be placed almost anywhere;

- that, per expert opinion, the Empire State Building and the Statue of Liberty, some of America's most important symbols and popular tourist attractions, were possible next targets (approximately a month after the attacks, New York City counterterrorism planners closed the observation decks of the Empire State Building and prohibited entrance to the Statue of Liberty);

- that suspension bridges in California, like the Golden Gate, would be attacked (Californians, who are no strangers to the devastating effects of earthquakes appeared most affected by this idea, which California governor Gray Davis even highlighted in a public statement);

- that Osama bin Laden had been seen in Salt Lake City (these sightings by Utah residents in January 2002 were called into the

FBI, which reassured tipsters that bin Laden was not in the United States, but somewhere in Afghanistan—that didn't stop a popular Canadian television satire from airing a weekly segment on Osama "sightings");

- that five Arab men, allegedly with terrorist connections, had sneaked into the United States from Canada in December 2002 (this story originated with the FBI, apparently from a Pakistani forgery suspect in Canadian custody; as the investigation unfolded, authorities discovered that the detainee had fabricated the entire story);

- that many United Parcel Service (UPS) uniforms were missing and might fall into the hands of Islamic fundamentalist terrorists already living in the United States (a story from February 2003); and

- that terrorist attacks would soon commence in the United States, especially around the weekend of February 14.

Government response to rumors and credible threats

The federal government issued its highest security threat in February 2003, after identifying what it called "credible threats of terrorism." This was almost simultaneous with the release of a video tape of bin Laden exhorting his followers and those sympathetic to al Qaeda to launch suicide attacks against the United States if it intervened in Iraq. It was also the first time the federal government suggested "practical measures" Americans could take in order to protect themselves (beyond simply being vigilant). In the event of a nuclear, chemical, or biological attack, Americans were advised to use duct tape and plastic to cover their doors and windows, and to have on hand a three-day supply of food. Many commentators and pundits thought this was a little unrealistic and impractical, but it did serve as a wake-up call for some Americans who had not already taken any action in light of these sorts of warnings.

The Department of Homeland Security, in a scene reminiscent of the old cold war–nuclear threat days, came up with a color-coded method of assessing potential threats and notifying the public. It quickly became tiresome, the public had a hard time figuring it out, and it was easily dismissed as ineffective. Even the irreverent and popular *Saturday Night Live,* a weekly television comedy show, spoofed the color-coding system.

Unfortunately, these announcements quickly grew to resemble the boy who cried wolf: the warning was offered, but no terrorist event—or even a foiled attempt—took place. In the meantime, the public became desensitized and let its guard down. But the government found itself in a "damned if you do, damned if you don't" position: it had to issue warnings to maintain legitimacy. In this kind of situation, the state must err on the side of caution, but increasingly the warnings and the officials who issue them lose legitimacy as the warnings become "background noise" to the pressures of daily life.

It appears that the federal government has now placed a disclaimer on these warnings, saying that they are "being issued out of an abundance of caution." When people and government agencies place some credence in them, it disrupts normal daily life, but the threat of the week quickly becomes tiresome and induces complacency—the opposite effect for which such warnings were created. In the end, this attitude ends up hindering, rather than raising, public awareness and preparedness about potential threats.

The inadequacies of Homeland Security

Another aspect to the failed warning system was a lack of trust in Homeland Security overall. Many people believe that Tom Ridge, former governor of Pennsylvania and the first director of Homeland Security, did not instill public confidence. He appeared awkward in the media and was considered to have had minimal impact. Perhaps this perception will change with the appointment of Michael Chertoff in his stead, but in the first four months since Chertoff's confirmation, he was relatively quiet compared to his predecessor.

The Department of Homeland Security, is in danger of becoming a good example of poorly thought-out government reasoning. Basic public administration theory dictates that adding another layer of bureaucracy has advantages and disadvantages (Ostrom 1976).

If the desired outcome is practical oversight—where calm, cool, collected reasoning is valued—then adding functional levels is a good suggestion. However, if the desired outcome is faster decision-making and action, then adding another layer of government bureaucracy is counterproductive. Traditionally, when there is a policy issue or crisis in the governments of advanced industrialized countries, in order to avoid confusion they establish what's called a "lead agency." For example, before 9/11, there was some coordination (albeit attenuated) between the FBI and the CIA. The FBI focused on domestic threats whereas the CIA focused on foreign ones. The 9/11 investigations pointed out a so-called intelligence failures, and the lead agency became a political scapegoat for "allowing" the attacks to occur. It was clear that memos of an impending major coordinated bombing had passed the desks of the national security advisor and the president. It seems that the threat or a proper response was not taken (Clarke 2004).

Every government agency wants to assign blame for 9/11 to another agency; this hunt is most prominent in *The 9/11 Commission Report*. It does not appear as if there is any middle ground to this debate, and it's unlikely that significant new information was uncovered. Though citizens are learning that the government knows more than it lets on, no single smoking gun exists, and blame must be shared among a number of agencies.

Conclusion

Unfortunately, many Americans fail to realize that the federal government, at the behest of the Bush administration, may be using the 9/11 disaster to strengthen and expand what can be called the "national security state." Several of the proposals that were hastily considered and passed were already formulated *before* 9/11, hidden in file cabinets for a considerable period of time, only to be dusted off and put into place later. To preserve our democracy and Western liberal freedoms, we need to avoid panicky or knee-jerk responses intended for more symbolic than practical reasons, especially if we are to avoid adverse unintended consequences that end up destroying or unnecessarily scaling back those freedoms.

In sum, we must refuse to be reactive and should insist on retaining our democratic values: "we must develop countermeasures to fight terrorism and to actively seek out terrorists. But let us do so in an intelligent and rational manner—we owe this much to ourselves and the country. If we do not act slowly, and wisely, the terrorists have already won."[10] Can we ever go back to the way we used to be? No. Are we any safer now than we were on September 11? Maybe. We have done much to protect ourselves, but more remains to be done—and there is still much more that we should *not* do.

Questions, Chapter 10

PART ONE: MULTIPLE CHOICE

1. Who introduced and documented the phenomenon that became known as crime-reporting waves?
    a. Miller
    b. Macklin
    c. Fishman
    d. Ross
    e. all the above

2. What is the current name of the new federal agency responsible for protecting American citizens?
    a. Office of Homeland Security
    b. Department of Homeland Security
    c. Transportation Safety Association
    d. Delta Force
    e. none of the above

3. With reference to the question above, who is the head of this organizational unit as of May 2005?
    a. George W. Bush
    b. George Tenant
    c. Thomas Ridge
    d. Michael Chertoff
    e. Tommy Thompson

4. What is a *hawala?*
    a. the head of an Islamic terrorist organization
    b. a type of Jewish bread
    c. type of Arabic food
    d. kind of bomb
    e. Islamic money exchange

PART TWO: SHORT ANSWER

1. List three factors that shape people's reaction to the events of 9/11.

2. What are three drawbacks with the Department of Homeland Security?

3. List three new safety precautions at airports implemented in the wake of 9/11.

4. What is the "threat of the week" syndrome?

PART THREE: ESSAY

1. Since 9/11, how has security improved at our nation's airports? How would you measure its effectiveness?

2. In the aftermath of 9/11, the United States has spent considerable resources on public safety. How can we ever maintain a balanced budget in the near future?

3. How can the United States minimize its perception of being overly aggressive or insensitive in matters of foreign policy?

CHAPTER ELEVEN

The Future of Terrorism

This chapter examines the future of terrorism, both in general and in light of the events of 9/11. It reviews the typical approaches toward the future of terrorism and provides an extended discussion of possible perpetrators, methods, and targets of terrorism. The chapter analyzes the potential for terrorism through weapons of mass destruction (WMD), cyberterrorism, and globalization. It concludes with a discussion regarding the relevance of the war in Iraq for possible terrorism. The paper also examines new procedures and technological innovations to combat terrorism.

Optimism or Pessimism?

There are two basic perspectives toward the future: optimistic and pessimistic. In terrorism studies, in an optimistic scenario, the frequency, intensity, and lethality of terrorism will subside until terrorism becomes a thing of the past. In the pessimistic alternative, terrorism will increase, and terrorists will eventually resort to utilizing more dangerous and destructive WMD. Between these two extremes lies the understanding that terrorism changes due to morphing, life cycles, and waves (Hewitt 2000; Rapoport 2003; Weinberg and Pedahzur 2003; Ross 2006).

In general, despite a worldwide effort to clamp down on terrorist groups and their activities, the frequency of terrorist acts will probably be greater than it has been in the past, for three reasons. First, governmental and bureaucratic intransigence will frustrate less powerful constituencies with grievances, who may then resort to terrorism. Second, countries wanting to avoid all-out warfare may secretly sponsor terrorism to achieve their goals. Third, weapons and communications technology will become more readily accessible to terrorists, as to the general public.

Bureaucratic intransigence

Large bureaucracies, like governments and corporations, often fail to address the continual unmet needs of domestic and/or indigenous groups and workers (Barak, 1991; Ross 2000a; 2000b). Both the increasing tendency toward bureaucratization and routinization (Ritzer 2000) mitigate oppositional organizations' ability to receive formal or informal access to and attention from government agencies. In other words, groups with grievances find it hard to make themselves heard by large bureaucracies. When their ability to work within the system is frustrated, they may be motivated to use violence in order to get their needs addressed.

Obsolescence of full-scale war

As many conflict theorists have argued, full-scale war is becoming obsolete and is being replaced by skirmishes, border clashes, and terrorism. Increasingly, militaries are becoming more sophisticated, destructive, and accurate in their targeting, and the resulting efficiency, thorough destruction creates increased military power. Governments, however, may be reluctant to use comprehensive military action out of fear of retaliation and its effects. This response may motivate some leaders to realize that military action itself is unnecessary: from certain countries, the *threat* of a military response alone may capitulate aggressors.

Available technology

Finally, advances in destructive and communication technologies have made equipment smaller, cheaper, and thus more portable and available to terrorist organizations. Individuals and groups who could not afford to mount a terrorist campaign in the past might have improved access to more sophisticated and deadlier weapons in the future. Improvements in communications may facilitate links among terrorist groups and improve coordination inside. This will lead to more extravagant, attention-seeking, destructive acts and to the possibility that terrorists will use more destructive technologies like nuclear, biological, chemical, and toxic weapons.

The Threat of Chemical, Biological, and Nuclear Terrorism

The United States is especially concerned about terrorists constructing, obtaining, and using weapons of mass destruction, and for good reason. Beginning in the late 1960s, security and terrorist analysts warned about the possibility of chemical, biological, and nuclear attacks by committed terrorists and their organizations (see Allison et al. 1996; Allison 2004; Zilinskas 1990; Tucker 1996; 1999). At the same time, they cautioned against mass hysteria, because terrorist organizations lacked the ability to develop, construct, or deliver WMD without injury or death to themselves or populations near them.

Although WMD, also known as asymmetric terrorism, are supposed to be confined to warfare between states, and a number of conventions controlling its use are in place, such as the Nuclear Non-Proliferation Treaty (NPT), the use of WMD by terrorists remains a source of concern for arms-control experts, public safety officials, and the public at large (Stern 1999). It is also understood that with the advent of suicide terrorism (see Pape 2003), fear of being killed while delivering a WMD is probably of less concern for some terrorists and their organizations. A number of incidents in the United States and elsewhere speak to the capability of terrorist groups using these techniques in relatively controlled settings.

Asymmetrical terrorist events in the United States

In 1972, "members of the Order of the Rising Sun, an American fascist group, obtained 80 lbs. of typhoid bacteria cultures they planned to feed into the water supplies of several cities" (Reeve 1999, 258). Although their intentions were not clear it was suspected that they were going to use this either for a terrorist attack or an extortion attempt. In 1984, individuals from the Rajneeshee cult, who owned a large tract of land in Oregon, poisoned local salad bars with *Salmonella typhimurium* so that residents would be ill and unable to take part in a critical vote (Miller, Engelberg, and Broad 2001). In 1985, members of the Covenant, the Sword and the Order, a neo-Nazi organization were "arrested with 30 gallons of cyanide they were hoping to use to poison the water in New York and Washington, D.C." (Reeve 1999, 258). And in 1995, three cases were discovered in which white supremist groups, or individuals with links to them, possessed deadly biological agents such as ricin and *Yersinia pestis*, which causes bubonic plague (Stern 1999, 8). In 1998, Larry Wayne Harris, once a member of a neo-Nazi organization, legally obtained anthrax and was accused of attempting to attack the New York City subway system. And in the fall of 2001, anthrax-laden envelopes were sent to members of Congress and the media. A total of 18 confirmed cases were uncovered and there were 5 anthrax-related deaths. While the culprit was not definitively identified many people feared it was the work of terrorists.

Asymmetrical terrorism outside the United States

In other countries, several incidents in which individuals and groups possessed materials or made threats of using WMD have given pause to counterterrorist planners. Among these is the previously mentioned 1995 sarin gas attack in the Tokyo subway by members of the Aum Shinrikyo religious cult. This incident left 12 dead and 12,000 injured. During the 1980s, the Animal Liberation Front (ALF) claimed to have placed rat poison in Mars-brand candy bars. Similar scares have occurred, all attributed to the ALF, of terrorists injecting "toxic mercury into turkeys" sold to supermarkets during the Thanksgiving and Christmas holiday seasons (Stern 1999, 66). And in 1995, Shamil Basayev, "the leader of a Chechen group," apparently "buried a packet of radioactive cesium" in a popular park in Moscow (Stern 1999, 67).

Causes of terrorist use of WMD

Stern identifies five reasons why terrorists, now more than ever, may resort to WMD.

1. Retribution, retaliation, and showmanship

WMD may help "terrorists seeking to conjure a sense of divine retribution, to display scientific prowess, to kill large numbers of people, to invoke the dead, or to retaliate against states that have used these weapons in the past" (Stern 1999, 8). Since WMD are rarely used, an attack of this nature will draw greater public attention and help place these terrorist groups in the history books.

2. Trend toward extreme violence

"A new breed of terrorists," Stern argues, "appears more likely than the terrorist of the past to commit acts of extreme violence" (Stern 1999, 8).

These individuals have less respect for human life and feel more committed to their ideals.

3. Availability of former Soviet material

The demise of the Soviet Union and its satellite states has created a black market of sorts in raw materials, weapons, and expertise (Stern 1999, 9).[1] Since the fall of the Berlin wall, it has been recognized that WMD are missing and that many nuclear scientists now working in free-market countries are willing to sell their services to the highest bidder.

4. General proliferation of WMD

Chemical, nuclear and biological "weapons are proliferating, even in states known to sponsor terrorism" (Stern 1999, 9).[2] According to intelligence analysts, countries like Iran and North Korea that feel threatened by the West either possess WMD or are in the process of acquiring or developing them.

5. Easier deployment of WMD

Finally, Stern argues, technological improvements have made it easier to carry out attacks (1999, 10). Delivery systems have vastly improved over the past decade enabling countries and rogue elements to fire WMDs from afar or sneak "dirty bombs" the size of a brief case into a country or a restricted security area.

Despite these new incentives, very few terrorist organizations have resorted to WMD. These obstacles remain: lack of technical sophistication, and the motivations and organizational efficiency of individual terrorists. According to Stern, "The technical hurdles would be considerable: acquiring the agent or weapon would present one set of difficulties; disseminating or exploding it would present another" (1999, 48). Others are less sanguine. According to Laqueur, "There is much reason to believe that if such attacks should be carried out in the near future, many, perhaps the great majority, will fail, or will have a smaller effect than anticipated. But it should also be clear that if only one out of ten, one out of a hundred such attempts succeeds, the damage caused, the number of victims will be infinitely higher than at anytime in the past" (2003, 227).

At the same time it takes a considerable amount of resources and organizational skills in order to mount and successfully complete a WMD attack. The 9/11 attacks, for example, required almost two years of planning before al Qaeda felt confident that it could be carried out (United States 2004)

The most immediate threat of future terrorism, however, is probably in connection with the American presence in Iraq.

Consequences of the War in Iraq

The United States' military (and political) efforts in Iraq could have one of three possible effects.

Stabilization of Iraq and the surrounding region

First, American involvement might help pave the way to stabilize Iraq and perhaps even the Middle East/Persian Gulf region as a whole, leading to a decrease in terrorism. If Western-style democracy manages to take hold, perhaps Iraq may serve as an example for the neighboring countries of Iran and Syria? On the other hand, it is reported that terrorists are flocking to Iraq to assist the anti-American insurgency and prove, once again, that the United States is not invincible.

Deterrence of states sponsoring or harboring terrorism

Second, the American occupation of Iraq may serve as a cautionary example to other states that have sponsored terrorism or provided safe haven to terrorists, compelling them to cease and desist lest the United States invade their country as well. Many commentators ascribe this rationale to Libya's 2004 voluntary cessation of its nuclear weapons testing program, its admission of responsibility for the Lockerbie attack of December 1988, and its normalization of relations with the United States.

Increased anti-Americanism in the Middle East

Then again, a possible third effect of the American presence in Iraq is increased hostility and resentment toward the United States—more of what we have seen already from both moderate Iraqis and citizens of other Middle Eastern countries, who believe Americans should not be there in the first place. American forces have had considerable difficulty restoring order; since the invasion, a phenomenal number of innocent civilians have been injured and killed.[3] Most Iraqis are still unemployed, and adequate food and medical care is lacking. Prisoners in Abu Ghraib are being held and questioned, and some have been tortured, in violation of the Geneva Convention (Hersh 2004). The American presence in Iraq—particularly because the United States did not receive the support of the United Nations, and the fact that, to date, no WMD have been found—is being perceived as yet another example of America using its power (and military might) in an arbitrary and inappropriate fashion. This reaction exacerbates each day the United States stays in Iraq.

How Can We Best Study the Future Course of Terrorism?

In the late 1990s, the Pentagon established a commission called "Terrorism 2000" to determine "the likely future of terrorism" (Reeve 1999, 259–60). Directed by Marvin Cetron, the president of Forecasting International, an Arlington-based consulting company, the study assembled approximately forty international experts to discuss the future of terrorism. As Reeve reports, "The group spent months investigating terrorism and turning its findings into a classified report that shocked the intelligence community. *Terror 2000* suggested the terrorist threat was increasing. International terrorists would launch major attacks on the West, . . . home-grown terrorists would become a major headache, and—most worrying—terrorists would increasingly turn to weapons of mass destruction" (1999, 259).

Missing, however, from these pronouncements, is the explanation of the methodology that futurists use, to determine the likelihood of any phenomenon, such as trend extrapolation, scenarios, mapping, and making better use of statistical modeling. In order to address these problems, a body of researchers skilled in advanced techniques should be assembled and an international center, similar to the one for data collection outlined in chapter 3, should be established in a politically neutral country such as Switzerland. This center must be committed to the systematic, nonideological, social-scientific study of terrorism. Ideally, it would bring together researchers from different academic disciplines who would have as their agenda pooling reference material, collecting and analyzing independent data sources to be shared among researchers,; and utilizing funds from public (nongovernmental) sources to study terrorism in the United States and elsewhere.

Future Causes of Terrorism

Around the world, small civil wars, population growth, natural disasters, conflicting values, and limited or unequal access to food, employment, and natural resources (through destruction and depletion) are prime motivators for mass migrations, refugee problems, and unaddressed grievances. Over time, these factors will place a greater burden on governments, and as we have learned, groups whose needs are not addressed by countries are more likely to resort to terrorism to make themselves heard.

Some of the phenomena listed above are due to the seemingly perpetual North–South and socioeconomic gaps identified by nongovernmental organizations and development and dependency theorists. All these factors, in combination, may fuel the future course of terrorism. But which individuals or groups might in the future continue or resort to terrorism?

Future Perpetrators

The spread of Islamic fundamentalism most likely will not end; it may, in fact, increase (Barber 1995; Huntington 1998; Juergensmeyer 2000). Secular governments like those in Algeria and the Philippines, or ones that are ruled by monarchs (such as Jordan and Saudi Arabia), are being challenged by indigenous religious fundamentalists who resort to violence to back up their demands (Buckley and Fawn 2003). It also does not appear that the Palestinian/Israeli conflict will end anytime soon; perhaps when new leaders emerge—when Ariel Sharon (the Israeli Prime Minister) steps down, or when Mahmoud Abbas (the current PNA leader), is capable of deterring Hamas and the al-Aqsa Martyrs' Brigade—there may be an opportunity for true peace. But until that time, the conflict will persist.

Fringe members of the anti-globalist movement may for a variety of reasons strike out with terrorism. The violent outbursts in Seattle (1999), Québéc City (2001), Gothenburg (2001), and Genoa (2001), during meetings of the World Bank and the International Monetary Fund, have led analysts to believe that some of the anti-globalist cadre will ramp things up in the years to come. Additionally, since the 1990s, particularly in the former Soviet republics, the number of nationalist and ethnic groups seeking independence from their home countries has increased. Tensions among certain nationalities (especially among Indians, Sikhs, and Pakistanis) are bubbling below the surface. The Pakistani army, in their efforts to root out suspected Taliban and al Qaeda members from the isolated tribes along the border with Afghanistan, is creating anti-Pakistani sentiments. In a strange twist, there has been talk of what is called the "Third Position," "a coalition between the extreme left and extreme right, between nationalism and socialism" (Laqueur 2003, 220). With this scenario these two ideological camps may find enough common ground to temporarily suspend their antagonism toward each other and form a short-term alliance to achieve a short-term mutual goal.

Finally, individuals and small groups with narrow issues from the ecology (Nilson and Burke 2002), animal-rights (Smith 1998), and anti-abortion movements may also resort to terrorism, if the situation presents itself. A new development in terrorist identity is that these violent actions are increasingly being committed by criminally, psychologically, and socially hardened but inexperienced youth with their own agendas. In sum, the number of possible perpetrators with grievances is considerable.

Future Targets

A substantial amount of recent public dialogue has been devoted to the possibility of cyberterrorism (e.g., Weimann 2004). This includes terrorists using the Internet to "ranging from psychological warfare and propaganda to highly instrumental uses such as fundraising, recruitment, data mining, and coordination of actions" (Weimann 2004, 1). This also includes attacking critical computer networks, and disabling a country's ability to counter terrorist groups. This threat is nothing really new and in many respects is overstated (Green 2002).

Solutions

The future is ultimately unpredictable. However, a number of changes should take place to minimize the possibility of terrorism or to lessen the amount of property damage, injuries, and deaths when political violence does strike. Most doctors diagnosing a sick patient suggest that a coherent and clear communication of the problem is half the battle to amelioration, but this has been often lacking in studies on terrorism. Thus, more definitionally and conceptually rigorous, nonideological, methodologically sophisticated, and theoretically appropriate approaches to understanding terrorism are necessary.

What won't help

Although bilateral treaties and cooperation among countries do occur in the fight against terrorism, the problem of sharing intelligence not only inside a country, between its own agencies, but also beyond its borders, between and among countries, looms large (Amit 1989). It is doubtful that this problem will be solved in the near future. Government agencies because of turf wars, scarce resources and/or the competition for this organizational input, or simply suspicion of the intelligence collection procedures and products are not willing to trust outsiders.

We have also learned, particularly in the cases of Libya and Cuba, that diplomatic and economic sanctions are not sufficient to deter countries from helping terrorist groups. States which are threatened or experience these kinds of responses can and do improve their relations with other countries and broker new alliances with others in order to get access to raw materials and finished products that are clearly lacking.

Poorly thought-out or designed technological fixes, like facial recognition systems derived from biometric screening, will probably not help in deterring or detecting possible terrorists. There are still too many problems with these tools to make them as useful as their inventors currently claim they are. The post-9/11 antiterrorism technology, as it currently exists, is subject to considerable error. Although this methodology may be appropriate for a controlled setting, its applicability to the real world is of limited value, and it is doubtful whether Transportation Security Administration (TSA) agents or administrators will find much merit in it. Law enforcement utilizes multiple screening systems, including driver's licenses, passports, fingerprints, DNA, and so on—in other words, they are not stuck with facial recognition only to catch the "bad guys." Another idea, proposed in the immediate wake of 9/11, was for national ID cards to be issued. This suggestion was hotly debated, its civil liberties infringements highlighted, and ultimately rejected as redundant.

Finally, target hardening will not deter the most dedicated individuals from attacking. But until more sophisticated antiterrorist measures are taken, it is the least risky first step in an antiterrorism strategy. "In truth, however," as Reeve points out, "there is often little the authorities can do to prevent terrorist attacks, particularly those by religiously motivated terrorists" (1999, 263). This is especially true when the advocates for terrorism speak from a theocracy some two thousand miles away.

What may help

What is going to win the day in the fight against terrorism? Clearly, a multipronged approach is most appropriate.

One way of minimizing future attacks is, if discernable and relatively painless, to address the legitimate grievances of the terrorists (Reeve 1999, 264). In April 2003, the United States finally announced that it would remove the nearly five thousand troops that have been stationed in Saudi Arabia since the 1991 Gulf War.[4] Although it is not completely clear that this has led to a cessation of anti-American terrorist attacks, it is probably a step in the right direction.

Another suggestion has been the timely collection and analysis of better intelligence, so that attacks can be prevented and perpetrators caught (Clarke 2004). But technologically gathered intelligence can only do so much. Thus, in terms of intelligence, countries will need to rely more on good informants. National security agencies' inability to cultivate appropriate sources and their lack of expertise in appropriate foreign languages make it difficult for them to obtain detailed and credible information on terrorist groups, especially when compounded by the secretive nature of antiterrorist organizations (Baer 2003). This information, however, needs to be gathered in a manner that protects civil liberties while not giving terrorists an unfair advantage. States are also well advised to build a functional national database to track suspected terrorists and to allow criminal justice agencies to develop the appropriate infrastructure for it to be useful. At a lower level, the personal motivations of law enforcement officers are often neglected; clearly, those officers who are truly attentive and care about their jobs are more likely to catch the "bad guys." Research needs to be initiated to determine what particular qualities or skills these individuals have and then try to improve the skills of current employees or seek out new hires with these qualities.

Some have suggested that now is the time for Americans to take a serious look at how they are viewed throughout the world. The United States should critically examine its foreign policy and revise it to avoid continuously aggravating other states (Pillar 2001; Johnson 2004). America must respect the sovereign powers of other countries and cannot continue to support authoritarian, totalitarian, or fascist regimes when it is (temporarily) convenient to do so. By the same token, the United States must not force democracy on those states that do not wish to have it, or perhaps are not ready to embrace its benefits. Unilateral decisions (or pacts made with a handful of states), similar to the invasion of Iraq, only reinforce the perception of the arbitrariness of American foreign policy. Major international relations decisions should be made with the increased cooperation of the member states of the United Nations and with the cooperation of other important nongovernmental organizations. It also would help America's image abroad if it would admit to the world that it has been on the wrong side of many of the conflicts. Since the cold war, on many continents, the United States has supported many authoritarian or fascist regimes (Ross 2000a; 2000b). This has led to numerous public displays of anger and frustration with American foreign policy that the media has been all too happy to present on prime time television.

These sentiments extend to American and transnational corporations. Although the United States provides aid to many less-developed countries, American interests are often quick to exploit these settings (Johnson 2004). They are continuously perceived to be exploitive and insensitive. For example, it is no secret that citizens in less-developed countries, working in sweatshop-like conditions, make brand-name products (Gap, Banana Republic, Nike, etc.) for consumers in advanced industrialized countries (Klein 2000). These economic decisions have long-term unintended consequences that many corporate directors, shareholders, and consumers are willing to overlook in the interests of expediency and temporary financial gain.

Most Americans are proud of their culture and the nation's progress, and rightly so. This stance, however, leads many to display an attitude of superiority. When traveling abroad, Americans need to learn more about the countries and cultures they visit and behave more sensitively. The problem of the "ugly American" has not been lost on many observers of anti-Americanism. Americans also need to be more humble and accommodating. American tourists, for example, should not expect things to be like they are back home (i.e., the United States) when they visit other countries. Unless other states contribute (either financially or materially) to the war on terrorism, the United States will continue to feel marginalized. In an effort to deal with the increased

Exhibit Box 24
Suggestions for the future
Dissemination and/or acceptance of international standards on definitions and concepts
Fostering of more rigorous, empirically derived research
Use of more sophisticated methods to test hypotheses
Creation of an international center in a nonpartisan country
Acquisition and use of better intelligence, both human and electronic
Minimization of aggressive foreign policy
Adoption of a policy of inclusion rather than exclusion
Recognition that terrorism is here to stay

expenditures for terrorism, perhaps the government should institute a terrorism tax. This way, the public will have more direct understanding with respect to where its money is going, and will perhaps force politicians to do something about our aggressive international posture (see Exhibit Box 24).

Tolerating Terrorism

Finally, although terrorism has created a considerable amount of controversy and has cost governments and corporations substantial resources, perhaps there is a tolerable level of terrorism with which a society can live (Gal-Or 1991). For example, during the 1960s and 1970s, citizens in advanced industrialized countries were constantly reminded through the media, educators, and personal experience that street crime was increasing. This created a furor of public indignation and governmental responses that manifested in a "war on crime." While the rate of crime has increased and decreased in a cyclical fashion since those times, and the methods by which we gather crime data and how we interpret it have been debated, the crisis of *response* seems to have abated, or been replaced by "the war on terrorism." No one has seriously posed the question of whether or not there are tolerable levels of violence that we can live with (Gal-Or 1991). Terrorist attacks are disruptive to the normal functioning of the government's, businesses', and individuals' daily lives. However, policymakers and practitioners, as much as possible, need to avoid simplistic responses that can create a more dangerous environment or lead to needless expenditure of resources.

Hopefully, the methodology, analysis, and suggestions outlined in this book will allow us to minimize the occurrence of terrorism and prevent researchers, policymakers, and practitioners from going down blind alleys or targeting as terrorists those individuals and groups who engage in legitimate advocacy, protest, and dissent. Needless to say, we must recognize that, in some constituencies, there is absolutely nothing the United States or any other country can do. In this case, neither accommodation nor eradication of terrorist enclaves will entirely eliminate this most salient form of political violence and crime. About the best we can do, at the very least, in this scenario is use our power to be informed, to seek out reliable information, and to question that which seems confusing or based on faulty reasoning.

Questions, Chapter 11

PART ONE: MULTIPLE CHOICE

1. What are the two basic perspectives when commenting on the future?
   a. internal and external
   b. optimistic and pessimistic
   c. international and domestic
   d. historical and predictive
   e. none of the above

2. From which groups have individuals been arrested with biological materials or weapons in their possession?
   a. Animal Liberation Front
   b. Aryan Nations
   c. Jewish Defense League
   d. Ku Klux Klan
   e. Order of the Rising Sun

3. Who identified five reasons why terrorists may resort to WMD?
   a. Hoffman
   b. Ross
   c. Schmid
   d. Stern
   e. Sterling

4. What was the name of the commission established by the Pentagon in the late 1990s?
   a. Scenarios 2000
   b. Terrorism 2000
   c. Targeting 2000
   d. names were used interchangeably
   e. none of the above

5. What is cyberterrorism?
   a. terrorists placing cyanide in the water system
   b. a specialized antiterrorist force
   c. terrorists attacking computer networks
   d. terrorism using cyborgs
   e. none of the above

PART TWO: SHORT ANSWER

1. Has terrorism replaced war?

2. What does a tolerable level of terrorism mean?

3. What is the antiglobalist movement?

4. What are three domestic terrorist groups that might engage in terrorism in the future?

5. List three weapons of mass destruction.

PART THREE: ESSAY

1. Why do you think it has taken the United States so long to capture bin Laden?

2. List three methods that analysts have not used in determining the future course of terrorism.

3. What do you think the United States can do, realistically, to stop terrorism?

4. In the future, will terrorists resort to WMD? If so, which types will they use and how?

5. What emerging groups and issues do you think will threaten the United States and Western powers?

6. Some analysts and observers have suggested that, in the future, Americans will simply have to tolerate a certain amount of terrorism. Do you agree or disagree with this statement, and why?

APPENDIX A

Pedagogical Suggestions

Although the subject matter of political terrorism is generally exciting in itself, here are some quick suggestions designed to bring added life into a class on this topic.

Bring a news article that mentions terrorism for discussion, perhaps every other class session. Photocopy enough for the entire class to read.

Discuss new policies implemented in the wake of 9/11, including on what sort of research they were built.

Integrate current videos, either documentaries or fictionalized accounts of terrorism.

Invite guest speakers (e.g., a representative from the Department of Homeland Security, someone who works in antiterrorism preparedness for a local law enforcement agency, or someone in the private security realm) and/or go on some sort of field trip to a private security facility.

Notes

Notes to Chapter One

1. One could also include public policy, international relations, ethics, communication, and journalism.
2. This attack led to the death of 259 people who were on board and 11 on the ground.
3. In an interesting hybrid of state terrorism, members of government agencies (typically police or military) may attack terrorist suspects or group and then blame the attack on terrorist organizations (Jenkins 2003, chapter 5).
4. According to Johnson, "Analysts invented the terms 'international terrorism' to refer to terrorist actions carried out by individuals or groups controlled by a sovereign state (e.g., Cuba or Libya) and 'transnational terrorism' to refer to terrorist actions carried our by basically autonomous actors (e.g., the Baader-Meinhoff gang)" (1982, 162). Over the years, this distinction has been ignored.
5. This is not to say that Palestinian attacks against Jewish settlers did not occur before this time.
6. All further references to terrorism subsume oppositional and political components unless otherwise indicated. Schmid's consensus definition of terrorism (1983, 100), with some modifications (Ross and Gurr 1989), is used.
7. This section draws on Ross (1993b).

8. There is no generally recognized acronym for this organization.
9. My thanks to Mark Hamm, personal communication, June 10, 1992, for this formulation.

Notes to Chapter Two

1. A handful of terrorism analysts (e.g., Vetter and Perlstein 1991, 31) include the "Thugs," an Indian group, as a terrorist organization that operated during this time period. The political motivations of the Thugs, however, is highly questionable.
2. It is important to understand that, although the four territories of the United Kingdom—England, Wales, Scotland, and Northern Ireland—share the same laws and currency, they are deloved (have home rule). This basically means that they have some powers to manage their own affairs but the majority of power remains in the central government in London.
3. These include the United States, Canada, the United Kingdom, France, Germany, the Netherlands, Belgium, Spain, Italy, Israel, and Japan.
4. On the rise of religious-based terrorism see, for example, Juergensmeyer (2000).
5. http://news.bbc.co.uk/1/hi/world/middle_east/1005081.stm
6. http://news.bbc.co.uk/1/world/middle_east/978626.stm
7. This section builds on Ross (1991a).
8. http://db.mipt.org/rand_68_97.cfm
9. http://www.state.gov/s/ct/rls/pgf.rpt
10. In June 2004, it came to public attention that the data presented in the 2003 annual report had serious problems and had underreported the amount of terrorism that occurred. The U. S. Department of State took responsibility, but argued, however, that in the interests of getting the report to the printer in time, data collection efforts were suspended before the year's end.
11. www.mipt.org
12. Why is this the case? Israel, because of its seemingly nonstop conflict with the Palestinians, and the Americans, French, and British largely because of their transnational corporations.
13. An in-depth discussion of content analysis will be provided in the chapter which reviews the contribution of the media to terrorism.
14. http://www.standrews.ac.uk/intrel/research/cstpv/pages/database.html
15. There is some attempt to build a comprehensive cross-national database, but details of this effort are sketchy (LaFree 2002).

Notes to Chapter Three

1. This chapter is drawn from Ross (1999), which takes as its point of departure Gibbs's (1989) oft-cited article "The Conceptualization of Terrorism." The author contends that the Gibbs article is too preoccupied with definitional and conceptual issues.
2. A direct discussion of rational-choice explanations is avoided as it is included under psychological motivation theories.
3. Depending on the circumstances, any of these actors can be audiences.
4. This factor may consist of such subcomponents as age, gender, and ideological persuasion (e.g., anarchist/communist, nationalist/separatist, and right-wing) (Post 1986).
5. As we have discussed, there are several different types of oppositional terrorism (domestic, international, state-sponsored). Thus, even finer differentiations could be made with these different geographic and actor dimensions.
6. In this context there are both hard and soft targets. The former are well protected while the latter are rarely secured.
7. Political support in the wider community for terrorist acts and objectives may prevent terrorists from antagonizing previously neutral and disinterested groups and from alienating many of the people on behalf of who they claim to act.
8. Several countries have been blamed for supporting terrorist organizations, including the former Soviet Union, Cuba, and Libya. This is more commonly referred to as the "conspiracy theory of terrorism." Many problems have been raised about the inclusion of certain states as benefactors of terrorism (e.g., Herman 1982, 64–65; Schmid 1983, 210–18), in particular that the conclusions are based on circumstantial evidence or on faulty reasoning (Bonante 1979). Additionally, many people forget that the United States supported Cuban counterrevolutionary groups that engaged in terrorism in the United States. Actions taken by this group in the United States fall under state-sponsored terrorism, not domestic terrorism.
9. The mass media have long been cited as a cause of terrorism (see chapter 8). The mass media can be used as a propaganda tool to help terrorists gain publicity; advertise their grievances; exaggerate their importance; create favorable public opinion; glorify themselves; diffuse knowledge about methods, technologies, and success; provide models for imitation; and provide information to their agents, especially in assault cases, as to the positions of counterterrorist forces. An alternative theory suggests that access to the media may cause terrorist attacks (Schmid and de Graaf 1982).
10. A similar but narrower argument is presented in Laqueur (1977) and Crenshaw (1981).

11. Closely connected to the availability of weapons, explosives, and materials is the knowledge about how to use them. See, for example, the section in this chapter dealing with learning.

12. Analysts must take into account the difficulty of integrating theories with fundamentally different underlying logics.

13. Many of these traits are connected, in whole or in part, with symptoms identified in the *Diagnostic and Statistical Manual of Mental Disorders* of the American Psychiatric Association.

14. The source of that frustration, whether relative or absolute deprivation, is not as important as how it translates into to frustration aggression (Gurr 1970).

15. These hypotheses are laid out in a unidirectional fashion. Perhaps with empirical testing, there might be some bidirectionality in these interactions. In other words, feedback is probably present but we should be able to see clearer after more research has been done.

16. This process builds upon Sutherland's (1947) concept of differential association and is similar to the pattern with individuals joining and staying in religious cults (Seligman and Conway 1995).

17. This point builds upon Burgess and Akers (1968), who applied learning theory and behavior modification to Sutherland's concept of differential association.

18. Crenshaw (1990, 8–11) expresses the same point but does not label it by its psychological terminology.

19. This position is not unanimously held. Post (1990), for example, takes issue with this perspective. Natasha J. Cabrera, personal communication, suggests that it is not so much that terrorists are rational, but rather that the consequences (death, arrest, etc.) may have little or no value to them.

20. The two available databases (Russell and Miller 1983; Cooper 1977) primarily include demographic variables, and the more psychologically oriented processes are not sufficient enough to test any but a handful of these hypotheses.

Notes to Chapter Four

1. This chapter draws on Ross and Miller (1997).

2. The effects of terrorism have been covered under the literature dealing with counter- and antiterrorism and are subsumed by the conflict literature on consequences, implications, outcomes, reactions, and responses.

3. See the literature on symbolic interactionism for a more detailed explanation.

4. In many cases, the idea of terrorist "groups" or "organizations" is a mis-
nomer. Many terrorist campaigns are carried out by loose collections of
individuals with similar goals who act individually, but use the same
name in concert. Several useful typologies of terrorist groups and campaigns, but not their effects, can be found in Wilkinson (1974, 32); Merari
(1978, 331–46), Waugh (1982, 35–67), Schmid (1983), and Schmid and Jongman (1988, chapter 3).

5. For theories of proactive and reactive responses to low-intensity conflict,
see, for example, Kitson (1971) and Everlegh (1978).

6. In any political system, various factions in the political arena are measuring, evaluating, and assessing the performance of the official government.
In addition, external political "forces"—opponents, dissidents, expatri-
ates, enemy states, and others—observe and study the conduct of a government under crisis conditions.

7. Occasionally terrorist organizations will attack other terrorist groups.
Alternatively, Schmid (1992, 97) identifies five actors: the terrorists; the
victims/hostages, the public/audience, the government, and the media
(editors and journalists). Our conceptualization here includes the media
as part of the public.

8. The "major" actors also have overlapping relationships. According to
Herman and O'Sullivan (1989), the public sector consists of "government
agencies and officials who establish policy and provide opinions and
selected facts about official acts," and the private sector involves "think
tanks, research institutes, security firms that deal in risk analysis, personal
and property protection and training, and a body of terrorism experts"
(55). Many of the institutes, think tanks, and lobbying organizations are
funded by private foundations, individuals, and governments.

9. Further iterations of this conceptualization should include the reactions of
supporters and allies of terrorists.

10. It must be appreciated that "not all hostages develop this, nor if it occurs
are all its features necessarily present. However, it seems to occur with
sufficient frequency for it to be regarded as an aspect of the hostage situation" (Taylor 1988, 21).

11. The reactions for the family are not placed in model form because of the
similarity between their reactions and those of the victims.

12. This is closely related to the commodification of culture (the marketing of
products) with the understanding that this later process is usually attrib-
utable to the business community, while the former is simply adoption.

13. Fanon (1963, 251), among others, outlined that repeated exposure to extra-
normal violence creates mental disorders called "reactionary psychosis."

14. Depending on the context, the media can be owned by the government (as in the Canadian Broadcasting Corporation) or private corporations (as in CNN).

15. A discrepancy often exists between what corporations are advised to do (e.g., maintain a low profile; cultivate a benevolent image; follow practical security measures) (Mitchell 1984) and what they actually manage to do. For a sample of research on the business community, see, for example, Alexander and Kilmarx (1979).

16. Some insurance companies have responded with kidnap and ransom policies (Fairer-Smith 1986; Morphew 1986; van Aartick 1987).

17. Such variables include the political culture, the role of the media, the general public's psychological state (including its perceptions of the threat versus the government's portrayal of the threat), and public support for the state's legal system and/or country. On the international scene, important factors sort into legal problems, such as extradition and asylum procedures, moral or ethical influences that restrain the authorities, and political considerations, including support to liberation movements and alliances with target states.

18. Should authorities not respond to terrorists and their threats, then the general public as well as other audiences may interpret this (accurately or otherwise) as a sign of weakness (Wilkinson 1986, 6). Even a non-response is a response. It is a decision not to do anything. The non-response approach will enhance terrorists' perceptions that the government is in no position to face or cope with the existing situation, much less to change or improve various conditions within the system. Furthermore, it will improve the terrorists' image in other audiences, even in foreign states where the central government cannot act (Laqueur 1986, 98). A prolonged situation of inertia will ultimately increase the general public's fear and reinforce their belief, in unprecedented future situations, that authorities are unable to act (Aston 1986, 74).

19. These documents include the Tokyo *Convention on Offenses and Certain Other Acts Committed onboard Aircraft;* the Hague *Convention on the Suppression of Unlawful Acts against the Safety of Civil Aviation;* the New York *Convention on the Prevention and Punishment of Crimes against Internationally Protected Persons Including Diplomatic Agents;* and the Bonn Economic Summit *Declaration on International Terrorism.* (July 17, 1978).

20. Three agreements or treaties with a regional scope have been adopted in an effort to combat international terrorism. These include the *Convention to Prevent and Punish Acts of Terrorism Taking the Form of Crimes against Persons and Related Extortion that are of International Significance* (OAS

Convention, February 2, 1971, Washington, D.C.); the *European Convention on the Suppression of Terrorism* (October 25, 1978, Bonn): and the *Dublin Agreement* on the application of the European Convention of 1980. The three conventions are strikingly different in their scope and basic purpose (Murphy 1985).

Notes to Chapter Five

1. See also http://domino.un.org/unispal.nsf
2. Although the relocation of the PLO headquarters to Tunis would insulate them from Israeli attack, it also meant that the leadership became increasingly out of touch with what was happening "on the street" in Palestinian areas. This also paved the way for the creation of the Intifada, largely an autonomous outgrowth.
3. See http://news.bbc.co.uk/1/hi/world/middle_east/978626.stm
4. See http://news.bbc.co.uk/1/hi/world/americas/1746777.stm
5. http://en.wikipedia.org/wiki/FARC
6. http://en.wikipedia.org/wiki/FARC
7. http://www.ict.org.il/inter_ter/org.cfm;   http://www.farcep.org/pagina_ingles
8. Frankel, G. 2005. IRA says it will abandon violence. *Washington Post*, Friday 29, 2005, pp. A1, A18.
9. http://www.henningcenterberkeley.edu/gateway/colombia.html

Notes to Chapter Six

1. In 1989, Pierce wrote *Hunter,* a follow-up book with a blueprint for attacking African Americans.
2. For more insight into this incident, see the movie *Talk Radio*. Produced by controversial filmmaker Oliver Stone and featuring a performance by Eric Bogosian, *Talk Radio* is loosely based on the talk shows of now-deceased KOA Denver radio host Alan Berg. During the early 1980s, Berg used to demean, belittle, and incite his audience, among whom were white supremacists and neo-Nazis. They eventually gunned him down in front of his home.
3. http://www.house.gov/reform/oversight/faln.htm
4. http://www.adl.org/extremism/jdl_chron.asp
5. For an alterative interpretation, see, for example, Jones and Israel (2001).

Notes to Chapter Seven

1. On August 27, 1998, the United States responded to the attack on the *USS Cole* by launching "80 Tomahawk cruise missiles from five warships in the Arabian Sea and two in the Red Sea" (Reeve 1999, 1), one to a pharmaceutical plant in Sudan, and another to a location in Afghanistan.
2. Council on Foreign Relations. Terrorism: Questions and Answers. Causes of 9/11: U.S. troops in Saudi Arabia.
   http://cfrterrorism.org/causes/saudiarabia.html
   http://cfrterrorism.org/causes/html
3. http://cfrterrorism.org/causes/saudiarabia.html
4. For further analysis of this interpretation, see, for example, Michael Moore's movie *Fahrenheit 9/11* (2004).

Notes to Chapter Eight

1. Many authors suggest that the media does not encourage terrorism (Picard 1986). For a competent analysis of the role of the media in terrorist campaigns, see Kelly and Mitchell (1981).
2. For a further discussion of this problem in connection with terrorism, see, for example, Schmid (1992).

Notes to Chapter Nine

1. This seems to be a regular feature of the current Palestinian-Israeli conflict.

Notes to Chapter Ten

1. It also did not help to have a handful of yet-unsolved anthrax threats, nor a youth who went throughout the American west leaving pipe bombs in rural mailboxes.
2. See the literature on symbolic interactionism for a more detailed explanation.
3. To the best of my knowledge, no similar studies were done of the other sites of attack: rural Pennsylvania and Washington, D.C. (the Pentagon is technically in Arlington, Virginia).
4. Josh White, 18 more detainees leave Guantanamo, *Washington Post*, 20 April, 2005.

5. Special thanks to David Charters for this observation (e-mail correspondence, March 10, 2004).
6. Report: Some INS targets disappeared, by Mary Beth Sheridan, *Washington Post*, 7 November 2001.
7. Ibid.
8. House committee approves anti-terrorism measure, *USA Today*, 4 October 2001.
9. See, for example, http://www.snopes.com/rumors
10. Personal correspondence with Jose Yepez, via letter March 2004.

Notes to Chapter Eleven

1. It has been suggested that the possibility of nuclear attack is present because of the lack of safeguards from former Soviet arsenals and nuclear power plants, poor economy in the states that made up the former Soviet Union, and the presence of organized crime, which can garner a considerable amount of money if individuals smuggle enriched plutonium (Reeve 1999, 257–58).
2. According to John C. Gannon, chairman of the CIA's National Intelligence Council, the types of biological weapons are proliferating. He says that "agents of increasing lethality are being developed that have the potential to cause massive casualties. . . . Rapid advances in biotechnology will yield new toxins or live agents, such as exotic animal viruses, that will require new detection methods and vaccines as well as other preventative measures. The CIA is also extremely concerned, Gannon admits, "that some states might acquire more advanced and effective CW agents, such as Russia's fourth-generation 'Novichok' against, which are more persistent and deadly" (Reeve 1999, 260–61).
3. As of June 24, 2005 there have been 1,918 fatalities of military personnel, including 1,730 Americans, 89 from the United Kingdom, and 99 from other countries (http://icasualties.or/oif). These figures do not include the numerous foreign civilian contractors who have been killed or injured, nor the numerous Iraqi soldiers and civilians, and foreign insurgents who have been killed or injured. Needless to say, these last numbers are considerably higher. .
4. http://news.bbc.co.uk/go/pr/fr/-/2/hi/middle_east/298457.stm

Bibliography

Adams, J. 1986. *The financing of terrorism.* New York: Simon & Schuster.

Aho, J. 1990. *The politics of righteousness: Idaho Christian patriotism.* Seattle: University of Washington Press.

Alexander, Y. 1973. *The role of communications in the Middle East conflict: Ideological and religious aspects.* New York: Praeger.

———. 1977. Communication aspects of international terrorism. *International Problems* 16: 55–60.

Alexander, Y. and R. Kilmarx, eds. 1979. *Political terrorism and business: The threat and response.* New York: Praeger.

Alford, R. H. 1967. Class voting in the Anglo-American political systems. In *Party systems and voter alignments,* ed. S. Rokkan and S. M. Lipset, 67–94. New York: Free Press.

Allison, G. 2004. *Nuclear terrorism: The ultimate preventable catastrophe.* New York: Times Books.

Allison, G. T., O. R. Cote, Jr., R. A. Falkenrath, and S. E. Miller. 1996. *Avoiding nuclear anarchy: Containing the threat of loose Russian nuclear weapons and fissile material.* Belfer Center for Science and International Affairs, John F. Kennedy School of Government, Harvard University.

Alon, H. 1987. Can terrorism be deterred? Some thoughts and doubts. In *Contemporary trends in world terrorism,* ed. A. Kurtz, 125–31. New York: Praeger.

American Psychiatric Association. 1995. *Diagnostic and statistical manual of mental disorders.* 4th ed. Washington, DC: American Psychiatric Association.

Amit, M. 1989. Diminishing the threat: Intelligence and the war against terrorism. *Israel Defense Forces Journal:* 8–10.

Anderson, T. A. 1993. *Dens of lions: Memoirs of seven years.* New York: Crown Publishers.

Arno, A. 1984. Communication, conflict, and storylines: The news media as actors in a cultural context. In *The news media in national and international conflict,* ed. A. Arno and W. Dissanayake, 1–20. Boulder, CO: Westview Press.

Arquilla, J. and D. Ronfeldt, eds. 2001. *Networks and netwars: The future of terror, crime and militancy.* Santa Monica, CA: RAND Corporation.

Aston, C. C. 1986. Political hostage-taking in Western Europe. In *Contemporary terrorism,* ed. W. Gutteridge, 57–83. New York: Facts on File Publication.

Atkinson, S. E., T. Sandler, and J. Tschirhart. 1987. Terrorism in a bargaining framework. *Journal of Law and Economics* 30: 1–21.

Avrich, P. 1986. *The haymarket tragedy.* Princeton, NJ: Princeton University Press.

Ayers, B. 2003. *Fugitive days.* New York: Penguin.

Babbie, E. R. 2001. *The basics of social research.* 2nd ed. Belmont, CA: Wadsworth.

Baer, R. 2003. *See no evil: The true story of a ground soldier in the CIA's fight against terrorism.* New York: Three Rivers Press.

Bandura, A. 1973. *Aggression: A social learning analysis.* Englewood Cliffs, NJ: Prentice Hall.

Barak, G., ed. 1991. *Crimes by the capitalist state.* Albany: State University of New York Press.

Barber, B. R. 1996. *Jihad vs. McWorld.* New York: Ballantine Books.

Beam, L. 1992. Leaderless resistance. *Seditionist* 12 (February 1992). http://www.louisbeam.com

Becker, J. 1978. *Hitler's children: The story of the Baader-Meinhof gang.* New York: Panther / Granada Books.

Bell, J. B. 1977. Trends in terror: The analysis of political violence. *World Politics* 29, no. 3: 447–81.

———. 1978. *A time of terror: How democratic societies respond to revolutionary violence.* New York: Basic Books.

———. 1997. *The secret army: The IRA.* 3rd rev. ed. New Brunswick, NJ: Transaction Publishers.

Bell, J. B. and T. R. Gurr. 1979. Terrorism and revolution in America. In *Violence in America,* ed. H. D. Graham and T. R. Gurr, 329–47. Newbury Park, CA: Sage Publications.

Berger, A. A., ed. 1979. *Television as an instrument of terror: Essays on media, popular culture and everyday life.* New Brunswick, NJ: Transaction Publishers.

Best, J., ed. 1989. *Images of issues: Typifying contemporary social problems.* New York: Aldine de Gruyter.

———. 1999. *Random violence: How we talk about new crimes and new victims.* Los Angeles: University of California Press.

Bill, J. A. and R. L. Hardgrave. 1981. *Comparative politics: The quest for theory.* Lanham, MD: University Press of America.

Blaise, C. and B. Mukherjee. 1987. *The sorrow and the terror.* Toronto: Penguin Canada.

Bodansky, Y. 1993. *Target America: Terrorism in the U.S. today.* New York: SPI Books.

———. 2001. *Bin Laden: The man who declared war on America.* Roseville, CA: Prima Publishing.

Bonante, L. 1979. Some unanticipated consequences of terrorism. *Journal of Peace Research* 16: 196–211.

Bowman, S. 1994. *When the eagle screams: America's vulnerability to terrorism.* New York: Birch Lane.

Breton, R. 1973. The socio-political dynamics of the October events. In *Québéc society and politics: Views from the inside,* ed. D. C. Thomson, 213–38. Toronto: McClelland and Stewart.

Bruce, Steve. 1993. Fundamentalism, ethnicity, and enclave. In *Fundamentalisms and the state,* ed. M. E. Marty and R. S. Appleby, 50–67. Chicago: University of Chicago Press.

———. 1995. Paramilitaries, peace, and politics: Ulster loyalists and the 1994 truce. *Studies in Conflict and Terrorism* 18: 187–202.

Buck, George. 2002. *Preparing for terrorism: An emergency services guide.* Albany, NY: Delmar Publishers.

Buckley, M. and R. Fawn, eds. 2003. *Global responses to terrorism: 9/11 Afghanistan and beyond.* New York: Routledge.

Bueno de Mesquita, E. 2005a. Conciliation, counter-terrorism, and patterns of terrorist violence. *International Organization* 59:145–76.

———. 2005b. The quality of terror in *American Journal of Political Science.* 49(3): 515–530.

Burgess, R. L. and R. L. Akers. 1968. Reinforcement theory of criminal behavior. *Social Problems* 14: 128–47.

Burke, J. 2003. *Al Qaeda: Casting a shadow of terror.* London: I. B. Tauris.

Canada. 1987. The report of the senate committee on terrorism and public safety. Special Committee of the Senate on Terrorism and Public Safety. Ottawa: Ministry of Supply and Services.

Carlton, D. 1979. The future of political substate violence. In *Terrorism: Theory and practice,* ed. Y. Alexander et al., 201–30. Boulder, CO: Westview Press.

Cauley, J. and E. Im. 1988. Intervention policy analysis of skyjackings and other terrorist incidents. *American Economic Review* 78, no. 2: 27–31.

Celmmer, M. 1987. *Terrorism, U.S. Strategy and Reagan Politics.* New York: Greenwood Press.

Chace, J. 1984. *Endless war: How we got involved in Central America—and what can be done.* New York: Vintage Books.

Chaliand, G. 1983. *Guerilla strategies: A historical anthology from the Long March to Afghanistan.* Berkeley: University of California Press.

Chermack, S. M., F. Y. Bailey, and M. Brown, eds. 2003. *Media representations of September 11.* Westport, CT: Praeger.

Chomsky, N. 1983. *The fateful triangle: The United States, Israel, and the Palestinians.* Boston: South End Press.

———. 2001. *9–11.* New York: Seven Stories Press.

Churchill, W. and J. Vander Wall. 1988. *Agents of repression: The FBI's secret war against the Black Panther Party and the American Indian movement.* Boston: South End Press.

Clark, R. P. 1983. Patterns in the lives of ETA members. *Terrorism: An International Journal* 6: 423–54.

Clarke, R. 2004. *Against all enemies.* New York: Free Press.

Clawson, P. 1989. Coping with Terrorism in the United States. *Orbis* Summer: 341–56.

Cline, R. S. and Y. Alexander. 1984. *Terrorism: The Soviet connection.* New York: Crane Russak.

Clutterbuck, R. 1983. *The media and political violence.* 2nd ed. London: Macmillan.

———, ed. 1986. *The future of political violence.* Oxford: Palgrave Macmillan Press.

Cohen, S. and D. Cohen 2001. *Pan Am 103: The bombing, the betrayals, the bereaved family's search for justice.* New York: Signet Books.

Cole, D. 2003. *Enemy aliens.* New York: New Press.

Coleman, W. D. 1984. *The independence movement in Québéc 1945–1980.* Toronto: University of Toronto Press.

Coll, S. 2004. *Ghost wars: The secret history of the CIA, Afghanistan, and Bin Laden, from the Soviet invasion to September 10, 2001.* New York: Penguin.

Conway, F. and J. Sigelman. 1995. *Snapping: America's Epidemic of Sudden Personality Change.* 2nd ed. New York: Stillpoint Press.

Cooley, J. 2002. *Unholy wars: Afghanistan, America and international terrorism.* New York: Pluto Press.

Coombs, C. C. 1996. *Terrorism in the twenty-first century.* London: Prentice Hall.

Cooper, H. H. A. 1977. What is a terrorist: A psychological perspective. *Legal Medical Quarterly* 1: 16–32.

Cordes, B. 1987. When terrorists do the talking: A look at their literature. *Journal of Strategic Studies* 10, no. 4: 150–71.

Corrado, R. R. 1981. A critique of the mental disorder perspective of political terrorism. *International Journal of Law and Psychiatry* 4: 1–17.

———. 1983. Ethnic and ideological terrorism in Western Europe. In Stohl 1983, 255–326.

Crelinsten, R. D. 1985. Limits to criminal justice in the control of insurgent political violence: A case study of the October Crisis of 1970. PhD diss., University of Montreal.

Crenshaw, M. 1981. The causes of terrorism. *Comparative Politics* 13, no. 4: 379–99.

———. 1985. An organizational approach to the analysis of political terrorism. *Orbis* 4: 465–89.

———. 1986. The psychology of political terrorism. In *The political psychology of contemporary problems and issues,* ed. M. G. Herman, 379–413. San Francisco: Jossey-Bass.

———. 1990. The logic of terrorism: Terrorist behavior as a product of strategic choice. In Reich 1990b, 7–24.

———. 1991. How terrorism declines. *Terrorism and Political Violence* 3, no. 1: 69–87.

———, ed. 1994. *Terrorism in context.* University Park: Pennsylvania State University Press.

Dartnell, M. Y. 2001. *Action Directe: Ultra-left terrorism in France, 1979–1987.* London: Frank Cass.

De Vault, C., with W. Johnson. 1982. *The informer: Confessions of an ex-terrorist* Scarborough, Ontario: Fleet.

Della Porta, D. 1992. Institutional response to terrorism: The Italian case. *Terrorism and Political Violence* 4: 151–70.

Delli Carpini, M. X. 1987. Television and terrorism: Patterns of presentation and occurrence, 1969 to 1980. *Western Political Quarterly* 40, no. 1: 45–64.

Denmark, R. A. and M. B. Welfling. 1983. Terrorism in sub-Sahara Africa. In Stohl 1983, 327–76.

Denzin, N. K. 1978. *The research act: A theoretical introduction to sociological methods.* New York: McGraw-Hill.

Dinges, J. and S. Landau. 1980. *Assassination on embassy row.* New York: Pantheon.

Dingley, J. 1999. Peace processes and Northern Ireland: Squaring circles. *Terrorism and Political Violence* 11, no. 3: 32–52.

———. 2001. The bombing of Omagh, 15 August 1998: The bombers, their tactics, strategy, and purpose behind the incident. *Studies in Conflict and Terrorism* 24, no. 6: 451–65.

Dobson, C. 1974. *Black September.* New York: Macmillan.

———. 1977. *The Carlos complex.* New York: Macmillan.

Dollard, J., L. W. Doob, N. E. Miller, O. H. Mowrer, and R. R. Sears. 1939. *Frustration and aggression.* New Haven, CT: Yale University Press.

Dowling, R. E. 1986. Terrorism and the media: A rhetorical genre. *Journal of Communication* 36: 12–24.

Dudziak, M. L., ed. 2003. *September 11 in history: A watershed moment?* Durham, NC: Duke University Press.

Duncan, R., B. Jancar-Webster, and B. Switky. 2002. *World politics in the 21st century.* New York: Longman.

Dyer, J. 1997. *Harvest of rage: Why Oklahoma City is only the beginning.* New York: Westview Press.

Ehrenfeld, R. 1992. *Narco-terrorism.* New York: Basic Books.

Elliot, P., G. Murdock, and P. Schlesinger. 1983. Terrorism and the state: A case study of the discourses of television. *Media, Culture and Society* 5: 155–77.

Emerson, S. 2002. *American jihad.* New York: Free Press.

Emerson, S. and B. Duffy. 1990. *The fall of Pan Am 103: Inside the Lockerbie investigation.* New York: Putnam.

Enders, W. and T. Sandler. 1993. The effectiveness of anti-terrorism policies: A VAR-intervention analysis. *American Political Science Review* 87, No, 4: 829–844.

Engene, J. O. and K. H. W. Skjolberg. 2002. Data on intrastate terrorism: The TWEED project. Paper presented at ISA Conference, March, New Orleans.

Epstein, E. C. 1977. The uses of "terrorism": A study in media bias. *Stanford Journal of International Studies* 12: 67–78.

Eubank, W. L. and L. Weinberg. 1994. Does democracy encourage terrorism? *Terrorism and Political Violence* 6: 417–35.

Evans, E. 1979. *Calling a truce to terror.* Westport, CT: Greenwood Press.

Everlegh, R. 1978. *Peace-keeping in a democratic society.* London: Churst.

Fairer-Smith, J. 1986. Forethought can stop a crisis from turning into a disaster. *ICC Business World* (July 1986): 24–26.

Fanon, F. 1963. *Wretched of the earth.* New York: Grove Press.

Farrell, W. 1982. *The U.S. government response to terrorism.* Boulder, CO: Westview Press.

Farrell, W. R. 1990. *Blood and rage: The story of the Japanese Red Army.* Lexington, MA: Lexington Books.

Fawn, R. 2003. From Ground Zero to the war in Afghanistan. In Buckley and Fawn 2003, 11–24.

Fernandez, R. 1987. *Los macheteros: The Wells Fargo robbery and the violent struggle for Puerto Rican independence.* New York: Prentice Hall.

Ferracuti, F. 1990. Ideology and repentance: Terrorism in Italy. In Reich 1990b, 59–64.

Fishman, M. 1980. *Manufacturing the news*. Austin: University of Texas Press.

Flemming, P. A., M. Stohl, and A. Schmid. 1988. The theoretical utility of typologies of terrorism: Lessons and opportunities. In Stohl 1998, 153–71.

Flynn, E. 1978. Political prisoners and terrorists in American correctional institutions. In *Terrorism and Criminal Justice*, R. D. Crelinsten, D. Laberge-Altmejd, and D. Szabo ed. 87–92. Toronto: Lexington Books.

Fournier, L. 1984. *FLQ: The anatomy of an underground movement*. Toronto: NC Press.

Fowler, W. 1981. Terrorism data bases: A comparison of missions, methods, and systems. Santa Monica, CA: RAND Corporation. N-1503-RC. RAND Report.

Friedland, A. and A. Merari. 1985. The psychological impact of terrorism: A double-edged sword. *Political Psychology* 6: 591–604.

Friedland, N. 1992. Becoming a terrorist: Social and individual antecedents. In Howard 1992, 81–93.

Friedlander. R. A. 1981. *Terrorism and the media: A contemporary assessment*. Gaithersburg, MD: International Association of Chiefs of Police.

Fuller, L. K. 1988. Terrorism as treated by *The Christian Science Monitor*, 1977–1987. *Political Communication and Persuasion* 5: 121–37.

Gal-Or, N. 1985. *International cooperation to suppress terrorism*. New York: St. Martin's Press.

———. 1991. *Tolerating terrorism in the West: An international survey*. New York: Routledge.

Gibbs, J. P. 1989. Conceptualization of terrorism. *American Sociological Review* 54: 329–40.

Gladwell, M. 2002. *The tipping point*. New York: Back Bay Books.

Glantz, J. and E. Lipton. 2003. *City in the sky: The rise and fall of the World Trade Center*. New York: Times Books.

Goffman, E. 1963. *Stigma*. Englewood Cliffs, NJ: Prentice Hall.

Goldstein, J. S. 1996. *International relations*. 2nd ed. New York: Addison-Wesley.

Grabosky, P. N. 1979. The urban context of political terrorism. In Stohl 1979, 51–76.

Graetz, B. and I. McAllister. 1987. Popular evaluations of party leaders in Anglo-American democracies. In *Political elites in Anglo-American democracies*, ed. H. D. Clarke and M. M. Czudnowski, 44–64. Dekalb: Northern Illinois University Press.

Green, J. 2003. The Myth of Cyberterrorism. *Washington Monthly* November (http://washingtonmonthly.com/features.2001/0211.green.html)

Griffin, M. 2003. *Reaping the whirlwind: Afghanistan, al Qa'ida and the Holy War.* London: Pluto Press.

Gross, F. 1972. *Violence in politics: Terror and political assassination in Eastern Europe and Russia.* The Hague: Mouton.

Gunaratna, R. 2002. *Inside al Qaeda: Global network of terror.* New York: Columbia University Press.

Gunter, M. 1986. *Pursuing a just cause for their people.* Greenwood, CT: Greenwood Publishing.

Gurr, T. R. 1966. *Cross-national studies of civil violence.* Washington, DC: American University, Center for Research in Social Systems.

———. 1970. *Why men rebel.* Princeton, NJ: Princeton University Press.

———. 1972. *Polimetrics: An introduction to quantitative macropolitics.* Englewood Cliffs, NJ: Prentice Hall.

———. 1979. Some characteristics of political terrorism in the 1960s. In Stohl 1979, 119–43.

———. 1988b. Empirical research on political terrorism: The state of the art and how it might be improved. In *Current perspectives on international terrorism,* ed. R. O. Slater and M. Stohl, 115–54. London: Macmillan.

———1989. Political terrorism: Historical antecedents and contemporary trends. In *Violence in America,* 2, T. Robert, ed., 201–30. Newbury Park, CA: Sage Publications.

———. 1990. Terrorism in democracies: Its social and political bases. In Reich 1990b, 86–102.

Gutmann, D. 1979. Killers and consumers: The terrorist and his audience. *Social Research* 46: 516–26.

Hacker, F. J. 1976. *Crusaders, criminals, crazies: Terror and terrorism in our time.* New York: W. W. Norton.

Hagy. J. W. 1969. Québéc separatists: The first twelve years. *Queen's Quarterly* 76: 229–38.

Hamilton, L. C. 1978. Ecology of terrorism: A historical and statistical study. PhD diss., University of Colorado.

Hamm, M. S. 1993. *Skinheads.* Greenwood, CT: Praeger.

———. 1994. *Hate crime: International perspectives on causes and control.* Cincinnati, OH: Academy of Criminal Justice Sciences/ Anderson Publishing Co.

———. 1997. *Apocalypse at Waco: Ruby Ridge and Waco revenged.* Boston: Northeastern University Press.

Handler, J. 1990. Socioeconomic profile of an American terrorist: 1960s and 1970s. *Terrorism: An International Journal* 13: 195–213.

Hansen, A. 2002. *Direct action: Memoirs of an urban guerrilla.* Vancouver: Between the Lines.

Harris, J. W. 1987. Domestic terrorism in the 1980s. *FBI Law Enforcement Bulletin* 56: 5–13.

Hart, A. 1984. *Arafat: Terrorist or peacemaker?* London: Sidgwick and Jackson.

Herman, E. S. 1982. *The real terror network.* Boston: South End Press.

Herman, E. S. and G. O'Sullivan. 1989. *The terrorism industry.* New York: Pantheon Books.

Hersh, S. 2004. *Chain of command: The road from 9/11 to Abu Ghraib.* New York: Harper Collins.

Hewitt, C. 1984. *The effectiveness of anti-terrorist policies.* Lanham, MD: University Press of America.

———. 1990. Terrorism and public opinion. *Terrorism and Political Violence* 2 (Summer): 145–70.

———. 2000. The political context of terrorists in America. *Terrorism and Political Violence* 12, nos. 3 & 4: 338–39.

Hippchen, L. J. and Y. S. Yim. 1982. *Terrorism, international crime, and arms control.* Springfield, IL: Charles C. Thomas.

Hocking, J. J. 1988. Counter-terrorism as counterinsurgency: The British experience. *Social Justice* 15, no. 1: 83–97.

Hoffman, B. 1987. Terrorism in the United States in 1985. In *Contemporary Research on Terrorism*, P. Wilkinson and A. M. Stewart, ed., 230–40. Aberdeen, UK: Aberdeen University Press.

———. 1998. *Inside terrorism.* New York: Columbia University Press.

Hoffman, B. and D. Claridge. 1998. The RAND–St. Andrews chronology of international terrorism and noteworthy domestic incidents. 1996. *Terrorism and Political Violence* 10, no. 2 (Summer): 135–80.

Holsti, O. R. 1969. *Content analysis for the social sciences and humanities.* Reading, MA: Addison-Wesley.

Holsti, O. R., R. A. Brody, and R. C. North. 1964. Measuring affect and action in international reaction models: Empirical materials from the 1962 Cuban Crisis. *Journal of Peace Research* 1: 170–89.

Homer, F. D. 1983. Terror in the United States: Three perspectives. In Stohl 1983.

Howard, L., ed. 1992. *Terrorism: Roots, impacts, responses.* New York: Praeger.

Hudson, R. A. 1999. The sociology and psychology of terrorism: Who becomes a terrorist and why? A report prepared under an Interagency Agreement by the Federal Research Division, Library of Congress. Washington, DC.

Hughes, M. 1990. Terror and negotiation. *Terrorism and Political Violence* 2, no. 1: 72–82.

Huntington, S. P. 1968. *Political order in changing societies.* New Haven, CT: Yale University Press.

————. 1998. *The clash of civilizations and the remaking of world order.* New York: Touchstone Books.

Im, E., J. Cauley, and T. Sandler. 1987. Cycles and substitutions in terrorist activities: A spectral approach. *Kyklos* 40: 238–55.

Ivianski, Z. 1985. The blow at the center: The concept and its history. In On *Terrorism and combating terrorism,* ed. A. Merari, 53–62. Frederick, MD: University Publications of America.

Iyad, A. with E. Rouleau. 1981. *My home, my land.* New York: Times Books.

Jager, H., G. Schmidtchen, and L. Süllwold, eds. 1981. *Analysen zum Terrorismus,* vol. 2. Oplanden: Westdeutscher Verlag.

Jenkins, B. 1974. *International terrorism: A new mode of conflict.* Santa Monica, CA: RAND Corporation. RAND Report.

————. 1979. The potential for nuclear terrorism. In *Studies in Nuclear Terrorism,* M. H. Greenberg and A. R. Norton, eds. Boston: G. K. Hall.

————. 1981. The psychological implications of media-covered terrorism. RAND Paper Series.

————, dir. 1982. Terrorism and beyond: An international conference on terrorism and low-level conflict. Santa Monica, CA: RAND Corporation Publication R-2716-DOE/DOS/DOS/R.S. Dec.

————. 1987. The future course of international terrorism. *Futurist* (July–August): 8–13.

————. 1992. Terrorism: A contemporary problem with age-old dilemmas. In Howard 1992, 13–27.

Jenkins, P. 1998. *Moral panic.* New Haven, CT: Yale University Press.

————. 2003. *Images of terror: What we can and can't know about terrorism.* Hawthorne, NY: Aldine de Gruyter.

Johnpoll, B. K. 1976. Perspectives on political terrorism in the United States. In *International terrorism, national, regional, and global perspectives,* ed. Y. Alexander, 30–45. New York: Praeger.

————. 1977. Terrorism and the mass media in the United States. In *Terrorism: Interdisciplinary perspectives,* ed. Y. Alexander and S. M. Finger, 157 –165 New York: John Jay Press.

Johnson, C. 1982. *Revolutionary change.* Stanford, CA: Stanford University Press.

————. 2004. *Blowback: The costs and consequences of American empire.* 2nd ed. New York: Henry Holt / Owl Books.

Jones, S. and P. Israel. 1998. *Others unknown.* New York: Basic Books.

Jones, J. and A. Miller. 1979. The media and terrorist activity: Resolving the First Amendment dilemma. *Ohio Northern University Law Review* 6: 70–81.

Joyner, N. 1974. *Aerial hijacking as an international crime.* Dobbs Ferry, NY: Ocean Public.

Juergensmeyer, M. 2000. *Terror in the mind of God.* Berkeley: University of California Press.

Kaplan, A. 1978. The psychodynamics of terrorism. *Terrorism: An International Journal* 1: 237–54.

Karber, P.A. 1971. Urban terrorism: Baselinedata and conceptual framework. *Social Science Quarterly* 52: 527–28.

Kehler, C. R., G. Harvey, and R. Hall. 1982. Perspectives on media control in terrorist-related incidents. *Canadian Police Journal* 6: 226–43.

Kellen, K. 1990. Ideology and rebellion: Terrorism in West Germany. In Reich 1990b, 43–54.

Kelly, M. J. and T. H. Mitchell. 1981. Transnational terrorism and the Western elite press. *Political Communication and Persuasion* 1, no. 3: 269–96.

Kersten, G. E. et al. 1987. Rule-based system to support negotiations. *Proceedings of the 31st International Conference on the Society of System Science,* Budapest.

Killyane, R. 1990. Target Medellin. *Soldier of Fortune* (June).

Kitson, F. 1971. *Low intensity operations: Subversion, insurgency, peace-keeping.* London: Farber.

Klare, M. T. 1996. *Rogue states and nuclear outlaws.* New York: Hill and Wang.

Klein, N. 2000. *No logo: Taking aim at the brand bullies.* Toronto: Vintage Canada.

Kramer, K. C. and J. L. King. 1986. Computer-based systems for cooperative work and group decision-making: Status of use and problems in development. *Proceedings of the Conference on Computer Supported Cooperative Work,* Austin, TX.

Krippendorf, K. 1981. *Content analysis: An introduction to its methodology.* Beverly Hills, CA: Sage Publications.

LaFree, G. 2002. Conceptual and methodological challenges to the criminological study of terrorism. Paper presented at the annual meeting of the American Society of Criminology, Chicago, November 14.

Langguth, A. J. 1978. *Hidden terrors.* New York: Pantheon.

Laplan, H. E. and T. Sandler. 1988. To bargain or not to bargain: That is the question. *American Economic Review* 78: 16–21.

Laqueur, W. 1977. *Terrorism.* Boston: Little, Brown.

———. 1986. Reflections on terrorism. *Foreign Affairs* 65, no. 1 (Fall): 86–100.

———. 2003. *No end to war: Terrorism in the twenty-first century.* New York: Continuum.

Lasswell, H. 1950. *National security and individual.* New York: McGraw-Hill.

———. 1962. The garrison hypothesis today. In *Changing patterns of military politics,* ed. S. P. Huntington, 51–70. New York: Free Press of Glencoe.

Laurendau, M. 1974. *Les Québécois violents.* Québéc: Les Editions Boreal Express.

Levin, A. and B. Morrison. 2001. Security plan proposed years ago. *USA Today,* October 5. A02.

Lichbach, M. I. 1987. "Deterrence or escalation": The puzzle of aggregate studies of repression and dissent. *Journal of Conflict Resolution* 31, no. 2: 266–97.

Lijphart, A. 1971. Comparative politics and the comparative model. *American Political Science Review* 65, no. 3 (September): 682–93.

———. 1975. The comparable-cases strategy in comparative research. *Comparative Political Studies* 8, no. 2 (July): 158–75.

Lillich, R. B. 1982. *Transnational terrorism: Conventions and commentary.* Washington, DC: Michie Company.

Livingstone, N. C. 1990. *The cult of counter-terrorism.* Lexington, MA: Lexington Books.

Livingstone, N. C. and T. E. Arnold, eds. 1986. *Fighting back: Winning the war against terrorism.* Toronto: Lexington Books.

Livingstone, N. C. and D. Halevy. 1990. *Inside the PLO.* New York: Quill / William Morrow.

Loftus, E. F. 1996. *Eyewitness testimony.* Boston: Harvard University Press.

Long, D. E. 1990. *The anatomy of terrorism.* New York: Free Press.

Loomis, D. 1984. *Not much glory.* Montreal: Deanu.

Mannheim, J. and R. C. Rich. 1986. *Empirical political analysis.* New York: Longman.

Marchetti, V. and J. D. Marks. 1974. *The CIA and the cult of intelligence.* New York: Laurel.

Marighela, C. 1971. Handbook (mini-manual) of urban guerrilla warfare. In *For the liberation of Brazil.* London: Penguin.

Martin, G. 2003. *Understanding terrorism: Challenges, perspectives and issues.* Thousand Oaks, CA: Sage Publications.

Martin, L. J. 1985. The media's role in international terrorism. *Terrorism: An International Journal* 8: 127–46.

Marx, G. 1990. *Undercover.* Berkeley: University of California Press.

Matwin, S. et al. 1987. Logic-based tools for negotiation support. *Proceedings of the 1987 Symposium on Logic Programming,* San Francisco, California.

Mazur, A. 1983. Bomb threats against American nuclear energy facilities. *Journal of Political and Military Sociology,* 11, no. 1: 109–121.

Melman, Y. 1986. *The master terrorist.* New York: Avon.

Merari, A. 1978. A classification of terrorist groups. *Terrorism: An International Journal* 1, nos. 3–4: 331–46.

Merton, R. K. 1938. Social structure and anomie. *American Sociological Review* 2: 672–82.

Michel, L. and D. Herbeck. 2001. *American terrorist.* New York: Harper Collins.

Mickolus, E. 1981. Combating international terrorism: A quantitative analysis. PhD diss., Yale University.

Midgley, S. and V. Rice, eds. 1984. *Terrorism and the media in the 1980s.* Washington, DC: Media Institute.

Midlarsky, M. I., M. Crenshaw, and F. Yoshida. 1980. Why violence spreads: The contagion of international terrorism. *International Studies Quarterly* 24: 262–98.

Miller, A., ed. 1982. *Terrorism, the media, and the law.* Dobbs Ferry, NY: Transnational.

Miller, J., S. Engelberg, and W. Broad. 2001. *Germs: Biological weapons and America's secret war.* New York: Simon & Schuster.

Miller, R. 1986. Acts of international terrorism: Governments, responses, and policies. *Comparative Political Studies* 19, no. 3 (October): 385–414.

———. 1990a. Responding to terrorism's challenge: The case of Israeli reprisals. *Virginia Social Science Journal* 25 (Winter): 109–23.

———. 1990b. Game theory and hostage-taking incidents: A case study of the Munich Olympic games. *Conflict Quarterly* 10, no. 1: 12–33.

Mishal, S. 1986. *The PLO under Arafat.* New Haven, CT: Yale University Press.

Mishal, S. and A. Sela. 2002. *The Palestinian Hamas: Vision, violence and coexistence.* New York: Columbia University Press.

Mitchell, T. H. 1984. Corporate security in an age of terrorism. *Canadian Business Review* 11, no. 1: 31–36.

———. 1985. Politically-motivated terrorism in North America: The threat and the response. PhD diss., Carleton University.

———. 1991. Defining the problem. In *Democratic responses to international terrorism,* ed. D. Charters, 9–16. Ardsley on the Hudson, NY: Transnational.

Monroe, C. P. 1982. Addressing terrorism in the United States, Annals, AAPSS, Vol. 463, September, 141–148.

Monti, D. 1980. The relation between terrorism and domestic civil disorders. *Terrorism: An International Journal* 4: 123–41.

Morf, G. 1970. *Terror in Québec.* Toronto: Clarke, Irwin.

Morphew, A. J. 1986. Terrorism and corporate insurance. *Management Review* 75, no. 11: 29–30.

Morris, B. 2001. *Righteous victims: A history of the Arab-Zionist conflict, 1881–2001.* New York: Vintage.

Murphy, J. F. 1985. *Punishing international terrorists.* Totowa, New Jersey: Rowman and Allanheld.

Netanyahu, B. 1986. *Terrorism: How the West can win.* New York: Avon.

Netanyahu, I. 2001. *Yoni's last battle: The rescue at Entebbe.* New York: Geffen Books.

Newman, D. 2003. The consequence or the cause? Impact on the Israeli-Palestine peace process. In Buckley and Fawn 2003, 153–64.

Nilson, C. and T. Burke. 2002. Environmental extremists and the eco-terrorism movement. *ACJS Today* 24, no. 5: 3–5.

O'Brien, S. P. 1996. Foreign policy crises and the resort to terrorism: A time series analysis of conflict linkages. *Journal of Conflict Resolution* 40: 320–35.

Ochberg, F. M and D. A. Soskis, eds. 1982. *Victims of terrorism.* Boulder, CO: Westview Press.

Ofri, A. 1984. Intelligence and counter-terrorism. *Orbis* 22, no. 1 (Spring): 32–41.

O'Neil, M. J. 1986. *Terrorist spectaculars: Should TV coverage be curbed?* New York: Priority Press Publications.

Oots, K. L. 1986. *A political organization approach to transnational terrorism.* Westport, CT: Greenwood Press.

Ostrom, E. 1976. Size and performance in a federal system. *Publius* 6, no. 2 (Spring): 33–74.

Pape, R. A. 2003. The strategic logic of suicide terrorism. *American Political Science Review* 97, no. 3: 20–32.

Parry, A. 1976. *Terrorism: From Robespierre to Arafat.* New York: Vanguard Press.

Pearlstein, R. M. 1991. *The mind of a political terrorist.* Wilmington, DE: Scholarly Resources.

Pearsall, R. B. (ed.). 1974. *The Symbionese Liberation Army.* Amsterdam: Rodopi.

Picard, R. G. 1986. News coverage as the contagion of terrorism dangerous: Charges backed by dubious science. *Political Communication and Persuasion* 3, no. 4: 385–400.

Picard, R. G. and P. D. Adams. 1991. *Characterizations of acts and perpetrators of political violence in three elite U.S. daily newspapers.* Terrorism and the News Media Research Project. (Center publication).

Picarelli, J. T. and L. Shelly. 2001. Methods not motives: The convergence of international organized crime and terrorism. *Police Practice and Review: An International Journal* 3 (Winter): 305–18.

Pillar, P. R. 2001. *Terrorism and U.S. foreign policy.* Washington, DC: Brookings Institute.

Pincus, W. 2002. Seized materials may help thwart future attacks. *Washington Post,* April 3. A14

Pitcher, B. and R. Hamblin. 1982. Collective learning in ongoing political conflicts. *International Political Science Review* 3: 71–90.

Poland, J. 1988. *Understanding terrorism.* Englewood Cliffs, NJ: Prentice Hall.

Posner, G. 2003. *Why America slept: The failure to prevent 9/11.* New York: Random House.

Post, J. M. 1984. Notes on psychodynamic theory of terrorist behavior. *Terrorism: An International Journal* 7: 241–56.

———. 1986. Hostilité, conformité, fraternité: The group dynamics of terrorist behavior. *International Journal of Group Psychotherapy* 36, no. 2: 211–24.

———. 1990. Terrorist psycho-logic: Terrorist behavior as a product of psychological forces. In Reich 1990b, 25–42.

Powell, W. 1971. *Anarchist cookbook.* New York: L. Stuart.

Preston, D. 2001. *The Boxer Rebellion.* Berkeley, CA: Berkeley Publishing Group.

Pysczynski, S., S. Solomon, and J. Greenberg. 2002. *In the wake of 9/11: The psychology of terror.* Washington, DC: American Psychological Association.

Rapoport, D. 1988. Messianic sanctions for terror. *Comparative Politics* 20, January: 195–213.

Rapoport, D. C. 2003. The four waves of rebel terror and September 11. In *The new global terrorism: Characteristics, causes, controls,* ed. C. W. Kegley, Jr., 36–59. Upper Saddle River, NJ: Prentice Hall.

Rapoport, D. and Y. Alexander. 1983. *The rationalization of terrorism.* New York: Pergamon.

Rashid, A. 2001. *Taliban.* New Haven, CT: Yale University Press.

Redlick, A. S. 1979. The transnational flow of information as a cause of terrorism. In *Terrorism: Theory and practice,* ed. Y. Alexander et al., 73–95. Boulder, CO: Westview Press.

Reeve, S. 1999. *The new jackals.* Boston: Northeastern University Press.

Reich, W. 1990a. Understanding terrorist behavior: The limits and opportunities of psychological inquiry. In Reich 1990b, 261–81.

———, ed. 1990b. *Origins of terrorism: Psychologies, ideologies, theologies, states of mind.* Cambridge, UK: Woodrow Wilson International Center for Scholars and Cambridge University Press.

Reid, E. F. 1983. An analysis of terrorism literature: A bibliometric and content analysis study. PhD diss., University of Southern California.

Ritzer, G. 2000. *The McDonaldization of society.* Thousand Oaks, CA: Pine Forge Press.

Rosen, E. 2000. *The anatomy of buzz.* New York: Doubleday.

Ross, J. I. 1988a. An events data base on political terrorism in Canada: Some conceptual and methodological problems. *Conflict Quarterly* 8, no. 2: 47–64.

———. 1988b. Attributes of domestic political terrorism in Canada, 1960–1985. *Terrorism: An International Journal* 11, no. 3: 214–33.

———. 1991a. The nature of contemporary international terrorism. In *Democratic responses to international terrorism,* ed. D. Charters, 17–42. Ardsely on the Hudson, NJ: Transnational.

———. 1991b. Review of *The cult of counterterrorism*, by N. C. Livingstone, Lexington, Mass.: Lexington Books, 1990 and *The "Terrorism" Industry*, by E. Herman and G. O'Sullivan, New York: Pantheon, 1991. *Contemporary Sociology* 5, No. 1: 731–33.

———. 1993a. The structural causes of oppositional political terrorism: Towards a causal model. *Journal of Peace Research* 30, no. 3: 317–29.

———. 1993b. Research on contemporary oppositional political terrorism in the United States: Merits, drawbacks and suggestions for improvement. In *Political crime in contemporary America: A critical approach*, ed. K. S. Tunnell, 101–20. New York: Garland Publishing.

———. 1994a. The psychological causes of oppositional political terrorism: Toward an integration of findings. *International Journal of Group Tensions* 24: 157–85.

———. 1994b. Low intensity conflict in the peaceable kingdom: Attributes of international terrorism in Canada, 1960–1990. *Terrorism: An International Journal* 14, no. 3: 36–62.

———. 1995. The rise and fall of Québéçois separatist terrorism: A qualitative application of factors from two models. *Studies in Conflict and Terrorism* 18: 285–97.

———. 1998. *Cutting the edge: Current perspectives in radical/critical criminology and criminal justice*. Westport, CT: Praeger.

———. 1999. Beyond the conceptualization of terrorism: A psychological-structural model of the causes of this activity. In *Collective violence: Harmful behavior in groups and governments*, ed C. Summers and E. Markusen, 169–94. Lanham, MD: Rowman & Littlefield.

———, ed. 2000a. *Controlling state crime*. 2nd ed. New Brunswick, NJ: Transaction Publishers.

———, ed. 2000b. *Varieties of state crime and its control*. Monsey, NY: Criminal Justice Press.

———. 2000c. *Making news of police violence*. Westport, CT: Praeger.

———. 2002a. *The dynamics of political crime*. Thousand Oaks, CA: Sage Publications.

———. 2002b. Terror in the aisles. Letter to the editor. *City Paper*, January 9. 5.

———. 2003. Defining terrorism: An international consensus, a critical issue after 9/11. In Shanty and Picquet 2003, 12–16.

———. 2004. Taking stock of research methods and analysis on oppositional political terrorism. *The American Sociologist* Summer: 26–37.

———. 2005a. Post 9/11: Are we any safer now? In *Terrorism: Research, readings, and realities*, ed. L. L. Snowden and B. C. Whitsel, 380–89. Upper Saddle River, NJ: Prentice Hall.

———. 2005b. Reacting to 9/11: Rational policy and practice versus threat of the week syndrome. In *After 9/11: Terrorism and crime in a globalized world,* ed. G. Walker and D. Charters, 306–21. Joint Publication of the University of New Brunswick's Centre for Conflict Studies and Dalhousie University's Center for Foreign Policy Studies.

———. 2005. *Will terrorism end?* Northborough, MA: Chelsea House Publishers

Ross, J. I. and T. R. Gurr. 1986. Ernesto (Che) Guevara. In *World encyclopedia of peace,* 401–02. Oxford: Pergamon Press.

———. 1989. Why terrorism subsides: A comparative study of Canada and the United States. *Comparative Politics* 21: 406–26.

Ross, J. I. and R. J. Miller. 1997. The effects of oppositional political terrorism: Five actor-based models. *Low Intensity Conflict and Law Enforcement* 6, no. 3: 76–107.

Rubin, J. Z. and N. Friedland. 1986. Theater of terror. *Psychology Today* 20: 18–28.

Rubner, M. 1987. Anti-terrorism and the withering of the 1973 War Powers Resolution. *Political Science Quarterly* 102, no. 2: 193–215.

Russell, C. A. and B. H. Miller. 1983. Profile of a terrorist. In *Perspectives on terrorism,* ed. L. Z. Freedman and Y. Alexander, 45–60. Wilmington, DE: Scholarly Resources.

Ryan, W. 1971. *Blaming the victim.* New York: Vintage Books.

Sandler, T. and J. L. Scott. 1987. Terrorist success in hostage-taking incidents. *Journal of Conflict Resolution* 31: 35–53.

Sandler, T., J. T. Tschirhart, and J. Cauley. 1983. Transnational terrorism. *American Political Science Review* 77, no. 1 (March): 36–54.

Sater, W. F. 1984. Violence and the Puerto Rican separatist movement. *Terrorism, Violence, and Insurgency Report* 5, Summer: 4–10.

Sayari, S. 1985. Generational change in terrorist movements: The Turkish case. Santa Monica, CA: RAND Corporation. Report

Sayre, R. 1984. The war of words: Can diplomacy be effective? In Livingstone and Arnold 1986, 85–94.

Scanlon, J. 1981. Coping with the media: Police media problems and tactics in hostage taking and terrorist incidents, *Canadian Police College Journal* 5: 129–48.

———. 1982. Domestic terrorism and the media: Live coverage of crime, *Canadian Police College Journal* 8: 154–178.

Schiller, H. I. 1989. *Culture Inc. The corporate takeover of public expression.* New York: Oxford University Press.

Schlesinger, P. 1981. Terrorism, the media and the liberal democratic state: A critique of the orthodoxy. *Social Research* 48: 74–99.

Schlesinger, P., G. Murdock, and P. Elliot. 1983. *Televising terrorism: Political violence in popular culture.* London: Comedia Publishing.

Schiff, Z. and E Ya'ari. 1989. *Intifada: The inside story of the Palestinian uprising that changed the Middle East equation.* New York: Touchstone.

Schmid, A. P. 1983. *Political terrorism: A research guide to concepts, theories, data bases and literature.* New Brunswick, NJ: Transaction Publishers.

————. 1992. Terrorism and the media: Freedom of information vs. freedom from information. In Howard 1992, 95–118.

————. 1996. The links between transnational organized crime and terrorist crimes. *Transnational Organized Crime* 2, no. 4: 40–82.

————. 1997. The problems of defining terrorism. In *Encyclopedia of world terrorism,* vol. 1, ed. M. Crenshaw and J. Pimlott, 12–22. Armonk, NY: M. E. Sharpe.

Schmid, A. P. and R. D. Crelinsten, eds. 1993. *Western responses to terrorism.* London: Frank Cass.

Schmid, A. P. and J. de Graff. 1980. *Insurgent terrorism and the Western news media: An exploratory analysis with a Dutch case study.* Leiden: Dutch State University.

————. 1982. *Violence as communication: Insurgent terrorism and the Western news media.* Beverly Hills, CA: Sage Publications.

Schmid, A. P. and A. J. Jongman. 1988. *Political terrorism: A new guide to actors, concepts, data bases, theories, and literature.* Rev. ed. New Brunswick, NJ: Transaction Publishers.

Schneier, B. 2003. *Beyond fear: Thinking sensibly about security in an uncertain world.* New York: Copernicus Books.

Sederberg, P. C. 1989. *Terrorist myths: illusion, rhetoric, and reality.* Englewood Cliffs, NJ: Prentice Hall.

————. 1991. Defining terrorism. Contending themes in contemporary research. *Annual review of conflict of knowledge.* New York: Garland Publishing.

Seidman, N. 1990. *Menachim Begen: His life and legacy.* New York: Shengold Publications.

Selzer, N. 1979. *Terrorist chic.* New York: Hawthorn Books.

Shaheen, J. G. 1984. *The TV Arab.* Bowling Green, OH: State University Popular Press.

Shanty, F. and R. Picquet. 2000. *International terrorism: An annual "event data" report, 1998.* Collingdale, PA: DIANE Publishing.

————, eds. 2003. *Encyclopedia of world terrorism.* Armonk, NY: M. E. Sharpe.

Shaw, D., and M. McCombs. 1972. The agenda-setting function of the mass media. *Public Opinion Quarterly* 36 (Summer): 176–87.

Sheridan, M. B. 2001. Report: Some INS targets disappeared. *Washington Post,* November 7. A10.

Shipler, D. 1986. *Arab and Jew.* New York: Times Books.

Sick, G. 1985. *All fall down: America's tragic encounter with Iran.* New York: Random House.

Silke, A. 1999. Rebel's dilemma: The changing relationship between the IRA, Sinn Fein, and paramilitary vigilantism in Northern Ireland. *Terrorism and Political Violence* 11, no. 1: 55–93.

Simon, H. 1982. *Models of bounded rationality.* Vols. 1–2. Cambridge, MA: MIT Press.

Simonsen, C. and J. R. Spindlove. 2004. *Terrorism today: The past, the players, the future.* 2nd ed. Upper Saddle River, NJ: Pearson Prentice Hall.

Skinner, B. F. 1938. *The behavior of organisms: An experimental analysis.* New York: Appleton-Century-Crofts.

Sloan, J. W. 1988. Political terrorism in Latin America. In Stohl 1988, 377–396.

Sloan, S. 1993. U.S. anti-terrorism policies: Lessons to be learned to meet an enduring and changing threat. *Terrorism and Political Violence* 5, no. 1 (Spring):

Smith, B. 1994. *Terrorism in America: Pipe bombs and pipe dreams.* Albany: State University of New York Press.

Smith, B. L. and K. Damphouse. 1996. Punishing political offenders: The effect of political motive on federal sentencing decisions. *Criminology* 34, no. 3: 289–321.

———. 1998. Terrorism, politics, and punishment: A test of structural contextual theory and liberation hypothesis. *Criminology* 36, no. 1: 67–92.

Smith, B. L. and G. Orvis. 1994. America's response to terrorism: An empirical analysis of federal intervention strategies during the 1980s. *Justice Quarterly* 10, no. 4: 663–83.

Smith, C. 1976. *Carlos: Portrait of a terrorist.* London: Sphere Books.

Smith, G. D. 1998. Single issue terrorism. *Commentary,* 74 (Winter). Publication of the Canadian Security Intelligence Service.

Snyder, M., ed. 1978. *Media and terrorism: The psychological impact.* North Newton, KS: Mennonite Press.

Sofaer, A. D. 1986. Terrorism and the law. *Foreign Affairs,* 64, no. 5, (Summer): 901–22.

Stafford, F. and M. Palacios. 2002. *Colombia: Fragmented land, divided society.* New York: Oxford University Press.

Sterling, C. 1981. *The terror network: The secret war of international terrorism.* New York: Holt, Rinehart, and Winston.

Stern, J. 1999. *The ultimate terrorists.* Cambridge, MA: Harvard University Press.

Stewart, J. 1970. *The FLQ: Seven years of terrorism.* Montreal: Montreal Star in cooperation with Simon & Schuster of Canada.

Stinson, J. 1984. *Assessing Terrorist Tactics and Security Measures.* Paper presented at the Detroit Police Department Conference on Urban Terrorism: Planning or Chaos?

Stohl, M. 1979. *The politics of terrorism.* New York: Marcel Dekker.

———. 1983. *The politics of terrorism.* 2nd edition. New York: Marcel Dekker.

———. 1988. *The politics of terrorism.* 3rd edition. New York: Marcel Dekker.

Süllwold, L. 1981. Station in der Entwicklung von Terroristen: Psychologische Aspekte biographischer Daten. In Jager, Schmidtchen, and Süllwold, Oplanden: Westdeutscher Verlag 2.

Sutherland, E. H. 1947. *Principles of criminology.* 4th ed. Philadelphia: J. B. Lippincott.

Talbot, R. 2003. Northern Ireland and the United Kingdom. In Shanty and Picquet 2003, 335–42.

Tanenbaum, R. and P. Rosenberg. [1979] 1994. *Badge of the assassin.* New York: New American Library.

Targ, H. R. 1979. Societal structure and revolutionary terrorism: A preliminary investigation. In Stohl 1979, 119–43.

Taylor, M. 1988. *The terrorist.* London: Brassey's Defense Publishers.

Tierney, J. J. 1977. Terror at home: The American Revolution and irregular warfare, *Stanford Journal of International Studies* 12: 1–9.

Thompson, L. 1986. *The rescuers—The world's top anti-terrorist units.* New York: Dell.

Thorton, T. 1964. Terrorism as a weapon of political agitation. In *Internal war,* ed. H. Eckstein, 82–88. New York: Free Press.

Toolis, K. 1997. *Rebel hearts: Journeys with the IRA's soul.* New York: St. Martin's Griffin.

Tovar, B. H. 1986. Active response. In *Hydra of carnage,* ed. U. Ra'anan, R. L. Pfaltzgraff, Jr., R. H. Schultz, E. Halperin, and I. Lukes, Lexington, MA: Lexington Press.

Townshend, C. 2002. *Terrorism: A very short introduction.* New York: Oxford University Press.

Tucker, J. B. 1996. Chemical/biological terrorism: Coping with a new threat. *Politics and the Life Sciences* 15: 167–83.

———. 1999. Historical trends related to bioterrorism: An empirical analysis. *Emerging Infectious Diseases* 5: 498–504.

Tuckman, G. 1978. *Making news: A study in the construction of reality.* New York: Free Press.

Turk, A. T. 1982. Social dynamics of terrorism. *Annals of the American Political Science Society* 463: 119–28.

———. 1989. Notes on criminology and terrorism. In *Advances in criminological theory*, vol. 1, ed. W. S. Laufer and F. Adler, 17–29. New Brunswick, NJ: Transaction Publishers.

Unger, C. 2004. *House of Bush. House of Saud: The secret relationship between the world's most powerful dynasties.* New York: Scribner.

United States Senate. 1985. Vice president's task force on combating terrorism. Government Printing Office.

United States. 1999. Clemency for terrorists. *Findings of the Committee on Government Reform,* November. www.house.gov/reform/oversight/faln.htm

———. 2002. Grossman outlines terrorist threat to Colombia. Testimony by Ambassador Marc Grossman, Undersecretary of State for Political Affairs before the Senate Committee on Foreign Relations Sub-committee for Western Hemisphere Affairs, April 24. State Department International Information Programs. http://usinfo.state.gov/topical/ pol/terror.htm

———. 2004. *The 9/11 Commission report.* New York: W. W. Norton.

Vallieres, P. 1972a. *White niggers of America.* Toronto: McClelland and Stewart.

———. 1972b. *Choose.* Toronto: New Press.

Van Aartick, P., Jr. 1987. Terrorism rises, cover demand rises. *National Underwriter* 91, no. 14, 6, 13: 16–17.

Vetter, H. J. and G. R. Perlstein. 1991. *Perspectives on terrorism.* Pacific Grove, CA: Brooks / Cole.

Von Tangen, P. 1988. *Prisons, peace and terrorism.* New York: St. Martin's.

Waite, T. 1993. *Taken on Trust.* Toronto: Harcourt.

Walter, E. V. 1969. *Terror and resistance.* New York: Oxford University Press.

Wardlaw, G. 1982. *Political terrorism: Theory, tactics, and counter measures.* New York: Cambridge University Press.

Waugh, W. L., Jr. 1982. *International terrorism: How nations respond to terrorists.* Salisbury, NC: Documentary Publications.

Weaver, D. H. and J. B. Mauro. 1978. Newspaper readership patterns. *Journalism Quarterly* 55 (Spring): 84–91.

Webster's. 1980. *Webster's New Collegiate Dictionary.* Toronto: Thomas Allen & Sons Limited.

Weimann, G. 1983. The theater of terror: Effects of press coverage. *Journal of Communication* 33 (Winter): 38–45.

———. 1987. "Terrorists or fighters"? Labeling terrorism in the Israeli press. *Political Communication and Persuasion* 2, no. 4: 433–45.

———. 2004. *How modern terrorism uses the Internet.* United States Institute of Peace Report, Washington, DC.

Weinberg, L. and P. B. Davis. 1989. *Introduction to political terrorism.* New York: McGraw-Hill.

Weinberg, L. and W. L. Eubank. 1987a. Italian women terrorists. *Terrorism: An International Journal* 9: 241–62.

———. 1987b. *The rise and fall of Italian terrorism.* Boulder, CO: Westview Press.

Weinberg, L. and A. Pedahzur. 2003. *Political parties and terrorist groups.* New York: Routledge.

Westcott, K. 2002. Who are the Hezbollah? BBC News World Edition, April 4. http://news.bbc.co.uk/2/hi/middle_east/1908671.stm

White, J. 1991. *Terrorism: An introduction.* Pacific Grove, CA: Brooks / Cole.

———. 2003. *Terrorism: An introduction.* 4th ed. Belmont, CA: Wadsworth.

Wilkinson, P. 1974. *Political terrorism.* New York: John Wiley and Sons.

———. 1977. *Terrorism and the liberal state.* New York: John Wiley and Sons.

———. 1981. Terrorism, the mass media and democracy. *Contemporary Review* 239 (July): 35–44.

———. 1986. Terrorism versus liberal democracy: The problem of response. In *Contemporary terrorism,* ed. W. Gutteridge, 3–28. New York: Facts on File Publications.

———. 2003. Implications of 9/11 for the future of terrorism. In Buckley and Fawn 2003, 25–36.

Williams, K. 2002. Scary movies. *City Paper,* January 2. 15–21.

Wilson, M. and J. Lynxwiler. 1988. Abortion clinic violence as terrorism, *Terrorism: An International Journal* 11: 263–73.

Wood, R. T. 1999. The indigenous, nonracist origins of the American skinhead subculture. *Youth & Society* 31, no. 2: 131–51.

Wurth-Hough, S. 1983. Network news coverage of terrorism: The early years. *Terrorism: An International Journal* 6: 403–22.

Zilinskas, R. 1990. Terrorism and BW: Inevitable alliance? *Perspectives in Biology and Medicine* 34: 1, 44–72.

Zohar, B. 2002. *The quest for the Red Prince.* Guilford, CT: Lyons Press.

Zwerman, G. 1988. Domestic counter-terrorism: U.S. government responses to political violence on the left in the Reagan era. *Social Justice* 16, no. 2: 31–63.

Index

Adams, Gerry, 134
Al-Aqusa Martyrs Brigade, 128
Al-Fatah, 124–128
Al Qaeda, 1–2,165–174, 188, 218–219, 227,
    243
Action reaction conflict model, 216
Anarchists/Anarchism, 14, 34
Animal Liberation Front/Army, 157, 238
Anti-Americanism, 240
Arafat, Yasser, 124, 127, 128
Armenian-related terrorism, 17, 37, 41,
    153–154
Aryan Nations, 149–151, 153, 177
Assassins (terrorist group), 33
Assassination (political), 11
Asymmetrical warfare (see WMD)

Baader-Meinhoff gang, 42, 62
Basque-related terrorism, 40–41
bin Laden, Osama, 167–176, 187, 215,
    227
Black Panther Party, 144, 145, 148
Black Militant terrorism, 147–148

Black September, 126
Bloody Sunday, 132
Bombings
    Dar es Salaam, 167, 172, 211, 213
    Jakarta, 176
    London, 206, 221
    Madrid, 176, 219
    Nairobi, 167, 172, 211, 213
    Oklahoma City, 152–153
    USS Cole, 173
Business community/Corporations,
    110–113, 221–222, 248

Causes of terrorism, 77–91, 242
Central Intelligence Agency, 170, 175,
    202–203, 232
Civil and Human Rights, 214
Colombia, 47, 129–130
Combating Terrorism/Counterterrorism,
    85, 201–212
Comparisons, 134–138
Conflict Theory, 95
Conlon, Gerry, 133

Contagion, 84, 186
Cooperation, 214, 227
Crime reporting wave, 216
Croatian-related terrorism, 152
Cuba, 154, 245
Cultural Industries/Commodification of Terrorism, 25, 107, 194–195

Dark Networks, 48
Data (on terrorism), 48–60
Definition of terrorism, 2–8
Department of Homeland Security, 203, 228, 231–232
Duma, 35

Eco-terrorism, 159–160
Effects of terrorism, 95–119, 175–178, 216–231
Emergency Legislation, 133, 202, 210

FARC (Columbia), 129–130
Federal Bureau of Investigation, 21, 166–167, 175, 189, 202–203, 221, 232
Front de Liberation du Quebec, 39–40
Future of terrorism, 235–248

Gaza Strip, 125
Globalization, 242–243
Gray area phenomenon, 47–48
Guerrilla organization, 11

Hamas, 46, 116
Hanafi Muslims, 149, 190
Hearst, Patricia, 105, 147–148, 187
Hezbollah, 45–46, 126
History of terrorism, 13–15, 31–48,

Ideology, 19–20, 41, 83
Infiltration, 213
Intelligence, 205, 245
Intifada, 46, 127
Italy, 43–44
Irish-related terrorism, 36–38, 41, 131–134
Islamic Muslim fundamentalism, 45–46, 170–171, 172, 242

Islamic Jihad, 46

Japanese Red Army, 42
Jewish Defence League, 16, 158–159

Kaczynski, Theordore, 78, 159–160
Koresh, David, 151–152
Ku Klux Klan, 149–150

Libya, 244
Laws, 114
Leaderless resistance, 161
Left-wing terrorism, 41–44, 143–149

McVeigh, Timothy, 151–152, 153, 175
Media, 109–110, 183–197
Middle East, 171–172, 220, 240
Military, 211
MIPT, 51, 66
Montoneros, 42
Morphing, lifecycles, and waves, 13–14, 235
Munich Massacre, 63, 110, 185

Narcoterrorism, 47, 129–130
National Identity cards, 227
Nationalism, 107–108, 220

Palestinian-related terrorism, 46, 124–128
Palestinian Liberation Organization, 17,
Pan Am Flight 103, 12, 103
PATRIOT Act, 222, 226
Police, 207- 209
Public Opinion, 193–194
Prison, 113–114
    Abu Ghraib, 241
    Guantanamo, 114, 218
Pro-life related terrorism, 157
Proximity to attack, 217
Puerto Rican- related terrorism, 154–156

RAND, 24, 49, 50, 65
Red Brigades, 42, 187
Research methods, 17, 22–25

Revolution, Algeria, 125
  Iran, 187, 192
  Nicaragua, 45
  Vietnam, 11
Right-wing terrorism, 44, 148–152
Rudolph, Eric Robert, 157–158

September 11, attack, 2, 8–9, 165, 167,
    170–178, 187, 217–218
Sicarri, 33
Skinheads, 16, 17
Social Revolutionary Party, 35
Sterling, Claire, 45
Stimulus-response conflict model, 96
Stockholm syndrome, 105
Studying terrorism, 243
Surveillance, 210–211, 223
Symbionese Liberation Army, 146

Taliban, 227, 243
Target Hardening, 117, 222, 224, 244
Technology, communications and
    weaponry, 185, 209, 236–237
Theocracy, 169
Theory (on terrorism), 20–22
Third Forces/SWAT teams, 117, 206, 207
Threat of the Week Syndrome, 221, 230–231
Transportation systems, 224–225

Treaties
  Anglo-American Peace Accord, 133
  Good Friday Agreement, 133
  Oslo Accords, 127
Trends, 52–59
Tupamaros, 41–42
Types of terrorism/terrorism typologies,
    10–13, 18–19, 98

United Freedom Front, 146–147
United States, State Department, 51

Victims, 102–106, 221

War
  Afghanistan, 168–169, 174, 229
  Gulf War, 174
  Iraq (2002–2005), 229, 240–241
  Lebanese Civil War, 126
  Six Days, 40, 125
Weapons of Mass Destruction, 56,
    227–228, 229, 237–238
Weathermen/Weather underground, 22,
    144–146, 147
Weaver, Randy, 151
West Bank, 125
World Trade Center Bombing (1983)
    166–167, 172

About the Author

Jeffrey Ian Ross received his Ph.D. at the University of Colorado. He is an Associate Professor in the Division of Criminology, Criminal Justice and Social Policy, and a Fellow of the Center for International and Comparative Law at the University of Baltimore. Dr. Ross has researched, written, and lectured on national security, political violence, political crime, violent crime, corrections, and policing for over two decades. His work has appeared in many academic journals and books, as well as popular magazines. In 2003, he was awarded the University of Baltimore's Distinguished Chair in Research Award.

Dr. Ross is also the author of *Making News of Police Violence: A Comparative Study of Toronto and New York City* (Praeger, 2000) and *The Dynamics of Political Crime* (Sage, 2002). He is the coauthor (with Stephen C. Richards) of *Behind Bars: Surviving Prison* (Alpha Books, 2002) and the editor of *Controlling State Crime* (2nd ed., Transaction Publishers, 2000), *Violence in Canada: Sociopolitical Perspectives* (2nd ed., Transaction Publishers, 2004), *Cutting the Edge: Current Perspectives in Radical/Critical Criminology and Criminal Justice* (Praeger, 1998), and *Varieties of State Crime and Its Control* (Criminal Justice Press, 2000). In addition, Dr. Ross is coeditor with Stephen C. Richards of *Convict Criminology* (Wadsworth, 2002) and coeditor with Larry Gould of *Native Americans and the Criminal Justice System* (Paradigm Publishers, 2005).

In 1986, Dr. Ross was the lead expert witness for the Canadian Senate's Special Committee on Terrorism and Public Safety. He created the first database on terrorism in Canada, which was later acquired by the Solicitor General of Canada. From 1995–1998, Dr. Ross was a social science analyst with the National Institute of Justice, a Division of the U. S. Department of Justice. His Web site is http://www.jeffreyianross.com